全球视野下的人工智能治理
（第一辑）

A Global Perspective of AI Governance
Vol. I

石谦 主编 李辉 谢旻希 副主编
上海市科学学研究所 策划

Chief Editor SHI Qian Vice Chief Editors LI Hui Brian TSE
Curated by Shanghai Institute for Science of Science (SISS)

同济大学出版社 · 上海
TONGJI UNIVERSITY PRESS | SHANGHAI

FOREWORD

AI will have a major impact on our future. It is the main driver of the information revolution that is occurring. The impact of the information revolution will be greater than the agricultural and industrial revolutions. Just as the industrial revolution eliminated jobs in agriculture, the information revolution will eliminate jobs in manufacturing. AI will change the nature of work, lifestyle, and the role of government.

We are already seeing its impact on transportation with self-driving cars, in social communication and translation between languages, and in many other areas as diverse as manufacturing, medicine, and agriculture, raising issues involving data ownership, fairness, bias, explainability, legal implications, affect recognition and social communication. AI governance is essential to ensure that AI systems remain beneficial and safe. This will require a deep understanding of the opportunities and limitations of AI.

A Global Perspective of AI Governance (Vol. I) is a compilation of the 2019 and 2020 Global AI Governance reports. The report is an important reading for AI scientists, social scientists, industrial leaders, policy makers, and people across different nations to ensure that the benefits of AI are equally available to all people.

The report is valuable as it provides a platform where people from different areas can consider the innovative thinking that exists around the issues so far. The articles report on progress that has been made including the Asilomar principles, Beijing AI principles, and the OECD principles on AI. The report also contains material on areas such as adding common sense to AI systems, differential privacy, and other areas that are essential to ensure that AI systems remain transparent and equitable. It is my belief that this book will create, in the public, a greater awareness of the critical decision-making needed to be addressed to achieve global justice.

John E. HOPCROFT
February, 2022

序言

人工智能对人类未来具有深远影响，它是正在发生的信息革命的主要驱动者。信息革命产生的影响，将远超农业革命和工业革命。就像工业革命减少了农业领域的工作，信息革命也将减少工业领域的工作。未来，人工智能将改变人们工作的性质、生活的方式，也可能改变政府所扮演的角色。

人工智能对社会的影响已经显现，出行方式正在被自动驾驶改变，不同语言之间的交流正在被智能翻译改变，制造业、医疗、农业等诸多行业也正在被各种人工智能技术改变。当然与此同时，人工智能也引起相应的社会问题，包括数据所有权、公正与偏见、算法透明度、算法的法律影响、对认知与沟通的重塑，等等。因此，人工智能治理将肩负重任——它将确保人工智能朝着有益且安全的方向发展。这也意味着人们对人工智能所带来的机遇与风险要有更深层次的理解。

《全球视野下的人工智能治理（第一辑）》是《2019全球人工智能治理年度观察》和《2020全球人工智能治理年度观察》这两份年度报告的浓缩。这两份报告对人工智能科学家、社会学家、产业界领袖、政策制定者、以及不同国家的人们具有重要的参考价值，旨在推动全世界每个人都能从人工智能发展中受益。

这两份报告的价值还体现在：它提供了一个交流平台，能够让来自不同领域的人获得人工智能最前沿的观点，它提到的阿西洛马人工智能原则、人工智能北京共识、OECD人工智能原则，都是本领域非常有价值的进展。这两份报告还提到应该在人工智能系统加入人类常识、差分隐私等，让人工智能保持透明度和公平性。我相信，这本书将提升公众对于决定全球正义的关键决策过程的认知。

约翰·霍普克罗夫特
2022年2月

PREFACE

Finding the Most Important "Advancements" in AI Governance

The impacts of artificial intelligence (AI) are becoming increasingly profound in all aspects of economic and social development. As those of any disruptive technology, such impacts are both positive and negative. Therefore, timely governance is required for the R&D and application of AI. However, AI features very broad impacts–you might say it is closely bound up with the future of almost everyone in the world. As a result, all countries, fields, industries and even many individuals have been paying close attention to AI governance from the outset.

Against the backdrop of pluralistic participation, we continuously identify new problems, offer new observations, and enact new measures with the hope of producing an effective AI governance solution as soon as possible. However, AI governance is such a complex issue that it is impossible to produce such a solution in a short time, and finding a consensus-based solution can be even more time-consuming. New problems, new observations, and new measures emerge constantly during the development of a consensus-based solution, posing a challenge to researchers, decision makers, and everyone interested in this issue. In this fast moving context, how can we identify the most noteworthy new problems, new observations, and new measures–the "three news" which are referred to as the "new advancements"–in AI governance?

Identifying New Advancements in AI Governance through "Idea Crowdsourcing"

We have found an effective way to summarize and share the existing research results and new advancements, namely "idea crowdsourcing", which means to invite representative experts around the world to extract information about the most critical advancements

前言

寻找人工智能治理领域最重要的“进展”

人工智能正越来越深刻地影响着经济和社会的方方面面。如同任何一种颠覆性技术，这些影响既有正面的，也有负面的——因此人工智能的研发和应用需要及时治理。而人工智能的特殊之处在于，它的影响面如此之广，甚至可以说与每个人都息息相关——因此，人工智能治理从一开始，就是各个国家、各个领域、各个行业乃至每一个人都密切关注的。

在多元参与的情况下，人们不断发现新的问题，提出新的观点，推出新的措施，从而希望尽快形成行之有效的人工智能治理方案。但是人工智能治理问题如此复杂，方案并非短时间内能够形成，共识性的方案更是需要时间。在最终形成共识性方案的过程中，新问题、新观点、新措施不断涌现，这也给研究者、决策者以及每一位关心这一问题的人带来了挑战：如何辨析出人工智能治理领域最值得关注的新问题、新观点和新措施——我们称这“三新”为“新进展”。

用“思想众包”的方式发现人工智能治理的新进展

为了更好地总结、分享已有的研究成果和新的进展，我们想到了一个办法：思想众包。邀请全球代表性专家，以他们深厚的专业功底和宽阔的分析视野，从纷繁复杂的人工智能治理进展中提取出最为关键的进展。基于这一思路，我们连续两年（2020 年、2021 年）发布了《全球人工智能治理年度观察》。报告的主体内容就是邀请全球代表性专家回答唯一的问题：您认为在过去一年（2019 年、2020 年）中，人工智能治理最重要的进展是什么？

关于 2019 年最重要的进展，我们邀请了全球 50 位专家进行回答和评述；关于 2020

in AI governance with their in-depth expertise and broad analytical view. To that end, we have released *AI Governance in 2019: A Year in Review* and *AI Governance in 2020: A Year in Review* for two consecutive years (2020 and 2021), which invited representative experts around the world to answer only one question: what do you think is the most important advancement in AI governance of the last year (in 2019 or 2020); the answers were compiled to be the main body contents of the reports.

We invited 50 global experts to answer the aforementioned question and make some comments for the most important advancements of 2019 and 52 for 2020. In terms of working background, the participating experts mainly covered five fields: science and technology, humanities and social sciences, the industry, national or regional policy communities, and international organizations.

Soon after the release of the reports, we received a large amount of feedback. Global industry peers re-posted the reports many times and made lots of comments on various social media and in professional communities. An expert from the Office of the President of the United Nations General Assembly specially sent a congratulations letter to us, and the Montreal AI Ethics Institute introduced *AI Governance in 2019: A Year in Review* as one of the highly recommended references in its report, *The State of AI Ethics*, which attracted wide attention to our reports from global industry peers. In China, our reports were also rated as one of the most important achievements of the years made by national think tanks. The positive encouragement from global industry peers has strengthened our belief that we need a platform for the exchange of information on "AI advancements". We hope that this platform can improve understanding of–and help to bridge–different viewpoints on the challenges and opportunities of AI governance, so as to effectively promote the global governance of this important technology.

This book is based on the aforementioned two annual reports. We hope that it can further consolidate the global wisdom collected in *AI Governance in 2019: A Year in Review* and *AI Governance in 2020: A Year in Review,* and record the most important advancements in global AI governance during those pivotal years.

Over 60 Authors around the World

This book is a curated collection of the 2020 and 2021 articles by over 60 of its authors, including John E. Hopcroft, professor at Cornell University and winner of the Turing Award; Stuart Russell, professor at the University of California, Berkeley, USA and co-author of *Artificial Intelligence: A Modern Approach* (with Peter Norvig), an AI textbook

年最重要的进展，我们邀请了全球 52 位专家进行回答和评述。这些专家的工作背景，主要涵盖五个方面：科技领域、人文社科领域、产业界、国家或地区的政策界和国际组织。

报告一经发布我们便收到了大量反馈。全球同行在各种社交媒体、专业社区中大量转载和评论。联合国大会主席办公室有关专家还专门给我们来信祝贺。蒙特利尔 AI 伦理研究所在其发布的全球同行广泛关注的《人工智能伦理现状》（*The State of AI Ethics*）中，将《2019 全球人工智能治理年度观察》作为其重点推荐的文献之一。在中国，我们的报告也被评为全国智库最重要的年度成果之一。全球同行的正向激励让我们更加相信，大家需要一个对“进展”进行交流的平台，全球人工智能治理的有效推进，需要这样一个互相交流、互通有无的平台。

本书，就是根据以上两份年度报告汇编而成的。我们希望以书的形式，进一步巩固这两年来《全球人工智能治理年度观察》所汇集的全球智慧，记录下 2019 年和 2020 年全球人工智能治理领域所取得的最重要的进展。

来自全球各地的 60 余位撰稿作者

2019 年的报告中有 50 位作者，2020 年的报告中有 52 位作者，其中有一些是重复的，共计 80 位。本书收录的则是其中 60 余位作者的文章。在这些作者中，有图灵奖得主、美国康奈尔大学教授约翰·霍普克罗夫特（John E. Hopcroft），被 116 个国家的 1,300 多所大学使用的人工智能教科书《人工智能：一种现代方法》（*Artificial Intelligence: A Modern Approach*）的编写者、美国加利福尼亚大学伯克利分校的教授斯图尔特·拉塞尔（Stuart Russell），中国外交部原副部长、希望全球人工智能领域“结伴同行，合作共赢”的清华大学战略与安全研究中心主任傅莹，呼吁发展中国家积极发声的联合国大会主席办公室高级顾问尤金尼奥·加西亚（Eugenio V. Garcia），等等。

从领域来看，专家中有人工智能领域的技术专家，他们介绍了针对人工智能治理最新的技术解决方案；有人文社会科学领域的学者，他们介绍了对于人工智能治理制度背后的理论基础的最新探索；与人工智能成果落地联系最紧密的产业界专家，则从企业实践的角度提供了一些最新的企业治理制度；国际组织的相关学者，则分享了协调各国人工

used by more than 1,500 universities in 130 countries; FU Ying, Former Vice Minister of Foreign Affairs of China, and Director of the Center for International Security and Strategy at Tsinghua University, who pursues "Benefit in Partnership" in AI at the global level; and Eugenio V. Garcia, Senior Adviser of the Office of the President of the United Nations General Assembly, who calls on the Global South to raise their voice.

We benefited from a wealth of expertise. Indeed, we have technical experts in AI, who presented the latest technical solutions to AI governance challenges; scholars specializing in humanities and social sciences, who introduced the latest discoveries about the theoretical foundation for AI governance systems; experts from the industry with the strongest connection to the materialization of AI achievements, who presented the latest corporate governance systems; scholars from international organizations, who shared their efforts to coordinate the AI governance systems of different countries and attempts to reach a consensus; and also scholars from countries and regions all over the world including Europe, Latin America, and Africa, who introduced the issues of the greatest concern and the new discoveries in their respective regions.

As Eugenio V. Garcia believes, AI is so important that international cooperation is required to jointly address related issues. In recent years, Garcia and other experts have been calling for increased representation of the Global South in the international discussions on AI governance. Therefore, you readers may find a distinct feature differentiating this book from other books about AI governance–it includes specially invited experts from Latin America to introduce the efforts that region, with a population of several hundred million, is making for AI governance.

Given that it is all the more necessary for China, a dominant country in terms of AI technologies and industry, to show the world its ideas about and specific efforts in AI governance, this book intentionally invited a number of Chinese experts to introduce the different dimensions of AI governance in China. In 2017, the State Council of China issued *The Development Plan for a New Generation of Artificial Intelligence* as China's national strategic plan on AI development, outlining its basic framework until 2030 and listing the active promotion of AI governance as an important task. In February 2019, the National New Generation AI Governance Expert Committee, consisting of experts from academia and industry, was established by China's Ministry of Science and Technology. Later that year, in June, the Committee released *The Governance Principles for a New Generation of Artificial Intelligence: Develop Responsible Artificial Intelligence*, addressing eight governance principles: harmony and friendliness/human-friendliness, fairness and justice, inclusiveness and sharing, respect for privacy, security and controllability, shared responsibility, open cooperation/collaboration, and agile governance. In Shanghai, AI has been designated as a priority development area and an efficient tool for future urban governance. However, the effective governance of AI is the key to ensuring the

智能治理制度并尝试达成共识的努力；来自欧洲、拉美、非洲等全球各国、各地区的学者，则介绍了自己所在地区最为关心的问题和新的探索。

正如尤金尼奥·加西亚先生所认为的，人工智能如此重要，因此全球需要团结，从而共同应对。加西亚等专家近些年大声疾呼，在国际人工智能治理的讨论中，不能忽视发展中国家的声音。因此，读者会发现本书相较其他人工智能治理书籍的一个特色——本书特别邀请了数位拉丁美洲的专家，介绍这个有着数亿人口的地区正在为人工智能治理所开展的工作。

中国作为人工智能技术和产业大国，更需要向世界展示其在治理方面的思路和具体工作，因此本书也特别邀请了多位中国专家，多维度地介绍中国的人工智能治理。2017 年，国务院发布了《新一代人工智能发展规划》，作为中国国家级的人工智能发展战略规划，它为中国 2030 年之前的人工智能发展描绘了基本框架，并把积极推动人工智能治理作为其中一项重要任务。2019 年 2 月，中国科技部牵头设立了由来自高校、科研院所和企业的相关专家组成的新一代人工智能治理专业委员会。2019 年 6 月，该委员会发布了《新一代人工智能治理原则——发展负责任的人工智能》，提出了和谐友好、公平公正、包容共享、尊重隐私、安全可控、共担责任、开放协作、敏捷治理八项治理原则。在上海这座超大型城市，人工智能是重点发展的未来产业，也是被寄予厚望的未来城市治理工具，而对人工智能进行有效治理是确保两者成功的关键。与此同时，国家层面也对上海的人工智能发展和治理寄予厚望。2019 年，上海被批复成为中国新一代人工智能创新发展试验区。在这个试验区的建设中，伦理治理是重要组成部分。国家层面希望上海能够先试先行，探索出成功经验并推广至全国。本书所邀请的中国专家，包括从国家层面到地方层面，从科学家到人文社科专家，从政策界、学术界到产业界，希望能够真正反映中国在人工智能领域的思考与探索。

基于“科学学”的组稿思路

本书的主编团队来自上海市科学学研究所。科学学，对于非中文读者来说，可能是一个比较难理解的名词。实际上，对于中文读者，它也是个比较少见的名词。这个单位是中国独特科技发展背景下的产物。上海市科学学研究所成立于 1980 年 1 月，是中国最早成立的科技创新智库之一。40 多年前，在中国改革开放伊始，科学技术刚刚被重新重视。

success of this strategy. In 2019, Shanghai was selected as the National New-Generation AI Innovation and Development Pilot Zone, which emphasized its pioneering role in exploring issues related to AI governance and ethics as well as developing innovative AI solutions. By including Chinese professionals from scientists to experts in humanities and social sciences, at both national and local levels, and from policy, academic, and industry communities, this book hopes to truly reflect China's various perspectives on and explorations of AI.

A Compilation Line Based on the "Science of Science"

The editorial team-in-chief of this book comes from Shanghai Institute for Science of Science (SISS). For non-Chinese readers, "science of science" may be an indigestible phrase. In fact, it is an uncommon one even for Chinese readers. Shanghai Institute for Science of Science emerged from China's unique context of scientific and technological development. Established in January 1980, SISS is one of China's earliest science and technology innovation think tanks. More than 40 years ago, at the beginning of China's reform and opening-up, the value of science and technology was just beginning to be recognized again. At that time, however, what the development patterns for science and technology and how they influenced the economy and society were major challenges of great urgency. The founders of SISS strongly urged study on the "science of science"–the science of studying science, to study the scientific laws. As the foundation of Shanghai Institute for Science of Science coincided with the "Third Wave" at the forefront of discussions in Western countries, the researchers swiftly translated the introduction, organized discussions, and presented views and proposals to relevant government departments. The results of their research greatly influenced China's national and Shanghai's local science and technology strategies.

Today, over 40 years later, China's science and technology strengths have been globally recognized. China's decision makers and researchers have already realized that there is a development pattern of science and technology and that China has been embracing strategic science and technology policies based on the awareness of science and technology laws for a long time. Despite the evolving era, however, we are still facing increasingly complex and intractable issues in the "science of science". In recent years, big data, the Internet, the Fourth Industrial Revolution, and emerging technologies such as AI have seen developments day by day, exerting profound, and even transformative influence in numerous areas, including on the economy, society, culture, ideology, and international relations.

但是，科学技术有着怎样的发展规律、对经济社会有着怎样的影响，在当时还是一个亟待解决的巨大难题。科学学所的创始团队，考虑到当时中国各界对科学的认知程度，大力倡导研究“科学学”——研究科学的科学，实际上就是研究科学规律的一门学问。在科学学所刚成立时，正遇上西方国家热议的“第三次浪潮”，研究人员迅速翻译介绍、组织讨论，并给政府部门建言献策。他们当时的研究成果深刻影响了中国国家层面和上海地方层面的科技战略。

40 余年后的今天，中国科学技术的实力举世瞩目。中国的决策者和研究者早已认识到科技发展是有规律的;中国的科技战略政策早已建立在对科技规律认识的基础上。但是，时代在发展，科学学问题依然存在，甚至更加复杂、更加棘手。近些年来，大数据、“互联网 +”、第四次工业革命以及人工智能等各种新兴技术日新月异，对经济社会乃至文化思想、国际关系等诸多方面带来深远的，甚至是重塑性的影响。

这些新的科技发展对科学学的研究提出了更高的要求，而人工智能议题就是当前科学学研究必须回应的问题之一。

见证全球人工智能治理体系的孕育形成

通读全球 60 余位专家对于人工智能治理进展的判断，作为主编，我们最大的感受是：在 2019 年和 2020 年这两个年份所代表的时代背景中，全球人工智能治理体系正在孕育形成——在技术领域，联邦学习等技术手段正在发展；在人文社科领域，关于人工智能治理的评估手段正在探索；在产业界，公司的人工智能治理制度正在形成；在众多国家和地区，人工智能治理原则正在被提出；在国际组织中，人工智能治理的全球协议正在赢得共识。而且，一个显著的趋势是，人工智能治理正在从原则走向实践。

当然，全球人工智能治理体系孕育形成的时代背景还有其特殊性：新冠肺炎疫情的暴发，让全球经济社会按下了“暂停键”。但是疫情下的全球人工智能治理并不是停滞不前的。疫情的特殊场景让各相关方，在部署人工智能应用时，更加认真思考人工智能对于整个社会的影响；在制定人工智能治理制度时，更加认真反思这些制度能否真的落地生效。

必须要说明的是，人工智能治理是一个全球性的议题，即使有几十位专家的参与，本书

The new developments of science and technology make higher demands of studying the science of science, and AI is currently one of the issues we must respond to within this field.

Being a Witness to the Formation of the Global AI Governance System

The deepest impression we editors in chief have gained from the experts' judgments about the advancements in AI governance is that the years 2019 and 2020 have been pivotal in shaping the premises of a global AI governance system. In terms of technology, AI techniques such as federated learning are developing; in terms of humanities and social sciences, evaluation criteria for AI governance are under exploration; in the industry, corporate AI governance and ethics processes are taking shape; in many countries and regions, AI governance principles are being proposed; and in international organizations, the global agreement on AI governance is gaining consensus. AI governance is unmistakably moving from principles to practice.

Certainly, there has also been a unique background against which the global AI governance system has been built: the outbreak of the COVID-19 pandemic. While the pandemic pushed the "pause button" for global economic and social development, global AI governance has not been stalled by the pandemic. On the contrary, the digital solutions developed during the pandemic have been making relevant parties consider more carefully the overall social impact of AI when deploying AI applications, and thinking more seriously about the effectiveness of AI governance systems at their development.

We must point out that AI governance is a global issue, which means it is impossible for this book to cover all important advancements even with the participation of dozens of experts. We hope that this book can be a basis triggering more discussions about the advancements in AI governance.

As the late Alan Turing said, "We can only see a short distance ahead, but we can see plenty there that needs to be done." It is our sincere hope that this book can serve as a launchpad for this consequential conversation of our generation and make a modest contribution to the new and important advancements in AI governance. Together, we can achieve more.

也不可能涵盖所有的重要进展。我们希望以本书为基础，引发大家关于人工智能治理进展更多的讨论。

正如已故的艾伦·图灵 (Alan Turing) 所说：“我们只能看到前方很短的距离，但我们可以看到有很多事情需要去做。”我们由衷希望，本书的出版能够成为更多对话的起点，为推动人工智能治理新的重要进展贡献一份绵薄之力。全球命题，我们共同解决。

CONTENTS

目录

PART II
INDUSTRIAL FRONTIER AND PROGRESS

PART III
POLICY RESEARCH AND IMPLEMENTATION

ASIA

NORTH AMERICA AND EUROPE

第三部分
政策研究与推进

亚洲

北美洲及欧洲

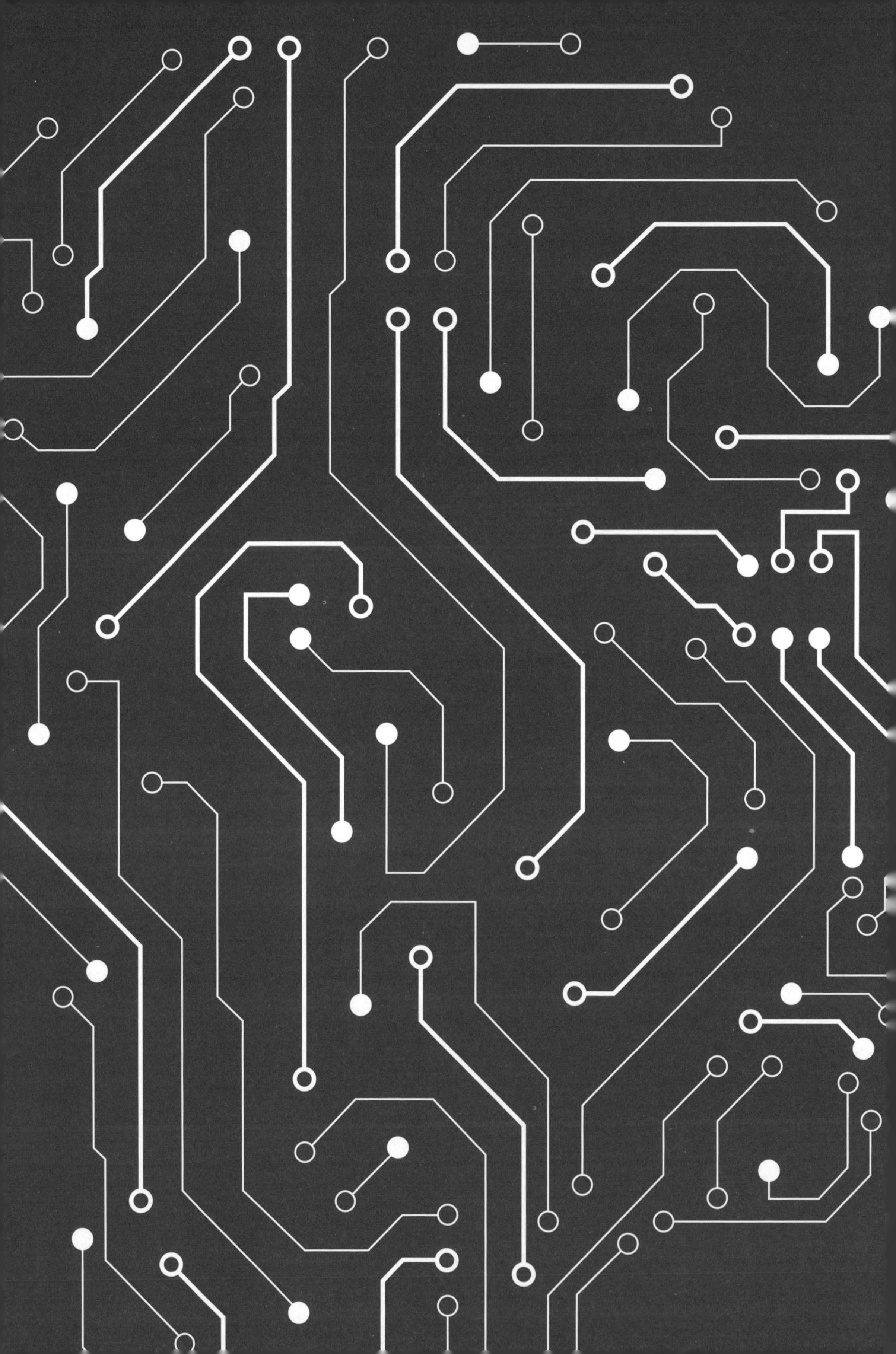

第一部分
PART I

发展趋势与思考
DEVELOPMENTAL TREND AND REFLECTION

人工智能治理是近几年学术研究中的一座“富矿”。科学家探索新的技术路线，人文社会学者探索新的分析框架。在这一部分，有若干位科学家介绍他们对人工智能治理的认识，以及从技术角度针对人工智能带来的问题所进行的探索。此外还有若干位来自哲学、法律、伦理、社会学等领域的专家，介绍他们认为人工智能带来的最需要讨论的社会问题，以及最新的分析框架和进展。

The field of artificial intelligence governance has been a fertile ground for academic research in recent years. Scientists are exploring new technical routes, while humanists and sociologists are seeking to build new analytical frameworks. In Part I, several scientists introduced their knowledge of artificial intelligence governance and explored ways of solving issues arising from artificial intelligence technology. We also invited experts in philosophy, law, ethics, sociology and other related fields to discuss social issues related to artificial intelligence of great concern, who also introduced the latest analytical frameworks and research progress in the field.

01

Issues on AI Governance

John E. HOPCROFT

AI will deliver great benefits and be a significant component of our environment. Oversight is important to ensure both responsible use of AI by organizations and faster economic growth. A number of issues are:

1. Update the legal system

For example, who will be responsible when a driverless vehicle is in an accident? Is it the owner, the manufacturer, or the developer of the AI system? Updating the legal system is important for companies to make investments.

2. Clarify data ownership

When we do a web search, the search company saves all searches by IP address. From this database, one can extract who we are, where we shop, what items we purchase. Looking at all searches from a single IP address also provides information about our gender, our hobbies, and other personal information. Will we allow search companies to sell this information?

3. Fairness

The impact of AI needs to be regulated so that all classes of people benefit, not just the rich and powerful.

4. Eliminating bias

AI systems are trained using data and bias in the data will impact the AI system. For example, if high level jobs are primarily held by men, an AI system is likely to primarily recommend men for high level jobs.

5. Explanability

Many AI system are black boxes and provide answers to queries but no explanation for the answers. If a system turns down an individual for a job, the individual may insist on a reason for the denial. Was it based on his qualifications or some other factors?

6. Face and affect recognition

Face and affect recognition has many important applications but it should not be used for some matters such as racial or ethnic origin, personality traits, or mental health.

关于人工智能治理的思考

约翰·霍普克罗夫特

人工智能（AI）对人类大有裨益，并将成为我们生活中的重要组成部分。监管是为了确保各组织负责任地使用 AI，并使其成为加快经济增长的重要手段。以下七个方面是我们需要考虑的问题：

1. 更新法律制度

   例如，无人驾驶汽车发生事故时，应由谁来负责？是车主、制造商，还是 AI 系统的开发商？特别是对公司而言，法律制度的更新对其投资决策具有重要意义。

2. 明确数据所有权

   我们在进行网络搜索时，搜索引擎公司会按照 IP 地址储存我们搜索的所有关键词。对这一数据库进行分析后，该公司就可以推断出我们的身份、购物地点，以及我们所购买的商品。甚至根据某一个 IP 地址对应的搜索记录，就能判断出我们的性别、爱好和其他个人信息。我们是否同意搜索引擎公司出售这些信息呢？

3. 公平性

   AI 应受到监管，并确保所有阶层的人都能享受其带来的乐趣，而不是只有富人和当权者受益。

4. 消除偏见

   AI 系统是通过数据进行训练的，因此源数据中的偏见会导致 AI 系统存在同样的偏见。例如，如果数据库中高级职位大多为男性，那么 AI 系统可能只会推荐男性作为高级管理者。

5. 可解释性

   许多 AI 系统用的都是黑箱算法，只会根据查询内容提供答案，而不会对答案做出解释。如果一个求职者被面试系统刷下来，他可能会坚持要求得到一个解释。那么他被拒绝到底是因为没有相关资质，还是其他的原因呢？

6. 人脸和情绪识别

   人脸和情绪识别技术有很多重要应用，但不应被用于识别种族或民族血统、人格特质或心理健康状况等。

7. Social network communication

Individuals use companies like Facebook and Twitter to communicate information or disinformation to large numbers of users. This can have a positive or negative impact on a nation. AI may be used to control what is communicated and will require AI governance.

These are a few of the issues that need to be thought about and regulated. Other issues concern safety in human AI interactions, security, ethical situations, etc. One also needs to consider at what level issues should be considered. Which issues are the prerogative of government and which should be developed by industry? The creation of an AI governance policy needs to include government, academy, and industry representatives.

7. **社交网络传播**

人们利用脸书（Facebook）和推特（Twitter）等平台向用户传递大量真实或虚假的信息。随之可能对一个国家产生正面或负面的影响。AI 可以被用于操控信息传播，故治理 AI 极其必要。

这些只是需要考虑和监管的一小部分问题。还有一些问题涉及人机交互的安全性、保障性和伦理困境等。人们还需要考虑应在什么层面上考虑相关问题，哪些问题应由政府负责，哪些问题应该由产业界处理。换言之，AI 治理政策的制定需要政府、学术界和产业界代表的共同参与。

02

Understanding AI for Governance

Bart SELMAN

It is exciting to see the recent significant level of activity around governance for AI. Good AI governance is vital for a proper transition of AI technology into our society. The goal is to keep human interests central and ensure that society truly benefits from AI technology.

In this statement, I would like to highlight a key challenge for developing proper AI governance. Good AI governance requires a deep understanding of both the opportunities as well as the limitations of AI methods. AI systems are starting to match or even exceed human performance on a range of cognitive tasks. However, it is essential to realize that these capabilities are often achieved in ways that are very different from how the human mind handles these tasks. A fundamental difficulty is that when we consider AI technologies, we tend to anthropomorphize the systems. In other words, we assume the systems perform cognitive tasks in a manner similar to ourselves.

Let me give an example. Machine translation based on deep learning approaches has made incredible advances in recent years. Current models provide reasonable translations between dozens of language pairs. However, rather counterintuitively, these translations are obtained without any real understanding of the text that is being translated. It is difficult for us even to imagine that one could translate between two languages without understanding either language. Nevertheless, this is what current language translation systems do–they operate in an almost alien way.

This "alien" mode of operation is also apparent in highly complex deep models trained for all types of data interpretation and decision–making tasks. It may seem reasonable to require the AI system to explain its decisions (i.e., "the right to an explanation"). However, researchers are discovering that attempts to provide explanations can easily lead to pseudo-explanations that may satisfy the human user but do not accurately reflect the system's internal decision-making process.

In general, we are seeing emerging AI systems that operate without the rich context of human knowledge and common sense that we take for granted. So, for example, in case of a medical emergency, we might instruct our self-driving car to ignore some traffic rules to take us as quickly as possible to the nearest hospital. A human driver would realize that this should be done without putting others in danger. However, this is part of our common sense but would need to be explicitly coded into a self-driving vehicle. To develop proper AI governance, we need to consider that AI technology often operates in a manner that is quite foreign to us. Good governance will therefore require close collaboration between AI researchers and policymakers.

二

人工智能治理从理解开始

巴特·塞尔曼

很高兴看到最近 AI 治理活动的水平显著提高。有效的 AI 治理对于 AI 技术在社会中的良好应用至关重要。AI 治理的目标是以保障人类利益为核心，确保 AI 技术能真正造福社会。

在本篇报告中，我将重点强调实现有效 AI 治理的关键挑战。良好的 AI 治理需要我们深入理解 AI 方法所带来的机遇及其局限性。在一系列认知型任务方面，AI 系统的表现正逐渐赶上甚至超过人类。然而，我们必须意识到，AI 系统获得这种能力的方式与人脑处理这类任务的方式大不相同。其中根本性的困境是，我们在考虑 AI 技术时，倾向于赋予这些系统人格化的特征。换言之，我们会假设 AI 系统执行认知型任务时采用的方法与人类类似。

基于深度学习方法的机器翻译近年来取得了长足的进步。当前的模型能在数十个语言之间进行合理、有效的翻译。令人惊讶的是，这些译文并非是在真正理解原文的基础上所获得的。我们甚至很难想象在未理解语言的前提下如何翻译两种语言。但这就是语言翻译系统的现状——以一种近乎陌生的方式运作。

在为各类数据阐释与决策任务训练的高度复杂的深度模型中，这种“陌生的”运作方式也十分明显。要求 AI 系统对其决策做出解释（即“有权获得解释”）似乎并无不妥。然而，研究人员发现，这类提供解释的尝试容易导致伪解释，即让使用者自身满意，却并未准确体现系统的内部决策流程。

总体而言，未掌握人类视为理所当然的知识和常识的新兴 AI 系统正在不断涌现。有鉴于此，以紧急医疗情形为例，我们可以指示自动驾驶汽车忽视某些交通规则，将我们尽快送往最近的医院，人类驾驶员能够意识到这种做法应以不会给他人带来危险为前提，这在人类的眼中是一项常识，却需要明确编写进自动驾驶汽车的代码中。为了实现合理有效的 AI 治理，我们需要注意，人类对于 AI 技术的运作方式往往是极为陌生的。因此，有效的 AI 治理需要 AI 研究人员与政策制定者的紧密合作才能实现。

03

From the Standard Model of AI to Provably Beneficial Systems

Stuart RUSSELL, Caroline JEANMAIRE

AI governance has made notable progress in the last few years. Important sets of principles have been published, notably the Asilomar Principles, the Beijing AI Principles, and the OECD Principles on AI. These focus particular attention on ensuring the robustness of AI systems in the short and long terms, an essential aspect of AI development.

Principles are a prelude for action; indeed, we have also seen instances of concrete action. In 2019, California became the first state to require all automated online accounts attempting to influence residents' voting or purchasing behaviors to openly identify as robots. This law is an important first step towards curbing deceptive new technology and making AI systems trustworthy; it is a step towards establishing a basic human right to know whether one is interacting with another human or with a machine. It will hinder the spread of misinformation. We hope this law will develop beyond commercial and voting issues to become a general right and serve as a precedent for other states and countries.

In 2019, AI regulatory frameworks have finally begun to emerge, advancing beyond mere "AI Principles." The proposed EU AI Act, currently nearing its final enacted form, replicates and broadens the California law that bans the impersonation of humans. It also considers risks to mental integrity from high-risk AI systems, potentially opening up social media and related systems to strong regulation. While those proposed changes are welcome, the Act does not address the risks of increasingly generalized AI systems that have multiple purposes, such as OpenAI's Generative Pre-trained Transformer 3 or Google's BERT. Regulators on both sides of the Atlantic have yet to verify risk assessment criteria and risk management strategies for those increasingly powerful systems. Processes to monitor and reassess technology for the appearance of "unknown unknowns" still need to be developed. Over 150 experts have signed the "Foresight in AI Regulation Open Letter" to the European Commission urging them to keep and strengthen the proposed regulation even though some groups may downplay potential risks related to AI.

In some areas, however, governance lags dangerously behind. There has been little progress in regulating Lethal Autonomous Weapons Systems (LAWS) such as autonomous (not human-piloted) drones and tanks. These technologies are designed to locate, select, and attack targets without human control. At the November 2019 meeting of member states of the Convention on Certain Conventional Weapons (CCW) at the United Nations in Geneva, diplomats could not

三

开发有益的人工智能系统

斯图尔特·拉塞尔，林晨力

近年来，人工智能治理进展显著。一系列重要的人工智能治理原则相继发布，其中尤以《阿西洛马人工智能原则》（Asilomar Principles）、《人工智能北京共识》（Beijing AI Principles）和《经合组织人工智能原则》（OECD Principles on AI）最为重要。以上原则都格外注重确保人工智能系统的短期和长期鲁棒性，而这也是人工智能发展的一个重要方面。

原则是行动的基础，现实中也确有一些具体行动的实例。2019 年，美国加利福尼亚州率先颁布法律，要求将所有试图影响加州居民投票或购买行为的自动在线账户公开标识为机器人。这项法律的颁布标志着我们在遏制新的欺骗技术，在确保人工智能系统可信度的进程上迈出了重要的第一步。同时，它也有助于我们了解一个人是在与另一个人还是一台机器互动，而这也是一项重要的基本人权。此外，该项法律还将阻止错误信息的传播。我们希望这项法律不仅仅局限于解决商业和投票问题，而是成为维护一般权利的利器，并为其他州和国家做出榜样。

2019 年，人工智能监管框架终于开始陆续出现，超越了单纯的“人工智能原则”。目前，欧盟提出的《人工智能法》（AI Act）的修订工作已接近尾声，该法案重申并拓展了加州法律中的内容，严禁人工智能模仿人类。同时，该法案还考虑到了高风险人工智能系统对精神健康的威胁，可能对社交媒体和相关系统施以严格的监管措施。虽然人们乐于看到上述变化，但该法案并不涉及解决日益普及的多用途人工智能系统（如 OpenAI 的生成预训练转换器 3 和谷歌的 BERT）带来的风险。大西洋两岸的监管机构尚未确定针对日益强大的人工智能系统的风险评估标准和风险管理策略。他们仍需制订相应的技术监督与再评估流程，以应对“无知而不自知”的情况。截至目前，已有超过 150 位专家在“人工智能监管展望公开信”上签名，力劝欧盟委员会不要听信一些可能对人工智能的相关潜在风险有所低估的团体的建议，而是应该继续实施并强化拟定的法规。

然而，在某些领域，人工智能治理工作严重滞后，带来了一些风险。例如，我们在管制（无需人类驾驶的）无人机和坦克等致命性自主武器系统（LAWS）方面进展甚微。此类技术可自动锁定、选择和攻击目标，而无需人类控制。2019 年 11 月，联合国在日内瓦举行《特定常规武器公约》

agree on a binding common approach towards this issue. In 2021, a proposal was developed that bans only weapons "designed to operate outside of any framework of human command and control"–a meaningless and empty category from the point of view of any plausible weapon design.

As we develop increasingly capable AI systems that become highly competent and self-sustaining, humans must ensure these systems remain beneficial and safe. Russell, one of the co-authors of this article, published a book on this topic in 2019: *Human Compatible: Artificial Intelligence and the Problem of Control* [1]. The problem of control over AI systems is not about the science fiction plot that preoccupies Hollywood and the media, wherein a humanoid robot spontaneously becomes conscious and decides to hate humans. Rather, it concerns the creation of machines that can draw on more information and look further into the future than humans can, exceeding our capacity for decision–making in the real world. With our present conception of AI and our technical approach, there is no plausible prospect of retaining control over machines more powerful than ourselves. To solve this problem, the research community needs to undertake a vast effort to shift the standard model in AI towards provably beneficial systems. The AI community is becoming aware of this issue, which makes us hopeful we will be able to achieve this transformation, but there is much work to do.

缔约国会议，但各国外交官未能在会上就这一问题达成具有约束力的共识。2021 年，有提案提出只禁用“可脱离任何人类指挥和控制框架运行”的武器，但就武器设计的合理性与可靠性而言，这一划分标准可谓不切实际且毫无意义。

随着功能日益强大、具有高度自我维持能力的人工智能系统的发展，人类必须确保这些系统始终安全且对人类有益。2019 年，本文作者之一拉塞尔围绕这一主题出版了《人类兼容：人工智能与控制问题》[1]（*Human Compatible: Artificial Intelligence and the Problem of Control*）一书。人工智能系统的控制问题并非是好莱坞和媒体一直关注的科幻故事情节：一个人形机器人实现了自我意识的觉醒，并决定憎恨人类。更确切地说，它是一个机器创造问题，即这些被创造出来的机器能比人类获取更多的信息，能看到更长远的未来，在现实世界中拥有比人类更强的决策能力。按照目前的人工智能概念和技术方法，我们不太可能继续控制比我们更强大的机器。为解决这一问题，科研界需要付出巨大的努力，以改变人工智能的标准模型，使其朝着对人类有益的方向发展。如今，人工智能界也开始意识到这一问题，这在一定程度上为我们实现上述转变增添了信心，但我们仍然任重而道远。

1. Russell, S. (2019). *Human Compatible: Artificial Intelligence and the Problem of Control*. Viking/Penguin.

04

The Importance of Federated Learning

YANG QIANG

As AI has moved out of the laboratory and into large-scale application, its potential ethical problems and impacts have gradually aroused public concern. In 2019, public discussions related to AI ethics focused on the protection and governance of user data privacy. Internationally, Facebook was fined $5 billion by the US Federal Trade Commission (FTC) for illegally leaking user data. Additionally, Google was fined tens of millions of euros by French regulators for breaching the GDPR because it made its privacy terms too complex for users to understand and too difficult for users to manage the ways their personal data were used. In China, data companies have been intensively investigated by regulators for the abuse and unauthorized sale of users' privacy data. A large number of data companies have been penalized with business suspensions, app removals and even criminal liabilities for serious cases. This series of events shows that, on the one hand, the public's awareness of the data rights related to personal privacy is gradually increasing, so these events have attracted wide attention in the media and the public. On the other hand, the shocking truths of these incidents indicate that the protection and governance of private data are seriously lagging if not missing.

When we trace these problems to their source, we see that they are caused by the objective incentives upon which AI technology heavily relies, requiring massive data collection. More important is the neglect of social responsibility and the subjective reckless behaviors of relevant stakeholders. Determining the knowledge and value of the data based on the premise of fully respecting and protecting user data privacy is an imminent challenge facing AI researchers.

Fortunately, 2019 also witnessed AI researchers realizing the seriousness of the problem and developing a set of solutions. Among them, federated learning, as a promising user data privacy protection scheme, has demonstrated unique advantages in promoting the implementation of industrial applications. Federated learning refers to a technical scheme of realizing the joint modeling of multiple participants by exchanging encryption parameters on the premise that the data are not out of the locality and are not shared. Its modeling effect is the same as, or not much different from, that of the aggregation modeling of an entire dataset. A variety of encryption techniques are used in the federated learning technology framework, such as secure multiparty computing, homomorphic encryption (HE), Yao's garbled circuit and differential privacy (DP). From the perspective of technology applications, currently, federated learning is being applied in fields such as small- and micro-enterprise credit, anti-money laundering, anti-fraud, insurance, and computer vision. In addition, it has been explored for application in fields such as smart medical treatment, autonomous driving, smart cities, and governance. In summary, federated learning can be regarded as an integrator of machine-learning and privacy protection technologies and as a universal privacy protection machine-learning technology with wide application prospects.

四

联邦学习的重要性

杨强

随着人工智能走出实验室，实现大规模应用，其潜在的伦理问题及影响逐渐引起公众的关注。回顾 2019 年，与人工智能伦理相关的公众讨论，集中体现在对用户数据隐私的保护及治理问题上。国际上，脸书因为非法泄露用户数据，而被美国联邦贸易委员会（FTC）处以 50 亿美元的罚款。谷歌因为其隐私条款难以被用户理解，使得用户难以管理个人资料被使用的方式，违反了《通用数据保护条例》（GDPR），而被法国监管机构开出数千万欧元的罚单。而在中国，数据公司因为滥用、售卖未经授权的用户隐私数据，被监管机构密集调查，大量数据公司受到停业、下架 APP 等处罚，情节严重者甚至面临刑事责任。这一系列的事件表明：一方面，公众对个人隐私相关的数据权利意识逐渐增强，而这些事件才在媒体和公众中引起广泛关注；另一方面，触目惊心的事件真相也表明，私人数据的保护和治理存在严重滞后和缺失。

追根溯源，这些问题的产生，虽有人工智能技术严重依赖于海量数据收集的客观诱因，但主要是相关利益方忽视社会责任，主观上肆意妄为导致的。如何在充分尊重和保护用户数据隐私的前提下，去挖掘数据背后的知识和价值，是人工智能研究者面临的一个迫在眉睫的挑战。

幸运的是，在 2019 年，我们看到人工智能研究者已经意识到问题的严重性并着手提出了一系列解决方案。其中，联邦学习作为一种大有希望的用户数据隐私保护方案，展示了其在推进产业应用落地上的独特优点。联邦学习是指在数据不出本地、数据不共享的前提下，通过交换加密参数，实现多个参与方联合建模的一种技术方案。联邦学习的建模效果与将整个数据集聚合建模的效果相同，或相差不大。联邦学习的技术框架用到了多种加密技术，如安全多方计算、同态加密（Homomorphic encryption）、姚式混淆电路和差分隐私（Differential privacy）等。从技术应用的角度看，目前联邦学习已经在小微企业信贷、反洗钱、反欺诈、保险、计算机视觉等领域落地应用。此外还在智慧医疗、自动驾驶、智慧城市、政府治理等领域有所探索。综上所述，联邦学习可以看作是机器学习技术与隐私保护技术的集大成者，并且是一种拥有广泛应用前景的通用型隐私保护机器学习技术。

05

Ungovernability of AI

Roman V. YAMPOLSKIY

In order to make future AIs beneficial for all of humanity, AI governance initiatives attempt to make AI governable by the world's governments, international organization and multinational corporations collaborating on establishing a regulatory framework and industry standards. However, direct governance of AI is not meaningful, and what is implied by the term is governance of AI researchers and creators in terms of what products and services they are permitted to develop and how. Whether it is possible to govern scientists and engineers working on AI depends on the difficulty of creating Artificial General Intelligence (AGI).

If computational resources and data collection efforts necessary to create AGI are comparable in cost and human capital to the Manhattan project conducted by USA to develop nuclear bomb technology, governments have a number of "carrots" and "sticks" they can use to guide researchers and to mold the future AI to their specifications. On the other hand, if it turns out that there is a much more efficient way to create the first AGI or a "seed" AI which can grow into a full-blown superintelligence, for example, by a teenager on a $1,000 laptop in their garage (an admittedly less likely, but nevertheless possible scenario), governments' attempts at regulation may be futile. We note that historical attempts at software governance (ex. spam, computer viruses, deep fakes) had only a very limited amount of success. With AGI as an independent agent, it may be ungovernable because traditional methods of assigning responsibility and punishment-based enforcement are not applicable to software.

Even presuming a, resource-heavy, favorable case for governance, we are still left with a number of established technical limits to AI predictability[1], explainability[2], and controllability[3]. It follows that AI governability, which requires, at least, those three capabilities for successful regulation is likewise only partially achievable, meaning smarter than human AI would be ungovernable by us in some important ways. Finally, even where AI governance is achievable, those in charge may be unwilling to take personal responsibility for AI's failures[4], or deliberate actions even if performed in the context of instituted governance framework. Consequently, a highly capable, creative and uncontrolled AGI may end up implicitly or even explicitly controlling some of the institutions and individuals, which we entrusted to govern such intelligent software.

五

人工智能的不可治理性

罗曼·亚姆波尔斯基

为了使未来的人工智能造福于全人类，人工智能治理倡议试图推进世界各国政府、国际组织和跨国公司间开展合作，以建立监管框架和行业标准，对人工智能进行治理。然而，对人工智能的直接治理是没有意义的，人工智能治理这个词所暗示的是对人工智能研究人员和创造者的治理，即对他们可以开发的产品和服务以及相关的方法进行管理。能否对从事人工智能研究的科学家和工程师实施管理取决于创建通用人工智能（AGI）的难度。

如果创建 AGI 所需的计算资源和数据收集工作在成本和人力资本方面与美国致力于开发核弹技术的曼哈顿计划相当，那么各国政府可以采取诸多软硬兼施的策略指导研究人员，并按照自己的标准塑造未来的人工智能。另一方面，如果事实证明有一种更有效的方法来创建第一个 AGI 或“种子”人工智能，该人工智能可由多种途径成长为一个全面的超级智能，例如，一名青少年在车库里用一台价值 1000 美元的笔记本电脑就可达成这一目的（可能性较低，但并非为零），那么政府所进行的监管尝试将可能是徒劳的。我们注意到，历史上在软件治理方面所做的尝试（例如垃圾邮件、计算机病毒、深度伪造）只取得了非常有限的成效。仅仅依靠 AGI 是无法实现治理的，因为传统的责任分配方法和基于惩罚的执行方法并不适用于软件。

即使假定一个资源丰富、有利的治理案例，我们仍在人工智能的预测力[1]、解释力[2]和控制力[3]方面面临一些既定的技术限制。因此，为实现人工智能的治理，我们至少需要这三种能力以确保成功监管，且同样也只能部分实现，这意味着比人类更聪明的人工智能在某些重要方面是我们无法治理的。最后，即使人工智能治理是可以实现的，那些负责人也可能不愿意为其失败承担个人责任[4]，即便是在既定治理框架的背景下执行经过深思熟虑的举措。由此会出现一个具有出色能力和创造力但不受控制的 AGI，最终可能会以隐性甚至显性的方式控制一些被我们委托以管理这些智能软件的机构和个人。

1. Yampolskiy, R. V. (2020). Unpredictability of AI: On the Impossibility of Accurately Predicting All Actions of a Smarter Agent. *Journal of Artificial Intelligence and Consciousness*, 7(01), 109-118.
2. Yampolskiy, R. V. (2020). Unexplainability and Incomprehensibility of AI. *Journal of Artificial Intelligence and Consciousness*, 7(02), 277-291.
3. Yampolskiy, R. V. (2020). On Controllability of AI. arXiv preprint arXiv:2008.04071.
4. Yampolskiy, R. V. (2019). Predicting Future AI Failures from Historic Examples. *Foresight*. 21(1), 138-152.

06

Emerging Institutions for AI Governance

Allan DAFOE, Alexis CARLIER

Much AI governance work involves preparation for a constitutional moment: an opportunity to create long-lasting, decision-shaping, institutions. Doing this well is a formidable task. It requires a fine balance. Institutions must constrain our actions today, yet preserve the freedom to adjust as circumstances change and our wisdom grows. Despite this difficulty, decisions must be made–and in 2020, multiple noteworthy institutions emerged. The research community has an opportunity to inform such decisions.

NeurIPS, one of the leading AI conferences, required that all paper submissions include a statement of the "potential broader impact of their work, including its ethical aspects and future societal consequences." For the 2021 conference, this has been changed to a "Checklist" in response to feedback from researchers, reflecting the value of the AI community engaging with governance initiatives. At the Centre for the Governance of AI (GovAI), we produced an (unofficial) guide to writing the NeurIPS impact statement. In a *Nature* Machine Intelligence paper, "Institutionalizing Ethics in AI through Broader Impact Requirements," we investigate the challenges and opportunities of such an initiative. Former GovAI affiliate Carolyn Ashurst ran a NeurIPS workshop examining how potential harmful impacts should affect the research community; GovAI founder Allan Dafoe, one of the co-authors of this article, discussed the requirement on a plenary panel at EMNLP, a top natural language processing conference.

Facebook's independent Oversight board began its work. The board's decisions are meant to be binding, acting as a "Supreme Court" for Facebook's content moderation. This is a commendable initiative, a rare case of a technology company (voluntarily) exposing itself to external constraints so as to improve technology governance. Researchers can support this endeavor by developing expertise to evaluate and advise the board, while the wider community–the public, media, non-profits, Facebook employees–can help hold the board and company accountable to their promising intentions.

The Partnership on AI created the "AI and Shared Prosperity Initiative," encouraging private AI actors to commit to an inclusive economic future. GovAI wrote the report which helped catalyze the initiative: "The Windfall Clause: Distributing the Benefits of AI," which proposes a policy instrument to lessen AI-induced inequality. Lead author and former GovAI researcher Cullen O'Keefe (now at OpenAI) is a member of the initiative's research group, and GovAI affiliate Anton Korinek serves on the Steering Committee.

六

新兴人工智能治理制度

艾伦·达福，亚历克西斯·卡利尔

许多AI治理工作都为迎接一个立宪时刻做准备,那就是一个建立持久有效的决策机制的机会。这并非易事，需要取得精妙的平衡。这种制度必须对我们目前的行动加以限制，但同时还需留有空间，以随形势变化和我们智慧的增加而进行调整。尽管有着上述困难，我们仍必须对此做出决定，况且在 2020 年出台了多个值得关注的制度。研究界现在也迎来了公布这些决定的机会。

作为国际人工智能顶级会议，神经信息处理系统大会（NeurIPS）要求所有论文提交需包含关于“其工作潜在的广泛影响，包括道德方面和未来社会后果”的声明。在 2021 年的会议上，结合研究人员的反馈，这项要求已被改为“检查清单”，反映出人工智能社区参与治理举措的价值。在 AI 治理中心（GovAI），我们编写了一份关于如何撰写 NeurIPS 影响说明的（非官方）指南。在即将发表于最新一期《自然》（*Nature*）期刊“机器智能”（Machine Intelligence）专辑上的论文《通过更广泛的影响要求实现 AI 伦理的制度化》(“Institutionalizing Ethics in AI through Broader Impact Requirements”)中，我们调查了此类举措所面临的挑战和机遇。前 GovAI 成员卡罗琳·阿瑟斯特（Carolyn Ashurst）举办了一场 NeurIPS 研讨会，研究潜在的有害影响对研究界造成的必然影响；GovAI 创始人艾伦·达福（Allan Dafoe）（本文的合著者之一）在自然语言处理国际峰会 EMNLP 的全体会议上就这一要求进行了讨论。

脸书的独立监督委员会也开始了运作。作为脸书内容审核的“最高法院”，委员会的决定是有约束力的。这是一项值得称赞的举措，是一家技术公司为改善技术治理（自愿）受外部约束条件控制的罕见个例。研究人员可以通过增进自身的专业知识对委员会进行评估并提供建议，从而为这项举措提供支持，更广泛的群体（公众、媒体、非营利组织、脸书员工）则可以帮助监督委员会和公司的相关责任的落实。

人工智能合作组织（Partnership on AI）创立了“AI 与共享繁荣倡议”，鼓励私有 AI 机构致力于构建一个拥有包容性经济的未来。GovAI 为推动该倡议撰写了报告《意外收获条款：AI 收益分配》(“The Windfall Clause: Distributing the Benefits of AI”)，提出了减少 AI

06

The aforementioned institutions are designed by humans, but AI systems could also help with governance. Bringing this about is one ambition of "Cooperative AI," a field recently outlined by Allan Dafoe, Thore Graepel, and other colleagues, in their paper "Open Problems in Cooperative AI" and associated *Nature* Commentary and NeurIPS workshop. We see an opportunity for the field of AI to explicitly focus on cooperation; and since institutions are central to cooperation, a promising avenue for Cooperative AI research is institutional design. Humans could determine an institution's goals, while AI systems serve as design tools and infrastructure for building new innovative institutions. We are excited to work together on these challenges with our colleagues in the AI governance community.

引起的不平等问题的政策工具。该报告的第一作者兼前 GovAI 研究人员卡伦·欧基夫（Cullen O' Keefe，现为 OpenAI 的研究科学家）是该倡议研究小组的一员，隶属 GovAI 的安东·科里内克（Anton Korinek）则担任指导委员。

上述制度均由人类设计，然而人工智能也能协助治理。实现这一目标是“协作式 AI”的宏愿之一，协作式 AI 是最近由艾伦·达福、托尔·格雷佩尔（Thore Graepel）等其他同仁在其论文《协作式 AI 尚待解决的问题》（“Open Problems in Cooperative AI”）和相关的《自然》评论及 NeurIPS 研讨会中提出的一个新领域。我们看到该领域在当下可以更专注于合作，并且由于制度是合作的中心所在，因此制度化设计是具有前景的协作式 AI 研究方式之一。人类可以确定制度的目标，而 AI 系统则可用作设计工具和基础框架，为新的创新机制的建立提供支持。我们很高兴能与 AI 治理界的各位同仁携手合作，共同应对这些挑战。

07

China's Initiatives: Applying Long-Term, Multidisciplinary Social Experiments to Explore the Social Impact of Artificial Intelligence

SU Jun

The "people-oriented" principle is the consistent aim of China in developing AI and other emerging technologies. The Chinese government and academia are highly concerned about the impact of AI on human society and are exploring AI social governance schemes to advance AI technologies that better serve the well-being of human beings. Encouragingly, China has taken a leading step in AI governance by conducting social experiments to explore its social impacts.

As the irreplaceable driving force of the S&T revolution, the opportunities and challenges resulting from AI have been widely recognized. The consensus has also been well established to remain vigilant in the face of the threats and risks of uncontrollable technological developments and severe social inequity.

In response to these challenges, we are supposed to not only advocate a responsible R&D and innovation value system but also strengthen the focus on ethical issues in the process of scientific and technological innovation. We should especially return to "humanism" and reinforce the research on social impact mechanisms, laws and trends and improve the social policy system for AI development from the perspective of the humanities and social sciences. Achieving effective AI governance requires a systematic knowledge and accurate understanding of the social formation and characteristics of the AI era. Establishing this recognition depends on the application of empirical research, especially the development of social experimental research.

Social experiments are a classic social science research method. They aim to observe people and organizations as the social, political or technological environment changes. These changes simulate the ideal experimental environment and permit the proposal and attestation of social science theories. Facing the new problems of social governance in the intelligence era, the Chinese government, academia and various sectors of society have committed to formulating, promoting and applying AI social experimental solutions in multiple arenas, including academic research, policy practice, and social impact.

七

中国倡议：采用长周期、多学科的社会实验方法研究人工智能的社会影响

苏竣

“以人为本”是中国发展人工智能等新兴技术的一贯宗旨。中国政府高层和学术界高度关注人工智能给人类社会带来的影响，努力探索人工智能社会治理方案，推动人工智能技术进步更好地服务于人类福祉。令人欣喜的是，2019 年，中国启动了利用社会实验方法研究人工智能社会影响的举措，在人工智能治理上迈出了领先的一步。

人工智能作为新一轮科技革命的重要驱动力量，全世界已经深刻认识到其技术发展与应用给人类社会带来的机遇与挑战。对人工智能所衍生出的技术失控、社会两极分化加剧等风险和威胁保持警惕，已成为大家的共识。

针对人工智能技术的风险与挑战，我们不仅需要积极倡导建立负责任的研发和创新价值体系，加强对科技创新过程中伦理问题的关注和控制，更应当回归“人文主义”，从人文社会科学的角度，加强对人工智能社会影响机理、规律与趋势的研究，完善和强化人工智能发展的社会政策体系。实现对人工智能的有效治理，需要我们对人工智能时代的社会形态和特征具有全面而系统的认知和把握。而这种认知的建立，有赖于以实践证据为基础的实证研究，特别是社会实验研究的开展。

社会实验是一种经典的社会科学研究方法，是以现实情境下的人、组织作为研究对象而开展的研究活动，目的在于通过一些社会、政治过程或技术变革导致的近似于理想实验的场景来研究社会科学的问题。面对智能化时代社会治理的新问题，中国学术界、政府、社会各界共同从社会实验实践的角度入手，致力于从学术研究、政策实践、社会影响等多个维度推动人工智能社会实验方案的形成、完善与落地。

2019 年，清华大学、浙江大学等单位的专家学者，在大量前期工作的基础上，针对人工智能社

07

In 2019, experts and scholars from Tsinghua University, Zhejiang University and other institutes combined their intellectual resources and took the lead in making policy suggestions to conduct long-term, wide-field, multidisciplinary AI social experiments based on abundant preliminary work.

Based on achievements from academic research, China's policy practices are rapidly taking shape and continually developing. In 2019, the Ministry of Science and Technology of China issued Guidelines for the Construction of the National New-generation Artificial Intelligence Innovation Development Pilot Area, which indicated that AI social experiments were being conducted nationwide. The guidelines propose different application scenarios–such as education, transportation, government administration, medical care, environmental protection, manufacturing, finance, and agriculture–and suggest the comprehensive objectives of social experiments, such as social risk prevention, organizational reinvention, data security, and technological adaptation.

Chinese society is reaching a consensus on the social governance of AI, and public support is increasing for social experimental schemes. In October 2019, the First National Conference on Artificial Intelligence Social Experiments was held at Tsinghua University in China. More than 100 experts and scholars exchanged and shared the latest research results of AI social experiments and discussed further research plans. *Guangming Daily* and other mainstream media have published articles such as "Exploring the Chinese Solution to the Social Governance of Artificial Intelligence," which has earned wide acclaim from all areas of society. The public foundation and social influence of AI social experiments are steadily increasing.

Evaluating China's initiatives and achievements in the social governance of AI, we have gained clarity that conducting AI social experiments could help us accurately identify the challenges and impacts of AI on human society, deeply understand the social characteristics and trends of AI and provide a scientific reference for the establishment of a humanistic intellectualized society.

会影响的问题，率先提出了开展长周期、宽领域、多学科人工智能社会实验的政策建议。

基于学术研究成果，中国的政策实践正在迅速形成、不断落实。2019 年，中国科技部组织制定了《中国新一代人工智能创新发展试验区建设工作指引》，将社会实验作为新一代人工智能创新发展试验区建设的重要工作，从教育、交通、政府、医疗、环保、制造、金融、农业等多个应用场景入手，从社会风险、组织再造、数据安全、技术适应等多个维度出发，在全国开展人工智能社会治理实验。

同时，中国社会对于人工智能社会治理问题的共识正在逐渐形成，公众对于社会实验方案的认可与支持也在不断加强。2019 年 10 月，第一届全国人工智能社会实验学术会议在清华大学召开，100 余名专家学者交流分享了人工智能社会实验的最新成果，研究讨论了人工智能社会实验的工作方案和行动计划。《光明日报》等主流媒体刊发了《探索人工智能社会治理的中国方案》等文章，获得社会各界的广泛赞誉。人工智能社会实验的公众基础与社会影响力与日俱增。

通过中国目前在人工智能社会治理上的举措与收获，我们更加明确，开展人工智能社会实验，有助于准确识别人工智能对人类社会带来的挑战和冲击，深入理解人工智能的社会影响特征与态势，深刻把握人工智能时代社会演进的规律，从而为建立有人文温度的智能社会提供科学的参考依据。

08

Interdisciplinary Approach to AI Governance Research

Petra AHRWEILER

Artificial Intelligence (AI), and especially the ethics of AI in areas of automated decision making, enjoys high priority in national policy strategies of many countries including China and Germany. International cooperation targets a joint research and governance network of a common AI-in-society ecosystem with shared ethical framing.

To improve AI algorithms for automated decision making depends to a large degree on the availability and quality of relevant training data. However, especially for high-risk decision contexts, empirical data is hardly available. Imagine automated decision making in case of an accident in a nuclear power station, a tsunami, or a terror attack in a megacity: Such events are, fortunately, too rare to produce sufficient training data. Furthermore, decision contexts involve people, who behave and interact in largely unpredictable ways according to their respective historical, cultural and social upbringing. Societal frameworks display much variety across the globe thus further restricting the utility of available training data in terms of generalizability and applicability.

Where then to get the models and the training data from to improve algorithms for better AI with a close fit to context-specific norms and values of world societies? This is where expertise of interdisciplinary research institutions such as TISSS Lab or the larger scientific community of the European Social Simulation Association ESSA comes in: for substituting missing empirical data, the innovative suggestion is to generate and exploit artificial data produced by simulations, which computationally represent the social environments AI algorithms have to operate in. In TISSS Lab, technical sciences cooperate with disciplines that are empirically researching, explaining, and anticipating human behaviour and societal developments, such as sociology, psychology, philosophy, law, and other social sciences. Realistically simulating social systems will provide sufficient high-quality training data to improve and validate AI algorithms in automated decision making. The starting international cooperation between Chinese SISS and German TISSS Lab to connect AI and social simulation can significantly further this line of cutting-edge research.

As recently emphasized by the World Artificial Intelligence Conference in Shanghai, cooperation –also transdisciplinary cooperation between science and other areas of society–is key to future progress. Perceptions, attitudes, discussions and acceptance of AI use vary between countries, as do the types and degrees of AI implementation, with reference to norms and values in-use, but also related to technology status, economic models, civil society sentiments, and legislative,

八

用跨学科方法探索人工智能治理研究

佩特拉·阿维勒

人工智能，特别是人工智能在自动化决策领域的伦理问题，在包括中国和德国在内的许多国家的国家政策战略中都受到高度重视。国际合作旨在基于共同的伦理框架，建立起人工智能社会生态系统中的联合研究和治理网络。

针对自动化决策的人工智能算法的改进，很大程度上取决于训练数据的可用性和质量。然而，在高风险决策环境下，很难获得有效的经验数据。想象一下在核电站发生事故、发生海啸或特大城市发生恐怖袭击时的自动决策算法，由于这类事件太少（当然，这是一件幸事），根本无法获得足够的训练数据。此外，个体也是影响自动决策算法的环境因素之一。由于每个人的背景、文化和社会教养不同，很难预测他们的行为和互动方式。因而社会框架在全球范围内表现出多样性，进一步限制了现有训练数据的通用性和适用性。

那么，我们可以从何处获得模型和训练数据以改进算法，使其更适合特定环境的标准规范和国际社会的价值观？这就是跨学科研究机构［如美因兹大学技术与创新社会学 / 社会模拟实验室（TISSS）和欧洲社会模拟协会（ESSA）大型科学社区］的研究内容所在。有一种创新建议是：生成和使用模拟产生的人工数据以弥补缺失的经验数据，而这些人工数据能够代表人工智能算法运行的社会环境。在 TISSS 实验室，技术科学与经验研究，以及解释和预测人类行为与发展的各个学科合作，例如社会学、心理学、哲学、法学和其他社会科学等，通过逼真的模拟社会系统提供足够高质量的训练数据，以改进和验证自动化决策中的人工智能算法。中国的上海市科学学研究所（SISS）与德国 TISSS 实验室开展国际合作，将人工智能与社会模拟结合起来，大大推进了这一前沿研究。

2019 年，在上海举行的世界人工智能大会治理论坛强调，科学与社会其他领域的跨学科合作是未来进步的关键。各国对使用人工智能的看法、态度、讨论和接受程度各不相同，运用人工智能的类型和程度也各不相同。这与各国的价值观及在使用人工智能时制定的规范有关，也与技术状况、经济模式、社会情绪以及立法、行政和司法特点有关。为使未来社会能建立更

executive and judicial characteristics. Building better, i.e. context-sensitive, ethically-acceptable, and socially-informed AI for future societies and realizing the international aspirations of global AI governance require the involvement of non-scientists, i.e. many relevant stakeholders and practitioners from all over the world and from all parts of society, in research. Here, the young partnership between SISS and TISSS Lab has already started to connect to participatory approaches within international funding schemes (e.g. cooperative research project AI FORA funded in the programme "Artificial Intelligence and the Society of the Future" of the German Volkswagen Foundation). Further funding schemes in this direction should be set on the policy agendas to promote progress in AI research and governance.

好的，即环境敏感的、伦理上可接受的、社会上知情的人工智能，并实现全球人工智能治理的国际抱负，需要来自世界各地和社会各阶层的许多利益相关者和实践者的参与。在这一方面，SISS 和 TISSS 实验室之间的新伙伴关系已经开始与国际筹资计划中的参与者相联系（例如，由德国大众基金会“人工智能和未来社会”项目资助的合作研究项目 AI FORA）。未来在这方面也应有更多的政策支持以推进人工智能的治理与研究。

09

Alignment Was a Human Problem First, and Still Is

Brian CHRISTIAN

Over the past decade we saw how deep learning made it possible for networks to perform complex tasks like identifying a face without the need for any manual "feature engineering". Something similar is beginning to happen in this decade with values.

To use a social network like Twitter as an example, instead of manually identifying ratios of comments to shares to likes that constitute "healthy" engagement on the platform, employees can simply identify certain communities as being "healthy" or "unhealthy". The system can then infer which specific metrics predict a healthy community. The platform can then be optimized in a way that promotes "healthy" engagement–potentially without any human ever explicitly defining what metrics, exactly, constitute "healthy" engagement[1].

As with many advances in technological capability, this alleviates one problem while emphasizing another. We end the problem of metrics, but we are left with the problem of judgment. Who, for instance, decides what constitutes "healthy engagement"? Who provides oversight? The engineering problem of specifying one's priorities numerically gives way to the human question of governance.

Etymology is often a surprisingly helpful guide to the present. The use of "alignment" in AI first came from computer scientist Stuart Russell in 2014. But he borrowed the term from the fields of economics and management science, which have been speaking for decades about how values and interests are "aligned" within and between organizations.

As the "alignment problem" between a system's engineers and an AI system they create begins to be "solved", our attention must turn to the larger question of alignment in its original sense: between that team of engineers and their managers, between the managers and the executives, between the executives and the shareholders, between the company as a whole with its regulators and its users.

The etymology reminds us that "alignment" has always been a problem that exists between humans and other humans. As we enter into the age of AI, this will be truer than ever.

九

一致性：人类永存的问题

布莱恩·克里斯蒂安

在过去的十年里，我们见证了深度学习如何使网络能够执行复杂的任务，如在不需要任何手动的“特征工程”的情况下识别人脸。类似的有价值的技术在过去十年间陆续出现。

以推特（Twitter）这样的社交网络为例，其员工无须手动识别平台上“健康”参与的评论、分享和点赞比例，即可简单确定特定社区的“健康”参与情况。然后，系统就可以推断出哪些具体的指标可以预测一个社区的健康度，接着相关人员便能以一种可促进“健康”参与的方式对平台进行优化——这一切都可能在没有任何人明确定义到底是哪些指标构成了“健康”参与的情况下完成[1]。

与许多技术能力的进步一样，这在缓解一个问题的同时又突出了另一个问题。我们解决了指标的问题，但判断的问题依然存在。例如，谁来决定什么是“健康”参与？谁负责监督？相比于用数字指明优先事项的工程问题，相关治理问题在当前更为重要。

在目前的情况下，词源学往往能提供意想不到的帮助。2014 年，计算机科学家斯图尔特·拉塞尔（Stuart Russell）首次在人工智能中使用“一致性”一词，但他是借用了经济学和管理科学领域的术语，这些领域几十年来一直在谈论如何在组织内部和组织之间实现“一致”价值观与利益的问题。

随着一个系统的工程师和他们创建的人工智能系统之间的“一致性问题”开始得到“解决”，我们必须把注意力转向更大的原始意义上的一致性问题：工程师团队和他们的经理之间、经理和高管之间、高管和股东之间、整个公司与其监管机构及其用户之间的一致性问题。

词源学提醒我们，“一致性”是人与人之间一直存在的一个问题。随着我们迈入人工智能时代，这将比以往任何时候都更符合现实情况。

1. Milli, S., Belli, L., and Hardt, M. (2021) From Optimizing Engagement to Measuring Value. Proceedings of the 2021 ACM Conference on Fairness, Accountability, and Transparency, 714-722.https://doi.org/10.1145/3442188.3445933.

10

SociAI Contract for 21st Century

Danil KERIMI

It is safe to say that 2020 has been nothing like the year we were expecting. Plans have been disrupted, travel postponed, and meetings conducted exclusively online. Inter- and intra-national, urban and rural, have and have-nots fault lines became wider than ever before. As the first truly global pandemic of the digital age, the COVID-19 crisis presented a stress test for our skills, policies, institutions and strategies. It forced us to throw away old assumptions, ask difficult questions and reminded to take nothing for granted.

Yet, the greatest advances in productivity growth normally follow periods of great disruption. While focusing on the short-term disruptions of the crisis and its mid-term consequences, we cannot lose track of long-term challenges facing humankind. We need to fully understand the impact of today's technological transformations on our future societies to avoid developing mitigation strategies later. If climate change taught us anything is that by the time global community gets to act, the challenge may require us to fundamentally rethink all our systems of production and consumption.

Urbanization, digitization and globalization are the megatrends that shaped societies in the last decades of 20th century and early 21st. Nowhere was this transformation felt more than in Asia. This year marked a new milestone in this evolution. The crisis forced us to doubt the livability of many cities around the world, question the design and ownership of key data driven services, and marked a new wave of globalization.

2020 also marked the official arrival of techlash in many parts of Asia. Algorithms that quietly enabled shifts in power dynamics were loudly scrutinized by many governments around the world. Wonky AI policy debates escaped the halls of universities and think–tanks to run wild in the ministerial corridors, corporate boardrooms, street corners, and private living rooms as more and more AI-enabled devices and services entrenched in our lives.

It is customary to differentiate between agricultural and industrial revolutions and their impact on our systems of production and consumption which in turn affect our environment, economies and societies. In the past centuries we have witnessed at least three agricultural and four industrial revolutions. With ever growing list of breakthroughs in and enabled by AI, happening against the backdrop of growing population, warming planet, competing superpowers and growing citizen consciousness, people around the world will see the emergence of a new social contract that is being written in front of our eyes. This social contract must include machine learning and human development, artificial intelligence and genuine empathy.

十

21世纪的社会人工智能契约

鲁子龙

可以肯定地说，2020年与我们的预期截然不同。计划被打乱、行程被推迟、会议完全在线上进行。国际和国内、城市和农村、贫富之间的差距空前扩大。作为数字时代第一个真正意义上的全球性疫情，新冠肺炎疫情危机为我们带来了一场关乎能力、政策、制度和战略的压力测试，提出了种种难题，迫使我们摒弃旧有的假设，警醒我们在各方面摆脱此前想当然的思维习惯。

然而，生产力的增长幅度在发生大动荡之后往往是最大的。在关注危机带来的短期混乱及其中期后果的同时，我们也不能忽视人类面临的长期挑战。我们需要全面了解当今技术变革对未来社会群体的影响，以免日后陷入被迫制定缓减措施的窘境。如果说气候变化给我们带来了什么启示，那一定是当全球社区开始着手应对气候挑战之时，我们可能需要从根本上对我们所有的生产和消费系统进行反思。

城市化、数字化和全球化是20世纪最后几十年和21世纪初的三大社会影响趋势，这种转变在亚洲最为明显。2020年是这一演变的新里程碑。疫情危机不仅迫使我们开始审视全球许多城市的宜居性和关键数据驱动型服务的设计和所有权界定，还掀起了一种新的全球化浪潮。

2020年也标志着技术后浪开始正式席卷亚洲许多地区。全球许多政府都仔细审视了算法悄然带来的权力动态变化。随着越来越多基于AI的设备和服务深植我们的生活，以往针对AI政策进行的严肃辩论不再局限于大学和智囊团，而是走进了部长级走廊、公司董事会会议室、街头巷尾乃至私人起居室等各种场所。

农业革命和工业革命都会影响我们的生产和消费系统，进而引发环境、经济和社会变革。人们习惯于对这两类革命进行区分界定。在过去的几个世纪里，我们至少目睹了三次农业革命和四次工业革命。在人口增长、全球变暖、超级大国竞争和公民意识不断增强的背景下，随着AI领域的突破和由AI推动的突破日益增加，我们所有人都将亲眼见证新社会契约的诞生。该社会契约必须同时涵盖机器学习、人类发展、人工智能和真正的移情。

第一次世界大战期间，现代专业公共管理硕士学位应运而生。公共管理学的目标是消除腐败和促进地方政府能力建设。普林斯顿大学伍德罗·威尔逊公共和国际事务学院和哈佛大学肯尼迪

10

The first modern professional master's degree in public administration was born during World War I with the aim of eliminating corruption and building the capacity of local governments. The Woodrow Wilson School at Princeton University and the Kennedy School at Harvard University were born during & shortly after the Great Depression, as countries were rethinking the social contract and citizens demanded better services. The past few months have demonstrated that we need future breed of professionals with a great grasp of policy and laws, business and society, humanity and technology.

政治学院分别诞生于经济大萧条时期和大萧条之后不久。当时，各国都在对社会契约进行反思，而公民们则希望得到更优质的服务。过去几个月的情况证明，未来我们需要培养在政策和法律、商业和社会，以及人文与技术领域拥有深厚积累的专家。

11

Artificial Intelligence Needs More Natural Intelligence

Markus KNAUFF

When AI was born, it was mainly a joint enterprise of computer science and psychology. The goal was to build machines that think like humans. The interdisciplinary collaboration even resulted in a new academic discipline, cognitive science, which studies information processing in all kinds of biological and technical systems. Today, the huge commercial success of deep learning has pushed this collaboration into the background of AI. In fact, the field is becoming increasingly anti-psychological. Deep learning systems are inspired by human learning, but today they learn in a very different way than humans. As a result, they can be easily fooled and produce many errors. Nevertheless, they are successful because they can discover latent patterns of relevance by analysing large amounts of data generated by humans. However, the limitations of this approach are already on the horizon. One reason is the devastating inability of AI systems to reason and draw inferences. Consider the following inferences:

1. If it rains, the street gets wet.
   It rains.
   Therefore, the street gets wet.

2. The spy is in Berlin or in Paris, but not both.
   The spy is in Paris.
   Therefore, he is not in Berlin.

Solving such inference lies in the core of intelligence and is trivial for most human beings. Yet, if you ask Alexa, Siri, or other virtual assistant AI systems you get answers that are complete nonsense. It is hard to imagine AI making further progress if it is unable to solve such easy problems. Here are some results from cognitive psychology that can help to build future AI system that comes closer to human-level intelligence:

1. When people think about the world, they mentally simulate real, hypothetical, or imaginary situations.
2. Human reasoning is defeasible, i.e., people retract previously drawn conclusions in light of new evidence.
3. For humans, logical connectives such as if, then, all, some, none, etc., have different meanings than in classical logic.

十一

人工智能需要更多的自然智能

马库斯·克纳夫

人工智能在其诞生伊始主要是一项计算机科学与心理学领域开展的合作项目，旨在创造出具备类人思维的机器。这一跨学科的合作甚至催生出了新的学科——认知科学，该学科研究所有生物和技术系统处理信息的方式。如今，得益于深度学习在商业上大获成功，这一合作继续向 AI 方向发展。然而实际上，该领域正逐渐背离心理学的规律。深度学习系统受人类学习启发而来，但时至今日，其学习方式已与人类大相径庭，其结果便是它们会很容易受骗并产生许多错误。即便如此，它们能够通过分析大量人类产生的数据，从而发掘其中潜在的关联模式，就这一点而言是成功的。然而，深度学习的局限性已初现端倪，原因之一便是 AI 系统完全无法进行推断并得出推论。请看以下推论：

1. 如果下雨，街道便会变湿。
   下雨了。
   所以，街道变湿了。

2. 间谍可能出现在柏林或巴黎，但不会同时出现在两地。
   间谍在巴黎。
   所以，间谍不在柏林。

处理上述推论是智能的核心所在，尽管这对于大多数人而言不值一提，但如果我们问 Alexa、Siri 或其他虚拟 AI 助手系统这类问题，通常只会得到毫无意义的回答。因此，很难想象如果无法解决如此简单的问题，AI 如何能取得进一步发展。以下是认知心理学得出的一些结论，有助于未来建立具备更接近人类智能水平的 AI 系统：

1. 当人思考这个世界时，他们会在脑海里模拟真实、假设或虚构的场景。
2. 人类推理是可以推倒重来的，即根据新的证据撤销之前得出的结论。
3. 对于人类而言，诸如“如果”“那么”“所有”“一些”“没有”等逻辑连接词的含义有别于古典逻辑。
4. 人类经常会通过快捷方式或试探性方法得出有用但在逻辑上不成立的结论。

4. Humans often use shortcuts and heuristics that lead to useful but logically invalid conclusions.
5. People can generate conclusions on their own rather than just evaluate them.
6. The discovery of an inconsistency often causes humans to abandon a previous belief. In this way, the cognitive system avoids the explosion of conclusions.
7. When multiple conclusions are possible, human reasoners prefer just one of them, but systematically ignore others. This is an instance of the principal of cognitive economy that guides many thinking, reasoning, and decision-making processes in human beings.

AI should incorporate such insights from cognitive psychology to develop systems that interact with humans and produce results that are understood and accepted by the user. Cognitive scientists have begun to implement computational reasoning systems that reflect these core principles of natural intelligence. AI should not lag behind these developments and become more psychological again to make technical systems more intelligent.

5. 人类更倾向于自行得出结论，而不仅仅是对相关结论进行评估。
6. 一旦发现某种矛盾,人类往往会抛弃之前信以为真的观念,从而避免认知系统得出过多结论。
7. 如果存在多个结论，人在推理时会倾向于选择其中一个而系统性地忽视其他结论。这便是认知经济学理论引导人类诸多思考、推理以及决策过程的实例之一。

这种认知心理学方面的洞察力应植入 AI 之中，以便开发出可与人类互动并能得出用户所能理解和接受的结论的系统。认知科学家已着手应用能够反映自然智能此类核心原则的计算推理系统。人工智能不应落后于这些发展，而应再次顺应心理学的规律，以使技术系统更加智能。

12

Towards Effective Value Alignment in AI : From "Should" to "How"

Gillian K. HADFIELD

How should we regulate AI? This is the question that has dominated the discussion of AI governance for the last several years. The question has taken the form of moral philosophical puzzles such as the trolley problem. It has been raised by activists and critics drawing attention to the dangers of discrimination and bias in algorithms and facial recognition technology. Concern about the impact of highly targeted political advertising on the stability of politics and social relationships has raised questions about whether we should regulate speech on social media platforms or constrain the collection of personal information. At the broadest level there is widespread agreement that AI should, as the European High-Level Expert Group on AI put it in 2019, "respect all applicable laws and regulations, ethical principles and values."

But how will that alignment of AI with our human values happen? In practice, what will ensure that AI is lawful and ethical?

It will not be enough to pass laws that say AI must follow the laws. Nor is it feasible to catalogue human values and ethics and embed them into our AI systems. Our world is far too complex, dynamic, and evolving for that.

As I have explored in my work and discuss in my book, *Rules for a Flat World: Why Humans Invented Law and How to Reinvent It for a Complex Global Economy*, long before the challenge of AI, our legal and regulatory systems have faced substantial limits in putting our policy choices–our "should"–into practice. The legal and regulatory technology that we perfected over the 20th century–legislation, regulation, regulatory agencies, courts, legal reasoning–is increasingly unable to keep up with the complexity, speed, and global nature of 21st century economies and societies. AI accelerates the rate at which the chasm between what we aim to do through law and regulation and what is achieved in practice widens.

While most AI governance projects in 2019 continued to focus on the "how should we regulate AI" questions, in 2019, a major new initiative began at the University of Toronto to shift the focus to "how can we regulate AI?". The mission of the Schwartz Reisman Institute for Technology and Society, under my leadership, is to do the fundamental cross-disciplinary research we need to build the technical, legal, and regulatory systems that can implement our politically–determined goals for AI. We will not ask, should facial recognition be regulated, for example. We will ask, if we put rules into place, such as non-discrimination or legitimate limits to surveillance, how can

十二

人工智能与人类价值观的有效统一：从“应该”到“如何”

吉莉安·哈德菲尔德

“我们应如何监管人工智能？”在过去几年中，这一问题一直是人工智能治理的关注焦点。该问题以道德哲学难题的形式出现，比如电车难题。人工智能的支持者和批判者也提醒人们注意算法和人脸识别技术中存在的歧视和偏见。针对性较强的政治广告可能对政治和社会关系的稳定产生重大影响，而对这种影响的担忧也引发了人们的思考，即我们是否应该有效监管社交媒体平台上的言论，或限制对个人信息的收集？正如欧盟人工智能高级别专家组在 2019 年所提出的那样，在最广义的层面上，人们普遍认为，人工智能应该“尊重所有适用的法律法规、伦理原则和价值观”。但该如何实现人工智能与人类价值观的统一？在实践中，怎样才能确保人工智能合法且合乎伦理？

由于世界的复杂化和动态化特征，仅通过制定法律来对人工智能进行约束远远不够，而将人类的价值观和伦理观一一列出，编入人工智能系统也是行不通的。

正如我的研究所发现的，并在《扁平世界的规则：人类为何发明法律，又如何再造法律以应对复杂的全球经济》（*Rules for a Flat World: Why Humans Invented Law and How to Reinvent It for a Complex Global Economy*）一书中讨论的那样，早在面临人工智能的挑战之前，我们的法律和监管体系在将政策选择——即我们的“应行之事”付诸实践方面，就已经面临着实质性的挑战。我们在 20 世纪制定的法律和监管技术——立法、监管、管理机构、法院、法律推理——越来越无法跟上 21 世纪经济和社会的复杂性、发展速度以及全球化程度。人工智能领域的发展进一步拉大了我们希望通过法律法规实现的目标与我们取得的实际成果之间的差距。

2019 年，尽管大多数的人工智能治理项目持续关注“我们应该监管人工智能”这一问题，但多伦多大学启动了一项新倡议，将重点转向“我们如何才能监管人工智能”。在我的领导下，施瓦茨·赖斯曼技术与社会研究所将进行基础的跨学科研究，以期建立起集技术、法律和监管于一身的体系，实现我们为人工智能设定的政治目标。例如，我们不会关注是否应该监管人脸识别系统，我们所关注的是，如果我们要落实规则，例如非歧视或合法的监控限制原则，我们应该如何确保人脸识别系统遵守这些规则？我们需要解决哪些技术挑战？在监管技术上可以

we ensure that facial recognition systems follow the rules? What technical challenges do we need to solve? What innovations can we develop in regulatory technologies? How can we build AI that helps to ensure AI stays within the bounds of what we, collectively, have decided is right or acceptable? How can we make sure that our efforts at value alignment are effective?

In 2020 and beyond, the Schwartz Reisman Institute will be aiming to broaden the global conversation about AI governance beyond "should" to "how". We will be aiming to contribute to the pool of knowledge and tools available to ensure that AI is deployed where we decide it should be and not where we decide it shouldn't be and that it follows the rules humans have set when it is.

十二

进行哪些创新？如何构建人工智能来帮助我们确保其处于我们普遍认为正确或可接受的范围内？我们如何确保在价值一致方面的努力不会付诸东流？

2020 年及以后，施瓦茨·赖斯曼研究所的目标是将有关人工智能治理的全球讨论从“应不应该治理”扩展到“如何治理”。我们将致力于发展现有的知识储备和工具库，以确保人工智能在许可之处得到应用，且遵循人类制定的规则。

13

Going Beyond AI Ethics Guidelines

Thilo HAGENDORFF

In the last years, discussions on AI ethics were omnipresent. Various academic, governance as well as industry initiatives have come up with their own AI ethics guidelines. News media were swamped with articles demanding for AI ethics. Additionally, countless commissions congregated to set up norms and standards. Besides the virulent discourse on AI ethics, the latest phase in AI ethics was also the time in which researchers and practitioners commenced to stress that abstract ethical principles are not worth much without putting them into practice. However, this is easier said than done. All over the world, ethics initiatives agree that privacy, fairness, transparency, safety, and accountability are the minimal requirements for building and using "ethical sound" AI applications. Nevertheless, what those tenets mean in day-to-day decision-making of organizations that develop and deploy such applications is rather unclear. At least empirical studies show that merely reading documents on ethical principles does not have any significant effect on practice.

The existence of ethics codes is only a tiny piece of the bigger puzzle of AI governance. If the aim is to strengthen the likelihood of ethical behavior in AI research and development, governance efforts first and foremost have to address measures for code enforcement, but also things like working climates or ethical cultures in organizations, virtue education, or the shift from competition to cooperation. Regarding the latter, the fierce competition and the related race rhetoric on "global leadership" in AI bears the risk of a reckless race for being first in accomplishing certain technical systems, especially in the context of military applications. This race is to the detriment of values like safety, privacy, or fairness. An important step towards achieving "trustworthy AI" is to attenuate competition in favor of cooperation between nations, companies, but also research institutes.

Future AI governance should focus on strengthening the ties between industry stakeholders but also governance initiatives themselves. This would have the effect of saving a lot of redundancy in deliberating governance tenets and principles. Moreover, in the future of AI governance soft laws should be increasingly translated into hard law, that gives clear rules for algorithmic non-discrimination, prohibitions for AI in high-stake areas, safety and privacy standards, as well as rules for dealing with labor displacement induced by AI applications.

十三

超越人工智能伦理准则

希洛·哈根多夫

近年来，关于人工智能伦理的讨论无处不在。学术界、政府部门以及产业界都提出了各自的人工智能伦理准则。新闻媒体上充斥着呼吁人工智能伦理的文章。此外，许多委员会聚集在一起制定规范和标准。暂且将有关人工智能伦理的恶意评论搁置，在人工智能伦理的最新发展阶段，研究人员和从业者愈发强调：抽象的伦理原则若不付诸实践，其价值就会大打折扣。然而，知之非难，行之不易。世界各地的伦理倡议组织一致认为，做到隐私、公平、透明、安全和负责任是构建和使用“合乎伦理的”人工智能应用程序的最低要求。然而，在开发和部署此类应用程序的日常决策中，我们需要制定什么样的伦理原则尚不明确。至少，实证研究表明，仅仅阅读有关伦理原则的文件对实践没有任何显著帮助。

制定伦理原则只是人工智能治理的第一步。如果要提高人工智能研发中合乎伦理行为的可能性，那么治理工作必须从这些方面入手：要保证伦理准则的执行；转变组织或工作环境中的伦理文化、美德教育；从竞争向合作的转变；等等。其中，人工智能领域的激烈竞争和与之相关的“全球领导地位”的竞争言论可能导致不计后果的竞争，为此人们通常力争最先完成某些技术系统，特别是在军事应用方面的系统。这种竞争对安全、隐私和公平等造成了巨大的损害。减少竞争，促进国家、公司以及研究机构之间的合作是实现“可信赖人工智能”的重要一步。

未来，人工智能治理应侧重于加强行业利益相关者之间的联系，同时也应关注治理举措本身。这将在商议治理原则时节省大量时间。此外，在未来的人工智能治理中，“软法”应当越来越多地转化为“硬法”，应当针对算法不歧视、在高风险领域禁止使用人工智能、安全和隐私标准以及人工智能应用导致的劳动力转移的处理方法等制定明确的规则。

14

Developing Responsible AI: From Principles to Practices

WANG Guoyu

In 2020, artificial intelligence continues to develop rapidly in the context of the global epidemic, while the ethical principles of artificial intelligence have become ever more abundant. By April 2020, more than 160 guidelines were included in the AI Ethics Guidelines Global Inventory developed by the nonprofit organization AlgorithmWatch. The publishing bodies involve various institutions and organizations, including governments, academia, enterprises, etc. Many of these ethical principles are directly titled "Responsible AI". Therefore, the development of responsible AI can be interpreted as an international consensus.

However, developing responsible AI requires not only principles and appeals but also actions and practices. To this end, it is necessary to clarify the subject and object of responsibility and the authority as well as to address the issues of who is responsible, for what, and to whom. For example, for issues resulting from AI applications such as privacy breaches, discrimination, and liability in autonomous driving, who is the responsible subject: the designer, the engineer, the corporate decision-maker, or the regulator? Is it the individual, the institution, or the state? When an action involves multiple subjects from different institutions, how should responsibility be allocated? When corporate interests and social ethics conflict, how should they be prioritized? In particular, when AI development involves national core competitiveness on the one hand and conflicts with ethical principles on the other, should it be developed (e.g., military AI applications) and how (e.g., facial recognition technology)? Who has the accountability authority, and how is it enacted? These questions cannot be avoided if the ethical principles of AI are to be implemented.

To answer these questions, we need to further theoretical discussion of these issues. However, more important is clarifying the issue of responsibility in the practice of developing AI and promoting the construction of responsible mechanisms and culture. To this end, the China Computer Federation (CCF) established an interdisciplinary "Committee on Ethics and Professional Conduct" (CEPC) in 2020, with computer experts and philosophers cochairing and acting as committee members. At the China National Computer Congress (CNCC) 2020, the committee held a special forum on "More Harmony for the World-Professional Ethics in Information Technology". On the one hand, analyzed at the theoretical level were not only the history and dimensions of computer and AI professional ethics in the era of information technology but also the theoretical path to develop responsible AI. On the other hand, also explored and discussed in depth were the path to the development of responsible AI, AI ethics

十四

发展负责任的人工智能：从原则到实践

王国豫

2020 年是全球疫情下人工智能继续飞速发展的一年，也是人工智能伦理原则不断丰富的一年。据非营利组织“算法监视”（AlgorithmWatch）所制定的全球人工智能伦理指南清单（AI Ethics Guidelines Global Inventory），截至 2020 年 4 月，其已收录伦理准则超过 160 部，发布主体涉及政府、学界、企业等各类机构和组织，其中许多伦理原则都直接以负责任的人工智能（Responsible AI）为标题。仅由此看来，发展“负责任的人工智能”已在一定程度上成为国际共识。

然而，发展“负责任的人工智能”不仅需要原则和呼吁，更需要行动和实践。为此，首先需要明确责任的主体和客体以及问责的主管（Instance），解决谁负责任（who），对什么事情负责任（what）和向谁负责（whom）的问题。比如，对于诸如人工智能应用中带来的隐私泄露、歧视和自动驾驶中的责任问题，谁是责任主体，是设计师、工程师还是企业的决策者或监管者？是个体还是机构或者国家？当一个行为涉及不同机构的多主体时，责任应该如何分配？当企业利益和社会伦理发生冲突时，如何进行优先排序？尤其是当一方面人工智能的发展涉及国家核心竞争力，另一方面与伦理原则发生冲突时，要不要发展（比如人工智能在军事上的应用）、怎么发展（人脸识别技术）？谁有权力问责、如何问责？如果要使人工智能伦理原则走向伦理实践，就不能回避这些问题。

要回答这些问题，还需要我们加深对这些问题的理论探讨。但是另一方面，更重要的是在发展 AI 的实践中厘清责任问题，推进负责任的机制建设和文化建设。为此，中国计算机学会于 2020 年成立了跨学科的“职业伦理与学术道德委员会”，由计算机专家和哲学家共同担任主席和委员。在 2020 年中国计算机学会的年会（CNCC）上，委员会举办了“为世界更和谐——信息技术中的职业伦理”专题论坛，一方面从理论层面对信息技术时代计算机和人工智能职业伦理的历史与维度、发展负责任的人工智能的理论路径等进行了分析，同时，也对在高校开展人工智能伦理教育的实践以及人工智能敏捷治理的框架等问题进行了深入讨论和交流。中国计算机学会青年计算机科学家与工程师论坛（CCF YOCSEF）也探讨了如何将公平、透明、可接受性与可持续发展等理念纳入第三代人工智能设计中去的问题。中国计算机学会正在尝试从伦理、机制、教育和技术四个层面推动人工智能的负责任原则转化为工程师的负责任实践。

education in universities and the framework of artificial intelligence agile governance. The Young Computer Scientists and Engineers Forum of the CCF (CCF YOCSEF) also discussed how to incorporate fairness, transparency, acceptability, and sustainable development into the design of the third generation of artificial intelligence. The CCF is trying to promote the conversion of the responsible principles of AI into responsible practices for engineers at four levels: ethical, structural, educational and technical.

To implement the development of responsible AI, it is also important to consider that AI cannot be viewed as merely an isolated, closed system of algorithms and technologies. The ethical issue of artificial intelligence operates in the sociotechnical system where humans and AI live in symbiosis and where technology and society interact to shape each other. The development of responsible AI needs to confront not only the technical ethics of AI and the professional ethics of engineers but also the uncertainty and socioethical challenges in the social context that include multiple dimensions such as economics, politics, and culture. In particular, AI must benefit society in the framework of global ethics. Therefore, it is necessary not only to awaken the moral sensibility of AI practitioners and strengthen the research on the responsibility and norms of AI in application scenarios but also to continue to promote international dialogne on AI ethics and the construction of transnational accountability mechanisms.

十四

要将发展“负责任的人工智能”落实到行动，还需要考虑的是，不能仅仅将人工智能看成是一个孤立的、封闭的算法和技术系统。人工智能的伦理问题是人与 AI 共生、技术与社会交互塑型的社会—技术系统中的伦理问题。发展“负责任的人工智能”需要面对的不仅是 AI 的技术伦理和工程师的职业伦理问题，而且还要面对社会的经济、政治和文化的多维度语境（context）下的不确定性和社会伦理挑战，特别是要考虑在全球伦理的框架下让人工智能造福社会。因此，不仅有必要强化人工智能从业人员的道德敏感性,加强人工智能在应用场景中的责任和规范研究，还必须继续推动人工智能伦理的国际对话和跨国问责机制的构建。

15

Governing Artificial Intelligence: From Principles to Law

Nathalie SMUHA

If 2019 was the year that AI governance debates shifted "from principles to practice", especially through the promulgation of ethics guidelines for AI, 2020 marked the year that this shift took a new turn, namely "from principles to law". It became increasingly apparent that the risks posed by the use of AI are too substantial to be left to non-binding guidelines, and the self-regulatory goodwill of private or public actors. This realization was spurred not only by media coverage of problematic AI applications and by vocal civil society organizations, but also by companies, some of which openly began to ask for binding rules that provide legal certainty, while enhancing citizens' trust. Consequently, policymakers examined more carefully the legal gaps impeding protection against AI's potential harms.

The most prominent step in this direction was taken by the European Union. Building on the work of its High-Level Expert Group on AI, in February 2020 the European Commission published a White Paper which maps a number of legal gaps in the EU legal order. One year later, the Commission put forward a proposal for an "Artificial Intelligence Act", imposing new obligations on AI providers and users to bridge those gaps. Beyond the EU, also the work of the Council of Europe's Ad Hoc Committee on AI (CAHAI) should be mentioned. In December 2020, the CAHAI published a Feasibility Study that examines potential elements of a legal framework for AI, focusing on human rights, democracy and the rule of law. It puts forward rights and obligations that could be included in a future binding instrument, such as an international convention.

Of course, it may well take years before these initiatives result in enforceable legislation. Moreover, they are still regional in scope, whereas many of AI's risks require a global approach. In addition, further interdisciplinary research is needed to better identify, understand and mitigate AI's adverse effects. The work is thus far from over. However, the path on which the abovementioned policymakers embarked is encouraging, and can hopefully set an example for others to follow. Going forward, I would like to raise three points to keep in mind.

First, AI policies and regulations should embrace a holistic perspective. AI systems do not exist in isolation, but are part of a broader socio-technical environment. This environment encompasses the numerous actors and processes that are involved in the lifecycle of AI systems, as well as the data they use and the infrastructure they run on. Governing AI hence also requires appropriate measures to govern data flows and digital infrastructures.

十五

治理人工智能：从原则到法律

娜塔莉亚·苏姆哈

如果说 2019 年是人工智能治理争辩焦点“从原则转向实践”的一年，突出表现在人工智能道德准则的颁布，那么 2020 年标志着这一转变发生了新的转折，即“从原则转向法律”。越来越明显的是，人工智能的使用所带来的风险实在过于庞大，仅靠无约束力指导方针、私人或公共行为主体善意的自我监管无法解决。这一认识不仅受到媒体对问题重重的人工智能应用的报道和敢于直言的民间社会组织的支持，也受到企业的推动，部分企业开始公开要求制定具有约束力的规则，以提供明确的法律依据，同时增强公民的信任度。因此，政策制定者更加仔细地审查法律漏洞，这些漏洞会导致某些人工智能的潜在危害无法被阻止。

在这一问题上，欧盟采取了最有力的举措。基于其人工智能高级别专家组的工作，欧盟委员会于 2020 年 2 月发表白皮书，描绘了欧盟法律秩序中的一些法律空白。一年后，委员会提出了“人工智能法案”提议，对人工智能供应商和用户施加新的义务，以填补这些空白。除欧盟外，欧洲委员会的人工智能特设委员会（CAHAI）的工作同样不可忽视。2020 年 12 月，CAHAI 发表了一份可行性研究报告，审查了人工智能法律框架的潜在要素，重点是人权、民主和法治，并提出了可纳入未来约束性文书（如国际公约）的基本权利和义务。

当然，这些倡议可能需要数年时间才能变为可执行的法律条款。此外，它们在范围上仍然是区域性的，而人工智能带来的许多风险需要通过一种全球性的方法来应对。此外，还需要进一步的跨学科研究来更好地识别、理解和减轻人工智能的不利影响。因此，工作还远远没有结束。然而，上述政策制定者所走的道路是鼓舞人心的，并有望为其他国家树立榜样。接下来，我想提出值得注意的三点。

首先，人工智能政策和法规应该具有整体性。人工智能系统不是孤立存在的，而是更广阔的社会技术环境的一部分。这个环境包括人工智能系统生命周期中涉及的众多行为主体和流程，以及它们使用的数据和运行所用的基础设施。因此，治理人工智能还需要采取适当的措施来治理数据流和数字基础设施。

Second, it must be ensured that the seats around the regulatory negotiation table are sufficiently diverse. Too often, the most marginalized individuals and communities are first in line to suffer the negative effects of AI applications, thereby entrenching and deepening inequities and problematic power relationships. Not only those who have something to gain, but also those who have something to lose should be represented in AI governance debates.

Finally, it is essential for policymakers to consider not only the individual harms that can arise from the use of AI, but also the collective and societal harms. When taking a long-term perspective, it becomes more visible how the delegation of human autonomy in not just one area but in ever more domains of our lives accumulatively, risks shaking the foundations of our moral, democratic and societal infrastructures. Only by acknowledging this risk can we take steps to tackle it.

十五

其次，必须确保人工智能监管谈判中的参与者足够多样化。通常情况下，面对人工智能应用的不利影响，最边缘化的个人和社区会首当其冲受到人工智能应用的不利影响，进一步加剧不平等和权力关系问题。在进行人工智能治理辩论时，不仅要让那些能够得利的主体参与，还应该让那些会有所损失的主体参与。

最后，政策制定者不仅要考虑使用人工智能可能造成的个人危害，还要考虑集体和社会危害，这一点至关重要。从长远的角度来看，人们越来越清楚地看到，人类自治权的下放不仅是在一个领域，而是发生在我们生活中越来越多的领域里，而这种放权累积起来便可能动摇人类道德、民主和社会基础设施的根基。只有承认这一风险，我们才能采取有效措施，妥善应对。

16

European Perspectives on the Anticipatory Governance of AI

Robin WILLIAMS

In his 1980 book, *The Social Control of Technology*, David Collingridge reflected upon the unanticipated risks that accompanied many emerging technologies. He highlighted a dilemma confronting attempts to control the undesired impacts of technology.

> *[...] attempting to control a technology is difficult, and not rarely impossible, because during its early stages, when it can be controlled, not enough can be known about its harmful social consequences to warrant controlling its development; but by the time these consequences are apparent, control has become costly and slow.*[1]

This insight has inspired the proposals for anticipatory governance of new and emerging science and technology, that reflect upon pathways for the development and use of technology and their potential impacts on health, the environment and social life. The UK Engineering and Physical Sciences Research Council today invites the researchers it funds to "anticipate, reflect, engage and act" to achieve Responsible Innovation.

> *Responsible Innovation is a process that seeks to promote creativity and opportunities for science and innovation that are socially desirable and undertaken in the public interest.*[2]

These ideas are closely related to European Union proposals for Responsible Research and Innovation. How then might these apply to Artificial Intelligence (AI)?

The success of private initiatives by firms like Google and Amazon has driven enormous public and policy interest in AI and has stimulated major public research and training investments worldwide to develop AI capabilities. These have been accompanied by compelling visions of the beneficial applications of AI: autonomous vehicles; care robots; advances in medical science and diagnosis etc. These expectations–sometimes unhelpfully informed by science fiction accounts–often run far ahead of currently demonstrated capabilities. Alongside this, growing concerns are being articulated about potential risks–for example to privacy and to autonomy. Complaints have been made about the lack of transparency of algorithmic decision-making systems in finance or in public administration and about algorithmic bias where these systems have been shown to disadvantage groups in ways which may conflict with equal opportunity

十六

对人工智能预期治理的看法

罗宾·威廉姆斯

大卫·科林格里奇（David Collingridge）在其 1980 年出版的《技术的社会控制》（*The Social Control of Technology*）一书中反思了许多由新兴技术带来的意外风险。他同时指出了控制技术的不良影响所面临的困境。

> *……试图控制一项技术是很困难的，通常也不可能做到，因为在技术的早期阶段，在其可以被控制时，我们对它的负面社会后果还不够了解，没有理由去控制它的发展；但当这些后果变得明显时，控制已变得成本昂贵，且见效缓慢了*[1]。

这一见解进一步激发了研究者对新兴科学技术进行预期治理的研究，这些研究反映了技术的发展和使用途径及其对健康、环境和社会生活的潜在影响。如今，英国工程与物理科学研究委员会正邀请其资助的研究人员“预测、反思、参与和行动”，以实现负责任的创新。

> *负责任的创新是一个过程，旨在促进创新、创造机遇，以推动科学和创新造福于社会和公众*[2]。

这些理念与欧盟关于负责任的研究和创新的提案密切相关。那么，如何将这些理念应用到人工智能中呢？

谷歌和亚马逊等私营企业倡议的成功，激发了公众和政策部门对人工智能的巨大兴趣，并刺激了全球范围的重大公共研究和培训投资，用以开发人工智能。这让人工智能在自动驾驶汽车、护理机器人、医学和诊断等领域的应用有着令人信服的前景。这些预期 —— 有些还只出现在科幻小说里——往往远远超出了目前人工智能所展示出的能力。与此同时，人们对隐私、自主权等潜在风险的担忧也在不断加剧。人们抱怨财务或公共管理等诸多领域的算法决策系统缺乏透明度，并且对算法偏见心存不满 —— 这些系统已被证明对弱势群体存在偏见，而这可能与有关男女平等和少数民族平等的法律相悖。这促使众人呼吁公平、道德、透明的机器学习系统的建立。至 2019 年，私营企业、研究机构和公共机构已经发布了 84 套指导原则[3]。

然而，伦理原则本身不会产生伦理结果。人工智能不是一个具有确定属性的“事物”。它指的是一组通用功能，适用于一系列设置，并在开发、使用和改进新工具和技术的快速周期中迅速进化。

legislation applying to women and ethnic minorities. This has inspired numerous calls for Fair, Ethical, Transparent Machine Learning systems. 84 sets of guidelines had been published by 2019 by private companies, research institutions and public bodies.[3]

However our research suggests that ethical principles per se will not deliver ethical outcomes. AI is not a "thing" with determinate properties. It refers to a general purpose set of capabilities, applicable to a range of settings, and advancing quickly through rapid cycles of developing, using and refining new tools and techniques. And the outcomes of AI are rooted not just in the design of these models but in the overall configuration of the algorithmic system. This includes the variables selected as proxies for intended outcomes, metrics and visualisations and above all in the data sets–and especially the training data for machine learning systems. And attempts to develop "unbiased" AI systems need to confront the fact that social inequalities in society are deeply embedded in the data available–there is no "view from nowhere".[4]

However, though there has been much discussion of the opacity of proprietary algorithmic systems, their operation is amenable to probing by those with moderate technical capabilities – for example submitting to recruitment algorithms job applications with different gender, age, racial identifiers. In this respect their operation and biases may be more readily made visible than traditional systems based solely on human judgement. Though it may be hard to "open the black-box" of algorithmic system, the performance of the black box under different circumstances can be made visible.

The pathway towards Responsible Innovation of Artificial Intelligence is thus through critically scrutinising AI components, configurations, and OUTCOMES–to open up the choices made by those developing/applying them in particular contexts and make them accountable.

Responsible Innovation is thus not a one-off task but a complex bundle of activities. It will best be achieved through interdisciplinary dialogue between AI practitioner communities, stakeholders and citizen groups–what Stilgoe has characterised as "constructively engaging with the contingencies" of AI practice.[5]

十六

人工智能的结果不仅植根于这些模型的设计中，还植根于算法系统的整体配置中。这包括被选为预期结果、标准和可视化指标的变量和上述所有数据集——特别是机器学习系统的培训数据。试图开发“无偏见”的人工智能系统需要面对这样一个事实，即社会中的不平等现象深深植根于现有的数据中，因此不存在“无中生有”的观点，算法中的偏见不过是反映了真实生活中的偏见[4]。

尽管人们对私有算法系统的不透明性进行了大量讨论，但即使技术能力一般的人也能很容易发现算法的运行方式——例如，向招聘算法提交带有不同性别、年龄和种族标识的求职信。在这一方面，相比于仅仅基于人类判断的传统系统，算法的运行方式和偏见可能更容易被发现。算法系统的黑箱虽然很难打开，但是黑箱在不同情况下的表现是能够被可视化的。

因此，通向负责任的人工智能创新的途径，是严格审查人工智能组件、配置和结果，进而观察人工智能开发者 / 应用者在特定环境下所做的选择，并使其负责。

所以，负责任的创新不是一次性的任务，而是一系列复杂的活动，最好通过人工智能从业者团体、利益相关者和民间团体之间的跨学科对话来实现——斯迪乔将其描述为“建设性地应对”人工智能实践中的“偶发事件”[5]。

1. David Collingridge (1980) *The Social Control of Technology* (p.19). London: F Pinter/New York: St. Martin's Press
2. https://epsrc.ukri.org/research/framework/ last sampled 25 August 2021
3. Jobin, A., Ienca, M. & Vayena, E. The global landscape of AI ethics guidelines. Nat Mach Intell 1, 389–399 (2019). https://doi.org/10.1038/s42256-019-0088-2
4. Lee F, Bier J, Christensen J, Engelmann L, Helgesson C-F, Williams R. (2019) Algorithms as folding: Reframing the analytical focus. Big Data & Society. doi:10.1177/2053951719863819
5. Stilgoe, Jack (2018) Machine learning, social learning and the governance of self-driving cars. *Social Studies of Science*, 48 (1) pp. 25-56. 10.1177/0306312717741687.

17

Artificial Intelligence Governance Requires "Technical Innovation + Institutional Innovation"

LI Xiuquan

The accelerated development and application of artificial intelligence are placing urgent demands on governance in terms of ethics, security, privacy, fairness, etc. New laws, institutional design and governance rules are needed to guide and standardize technological development. The issue of artificial intelligence governance is a matter not only of system design but also of technology research and development. The increasingly urgent requirement for technological innovation in artificial intelligence governance needs to be addressed.

Each type of governance problem contains many technology innovation needs. The current big data-driven machine-learning methods represented by deep learning rely on a black box model. The internal structure and mechanism of the model are not transparent to users and lack transparency for increasingly large and complex machine intelligence. When there is an error, the origin and explanation are difficult to trace, which results in great difficulties to the system designer in terms of legal and normative design. Research on more transparent model algorithms and the development of interpretable, understandable, and predictable intelligent algorithms will provide technical approaches for solving the dilemma of responsibility identification to overcome ethical constraints.

Similarly, sample attacks, sensor interference, and deep-learning framework vulnerabilities may result in challenges to the security of intelligent systems. A safe and reliable artificial intelligence system should have strong security performance, should effectively respond to various deliberate attacks, and should avoid security accidents caused by abnormal operations and malicious attacks. Governance over issues such as privacy violations and discrimination or prejudice also requires technological innovations–such as user privacy data desensitization, federated learning, and small data incremental learning–to cope with these risks and challenges and enhance public trust in AI technology.

To meet the challenges of artificial intelligence governance, in 2020, technological and institutional innovation are increasingly integrating. Artificial intelligence technology developers are devoting increasing energy to the development of technical solutions to security, privacy, and fairness issues. In the future, the development of responsible artificial intelligence technology should become the next important direction for theoretical innovation and technological development. Governance problems must be solved through technological approaches, and responsibility must be shared with legal and administrative parties to jointly guarantee the healthy development of the AI industry.

十七

人工智能治理需要“技术创新 + 制度创新”

李修全

人工智能的加速发展和应用正在对伦理、安全、隐私、公平等各方面治理提出迫切需求，需要新的法律、制度设计和治理规则引导和规范技术发展。人工智能治理问题既是制度设计问题也是技术研发问题，应对人工智能治理对于技术创新的需求日益迫切。

每一类治理问题都蕴含大量的技术研发需求。当前以深度学习为代表的大数据驱动的端到端的机器学习方法，采用黑箱模式，模型内部结构和机理对用户不透明，无法对越来越庞大和复杂的机器智能进行理解，“智能”行为出现错误时就无法做出溯源和解释，给制度设计者进行法律、规范设计带来非常大的困难。研发更具透明性的模型算法，开发可解释、可理解、可预测的机理型智能技术，将为解决责任认定困境、实现伦理约束等治理问题提供技术途径和实现可能。

同样，样本攻击、传感器干扰、深度学习框架漏洞，都可能给智能系统安全带来冲击和挑战。安全可靠的人工智能系统应具有强健的安全性能，能有效应对各类蓄意攻击，避免因异常操作和恶意攻击导致安全事故；隐私侵犯和歧视或偏见等问题的治理，也需要从数据采集、数据保存、知识处理等各环节的技术本源入手破解，用户隐私数据脱敏技术、联邦学习和小数据增量学习正在为应对这些风险挑战提供有益探索，将通过技术创新增强社会公众对技术的信任。

为应对人工智能治理挑战，技术创新与制度创新的融合在 2020 年走向深化，人工智能技术研发者开始将越来越多的精力投入到研发应对安全、隐私、公平问题的技术解决方案。未来，发展负责任的人工智能技术应该成为科研界下一步理论创新和技术研发关注的重要方向，通过技术途径破解治理难题，更需与法律、行政各方强化责任共担，携手应对，共同保障人工智能产业健康发展。

18

Three Modes of AI Governance

YANG Qingfeng

An article on AI governance caught my attention. This article noted that AI governance is "an unorganized area".[1] James Butcher overviewed the practice of different stakeholders in AI governance activities. According to this article, the key point is to maximize benefits and minimize risks. Public and nonpublic sectors have different responsibilities in AI governance.

AI governance is certainly a new field waiting to be explored. Controversy remains over the understanding of what constitutes AI and AI governance. Therefore, the primary issue is to clarify these two definitions. I distinguish three modes of governance based on the AI definition: governance based on governmental bodies, technologies, and humanistic values.

The first type of AI governance is based on governmental bodies. In this view, AI is considered a tool related to different bodies. AI is used by governments, companies, individuals, etc. Safety and reliability are the keys to its good or rational use. However, problems arising from rational use are ignored in this view.

The second type of AI governance is based on human values. AI is seen as an embodiment of human values. AI must follow human values such as responsibility, safety, fairness and trust. AI governance is focused on the design process and how to guard against or embed human values as agents. The ethical framework and decision-makers are emphasized. Through the glass box, we can "implement transparent moral bounds for AI behavior".[2]

The third type of AI governance is based on technologies. AI in this view is regarded as a technology or technological system. This view is useful for addressing philosophical, technological and other problems entangled between AI and society. In this view, AI governance focuses on how to tackle such problems as the societal and humanistic impact of AI. In 2019, the Partnership on AI (PAI) has discussed the influence of AI on people and society, especially the algorithmic biases and errors in AI.

Logically, AI governance has transitioned from a "use context" to a "prediction context". Most studies have focused on entities that use and design AI. Rational or responsible use is the inevitable path. However, AI has strong autonomy and the ability to learn. Algorithms have been used to predict future human behavior. The basic problem is addressing the relationship between AI and humans. Coexistence is a good relational model. Some technological problems, such as AI algorithmic bias, are more important. Many media have expressed concern about an AI bias

十八

人工智能治理的三种模式

杨庆峰

一篇讨论人工智能治理的文章吸引了我的注意。这篇文章指出人工智能治理是一个“无组织的领域”。[1] 作者詹姆斯·巴彻（James Butcher）回顾了人工智能治理活动中各个利益相关方的做法。根据这篇文章，关键点是最大化福利和最小化风险。公共部门与非公共部门在人工智能治理中有着各自不同的责任。

人工智能治理无疑是等待开拓的新领域。产生这种状况的原因是对于人工智能及其治理的理解有争议。因此首要的问题是澄清人工智能和人工智能治理。作者根据人工智能定义区分了三种治理类型。这些类型分别是：基于机构实体、基于人类价值和基于技术的治理。

第一类是基于机构实体的人工智能治理。人工智能被看作是与不同实体有关的工具，政府、公司和个人等不同实体使用着人工智能。良好使用或者理性使用的关键是安全和可靠。然而，这一观点可能会忽略来自理性使用的问题。第二类是基于人类价值的人工智能治理。人工智能被看作是人类价值的具身化。人工智能需要遵循诸如责任、安全、公平和信任等价值观念。人工智能治理聚焦设计过程中如何把人类价值嵌入到智能体中。这一过程强调伦理框架和伦理决策者的作用。借助“玻璃箱”，我们可以“提升指向人工智能行为的透明的伦理范围”。[2] 第三类是基于技术的人工智能治理。人工智能被看作是技术或者技术系统。这种观点有助于考虑哲学问题、技术问题和纠缠在人工智能与社会中的一些问题。在这一观点中，人工智能治理聚焦何处理诸如人工智能的社会和人文影响等问题上。2019 年 Partnership on AI（PAI）已经讨论了人工智能对于人和社会的影响，尤其是人工智能中的算法偏见和错误所带来的影响。

从逻辑上看，人工智能治理经历了从使用语境向预测语境的转变。大多数研究关注使用和设计人工智能的实体。理性使用或者负责任地使用成为不可避免的路径。但是，人工智能具有很强的自治能力和学习能力。算法已被用来预测人们的行为。基本问题是处理人工智能与人的关系。共在是一种好的关系模式。诸如算法偏见之类的技术问题更待解决。许多媒体都关注算法偏见问题，众多组织和政府也越发重视人工智能偏见所带来的影响。可解释的和没有偏见的算法变

arising from algorithms. Many governments and organizations are also becoming increasingly concerned about AI bias. Explainable and unbiased algorithms are possible directions. How we use AI tools to predictively represent the status of major social practices and predict its development is a question that needs to be considered. BlueDot may be a good case.[3] It has sent us many real-time infectious disease alerts.

成可能的方向。如何使用人工智能让我们对重大社会实践的状况给予预测性表征以及预测它的发展成为我们需要考虑的问题。也许蓝点公司（BlueDot）是一个很好的例子[3]，它已经对许多即时的流行病发出了警告信号。

1. James Butcher & Irakli Beridze (2019) What is the State of Artificial Intelligence Governance Globally? The RUSI Journal, 164:5-6, 88-96, DOI: 10.1080/03071847.2019.1694260
2. Tubella A A, Theodorou A, Dignum V, et al. Governance by glass-box: Implementing transparent moral bounds for AI behaviour. arXivpreprint arXiv:1905.04994, 2019.3. Jobin, A., Ienca, M. & Vayena, E. The global landscape of AI ethics guidelines. Nat Mach Intell 1, 389–399 (2019). https://doi.org/10.1038/s42256-019-0088-2
3. 多伦多人工智能创业公司 BlueDot 于 2019 年年底就发出了关于新冠疫情即将爆发的警告
BlueDot, a Toronto-based artificial intelligence platform, has spotted COVID-19 at the end of 2019.

19

An Important Issue of International Relations: AI Governance

CHEN Dingding

As a new round of industrial revolution sweeps the world, artificial intelligence has become the core direction of industrial change. Artificial intelligence is a new engine of economic development, a new focus of international competition, and a new opportunity for social construction. In recent years, as artificial intelligence has continued to increase in popularity at the technological level, its urgency is also emerging at the governance level.

As the focal point of the fourth scientific and technological revolution, achievements in the field of artificial intelligence affect the overall national strength of a country. In recent years, countries have conducted a series of cooperative and competitive interactions around artificial intelligence. To ensure healthy competition in the field of science and technology and to continually stimulate innovation, the global governance of artificial intelligence has become an important concern in international relations. Technology competition, trade conflict, information security, and ethical responsibility are all issues in the field of artificial intelligence. The absence of governance norms is not conducive to the positive effects of technology on human society and may even result in disorder and chaos.

In recent years, countries have strived to promote AI governance to keep pace with technological development by holding forums, publishing reports, and formulating specifications. However, differences among countries in terms of governance philosophies, development stages, and technological development levels pose numerous obstacles to consensus. As major powers in the world today, China and the United States should play a leading role in shaping the international order, working with other countries to formulate norms. The two powers are expected to lead the all-dimensional governance of artificial intelligence under the principle of "science and technology for good". Moreover, they should lead countries to jointly respond to challenges in the development process and promote the maximum application of technological achievements on a global scale. At the same time, the development of artificial intelligence remains at an unsaturated stage, and much room remains for cooperation between China and the United States. The two countries should fully recognize their interdependence in this industry chain and the broad future prospects of this field so they can jointly promote the orderly development of the artificial intelligence industry.

十九

人工智能治理成为国际关系的重要议题

陈定定

随着新一轮产业革命席卷全球，人工智能成为产业变革的核心方向。人工智能是经济发展的新引擎，是国际竞争的新焦点，是社会建设的新机遇。近年，人工智能在科技层面的热度持续攀升，其在治理层面的紧迫性也逐渐显现。

作为第四次科技革命的核心，人工智能领域的成果影响着一国综合国力水平，世界各国都对人工智能领域的发展给予了高度的重视，力争在这一关键领域取得先发优势。近年，各国围绕人工智能开展了一系列合作与竞争互动，为保证科技领域的良性竞争，不断激发创新活力，人工智能全球治理成为国际关系研究的重要关切。技术竞争、贸易冲突、信息安全和伦理责任等都是人工智能领域亟待达成全球共识的议题。治理规范的缺失，不仅不利于发挥技术对人类社会的正面效应，甚至可能带来无序和混乱。

近年，各国通过举办论坛、出版报告和制定规范等多种方式，力求推动人工智能治理跟上技术发展的脚步。但各国在治理理念、发展阶段和技术水平等层面的差异，为共识达成设置了重重障碍。作为当前世界的主要大国，中美两国在国际秩序塑造过程中应进一步发挥带头作用，协同各国加入规范制定，以“科技向善”引领人工智能全方位治理，共同应对发展过程中面临的挑战，并促进技术成果在全球范围内的最大化应用。与此同时，人工智能发展仍处于不饱和阶段，中美仍有很大的合作空间，两国应充分认识双方在该产业链中的相互依存关系，以及该领域广阔的前景，共同推动人工智能产业有序向前发展。

20

From Diversity to Decoloniality: A Critical Turn

Malavika JAYARAM

There is no shortage of frameworks for AI governance, yet their utility and legitimacy are not universally accepted. In addition to claims that the proliferation of principles and guidelines is about "ethics washing" rather than representing a commitment to real change and that it furthers the case for industry self-regulation rather than the enforcement of legally binding rules, a more fundamental set of questions is emerging about the values and norms that are embedded and reified in these frameworks and, equally importantly, those that are not.

It has become increasingly common–fashionable even–to look to multiple sources of values, such as Shintoism or Ubuntu philosophy, in an attempt to make the AI governance discourse more "inclusive". This trend, however well intentioned, is often restricted to a cosmetic exercise, cherry-picking concepts and anecdotes without engaging more critically with the structures and histories that they embody or with the dominant narratives and patterns of power that AI systems can internalize and amplify. These philosophies are often coopted and remixed by scholars and actors with privilege on stages and in spaces that either remain closed to the cultures and communities from which they borrow or appropriate or that fetishize them to perform diversity.

A growing body of scholarship rejects the idea of "inclusion" as paternalistic and inequitable. Who is doing the including? Into what? On what terms? How does doing so entrench and reproduce pre-existing power dynamics? This scholarship offers decolonial theory as a lens through which to understand the residue of colonizer–colonized relationships that continues to shape and produce digital technologies, including AI.

Colonial histories were built on land grabs and on the exploitation and dispossession of material resources. The effects of colonialism endure even today, continuing the process of appropriation and extraction: the survival of these power dynamics and structures is referred to as coloniality. Scholars have conceptualized data colonialism as a digital emanation of these colonial practices as human behaviors and interactions, represented by data, are mined and manipulated for material gain. The movement to decolonize data includes, among other things, efforts to preserve the sovereignty and autonomy of data that does not fit neatly into Western parameters, to have indigenous and marginalized communities control their information and their stories, and to decolonize research methodologies and practices.

To the extent that AI embeds and amplifies data colonialism at scale, it has a disproportionate

二十

从多样性到去殖民性：一个关键的转折

马拉维卡·杰亚拉姆

虽然我们并不缺乏 AI 治理框架，但是这些框架的效用和合理性并未受到广泛认可。有人认为层出不穷的原则和指导方针是一种“道德清洗”，而非对真正变革的承诺；它们进一步推动了行业的自我监管，而不是强制执行具有法律约束力的规则。除了这种声音之外，一系列更加基本的问题也逐渐浮出水面，这些问题有关融入这些框架并在其中具现化的价值观和标准，以及尚未融入并具现化但同等重要的价值观和标准。

为了让有关 AI 治理的讨论更具包容性，关注诸如神道教或乌班图理念等多种价值观来源的做法日益普遍，甚至成为了一种流行趋势。但是，无论初衷多么好，这种趋势往往都限于表面功夫、经过专门筛选的概念以及趣闻轶事，而没有以更严谨的态度考察这些理念所体现出的权力结构和历史，或可由 AI 系统内化和放大的主导叙事和权力模式。这些理念往往由拥有特权的学者和行为主体在相对于他们所借鉴或适合的文化和社区保持封闭的舞台和空间中，或让他们沉迷于追求多样性的舞台和空间中共同挑选和混合。

越来越多的学者开始拒绝包容性，因为他们认为，“包容性”这一概念带有一种不平等的家长式作风——谁在进行融合工作？融入什么之中？融合的条件是什么？它如何巩固和再现既存的权力动态？他们还提出了殖民主义理论，让人们透过其理解殖民者与被殖民者之间关系的残余，而这种关系正持续影响并产出包括 AI 在内的数字技术。

殖民的历史建立在对土地的掠夺、对物质资源的剥削和剥夺之上。殖民主义直至今日还在造成影响，继续着侵吞和榨取的过程：这种权力动态和权力结构的留存被称为“殖民性”。随着人们开始挖掘和操纵由数据代表的人类行为和互动以获得物质利益，学者们已经提出了“数据殖民主义”的概念作为这些殖民行为的数字化表现。数据去殖民化工作包括努力维护并不完全符合西方标准的数据的主权和自主权，让当地和边缘化社区管控其信息和案例以及实现研究方法和实践非殖民化。

AI 大规模嵌入和放大数据殖民主义的程度这一情况对意义的产生，以及现实甚至算法“真相”的建构造成了极其严重的影响。因此，它具有削弱甚至消除其他知识生产和意义建构系统的

impact on the production of meaning and the construction of reality, even of algorithmic "truth". As such, it contains the capacity to diminish or erase other systems of knowledge production and sense-making. The turn to decolonial AI consists of a conversation about resisting, undoing and providing alternatives to the dominant values, assumptions and biases that make AI systems oppressive, inequitable, and unsustainable. As scholars continue to identify and study sites of coloniality–such as predictive policing, welfare systems, and identity cards, which embed and perpetuate colonial histories and stereotypes about race, criminality, and poverty–the field of AI governance will expand from one that enshrines a narrow, homogenous idea of universal values to one that supports a genuinely pluralistic set of imaginaries and possibilities. This turn from diversity to decoloniality promises greater opportunities for a humane approach to living with, or without, AI.

能力。转向去殖民化 AI 需要的是一场对话抵制和消除使 AI 系统不公平、不平等和不可持续的主流价值观、主观臆断和偏见，并为其提供替代方案。随着学者们继续识别和研究殖民性孳生的温床，例如嵌入并延续了有关种族、犯罪和贫穷的殖民历史和刻板印象的预测性政策、福利制度以及身份证明，AI 治理将从一个恪守狭义、同质的普遍价值观念的领域，扩展为一个能为一套真正多样化的假想和可能性提供支持的领域。这一从多样性走向去殖民性的转变，为以人性化的方式与 AI 共存或在没有 AI 的情况下生活提供了更大的机会。

21

Mitigating Legacies of Inequality: Global South Participation in AI Governance

Marie-Therese PNG

In a historic year shadowed by the COVID-19 pandemic and global protests for racial justice, it is unsurprisng that the historic arc of structural inequality has been spotlighted in AI governance.

AI governance initiatives recognise their responsibilities in ensuring AI deployment and regulation do not "lock-in" intra and international inequalities. Accordingly, we see greater efforts towards heterogeneous representation in constructing guardrails to protect those most exposed to systemic harms. For example, the UN Secretary-General's 2020 Roadmap for Digital Cooperation called for greater participation of the Global SouthAI governance, to rebalance the situation led by North America, Europe and China.

As Jasanoff and Hurlbut advocate, we must be aware of "who sits at the table, what questions and concerns are sidelined and what power asymmetries are shaping the terms of debate".[1] Strategies for harms mitigation cannot be defined by those who benefit from AI systems, but by those who know and experience the costs.

For instance, Dr. Eugenio Vargas Garcia identifies that though lethal autonomous weapons are likely to be deployed first in conflict zones in low/middle-income countries, many of these regions are completely absent in the regulatory discourse. Exporting harms of AI systems to marginalised populations or low/middle-income countries via beta-testing is a well documented commercial or development practice.

In order to convene effective stakeholder coalitions to mitigate harms, we must first identify structural barriers to meaningful political participation of Global South stakeholders. If Global South state actors cannot act unilaterally to protect their interests, or civil society is not empowered to inform contextualised governance, AI governance initiatives will enact what Professor Ruha Benjamin terms "techno-benevolence"–interventions that intend to address inequalities, but instead reproduce or deepen dependency and extractivism. Moreover, policies will be replicated across jurisdictions in ways that are incompatible with the goals and constraints of developing countries.

廿一

减轻历史遗留的不平等问题：发展中国家在人工智能治理上的参与

方淑霞

在一个被新冠肺炎疫情和全球反种族歧视抗议所笼罩的历史性年份，结构不平等的历史轨迹在人工智能治理中受到关注不足为奇。

人工智能治理倡议认识到，它们有责任确保人工智能的部署和监管不会“锁定”内部和国际不平等。因此，我们构建壁垒保护易受系统性伤害的人时，在确保代表方的多样性方面做出了更大的努力。例如，联合国秘书长 2020 年数字合作路线图呼吁南半球国家更多地参与人工智能治理，以重新平衡北美、欧洲和中国在此方面的主导地位。

正如贾萨诺夫和赫尔伯特所提倡的，我们必须意识到“谁坐在谈判桌旁、哪些问题和担忧被搁置一旁、哪些权力不平衡现象正在影响着辩论的内容”。[1] 减轻危害的策略不能由那些受益于人工智能系统的人来确定，而必须由那些了解并付出过代价的人来确定。

例如，尤金尼奥·加西亚（Eugenio Vargas Garcia）博士指出，尽管致命性自主武器可能首先部署在中低收入国家的冲突地区，但其中许多地区完全没有监管方面的话语权。通过贝塔测试将人工智能系统的危害输出到边缘化人群或中低收入国家是一种有据可查的商业或发展实践。

为了召集利益相关者组成有效联盟以减轻危害，我们首先必须查明阻碍发展中国家的利益相关者在政治方面进行有效参与的结构性障碍。如果南半球国家不能单方面采取行动来保护自己的利益，或者市民社会未被授予权力进行情境化治理，那么人工智能治理倡议将实施鲁哈·本杰明（Ruha Benjamin）教授所说的“技术恩税”，即旨在解决不平等问题，却再现或加深了依赖性和榨取主义的干预措施。此外，相关政策还将以不符合发展中国家的目标和制约因素的方式在各司法管辖区推广。

在 DeepMind 的《去殖民化人工智能》（“Decolonial AI”）论文中，我和我的合著者沙基尔·莫赫德（Shakir Mohamed）博士、威廉·艾萨克（William Isaac）博士提出，如果不看人工智能

21

In DeepMind's 2020 Decolonial AI paper, my co-authors Dr. Shakir Mohamed, Dr. William Isaac, and I posit that we cannot understand present AI inequalities, or anticipate their futures, without looking at their historic trajectories. The first-mover advantages and exclusionary path dependencies we see today are, in part, living relics from our colonial histories. When we seek to increase Global South representation, we recognise that "Global South" describes a geography which emerged from legacies of colonialism.

The existence of international coalitions such as the G77 and Non Aligned Movement, key in the decolonisation and independence movements in Africa, Asia, Latin America and other regions, affirm the continuities of colonialism in contemporary global inequality. Today, these coalitions represent two-thirds of UN membership, and 55% of the global population. They are a platform for Global South countries to articulate collective interests and promote South-South cooperation.

In 2020 Professor Ulises Mejias proposed a Non Aligned Technology Movement, with a primary goal of transitioning from technological governance, and economic systems that reinforce dependency dynamics, to systems that support the self-determination of developing countries. Such ethos is a pre-requisite for meaningful Global South participation, robust risk mitigation, and preventing locked-in inequalities.

不平等现象的历史轨迹，我们就无法理解当前的人工智能不平等现象，也无法预测它们的未来。我们今天看到的先发优势和排他性路径依赖在某种程度上是从我们的殖民历史中遗留下来的。当我们寻求增加发展中国家的代表性时，我们认识到“发展中国家”描述的是殖民主义遗留下来的一种地理现象。

七十七国集团和不结盟运动等国际联盟的存在，是非洲、亚洲、拉丁美洲和其他区域非殖民化和独立运动的关键，证实了殖民主义在当代全球不平等中的持续性。如今，这些联盟占联合国成员国的三分之二、全球人口的55%。它们是发展中国家阐明集体利益和促进南南合作的平台。

2020年，乌利塞斯·梅杰斯（Ulises Mejias）教授提出了一项不结盟技术运动，其主要目标是从加强依赖程度的技术治理和经济系统过渡到促进发展中国家自主能力的系统。这种精神是发展中国家有效参与、降低风险，以及防止陷入不平等僵局的先决条件。

1. Jasanoff, S. and Hurlbut, J. B. (2018). A global observatory for gene editing. Nature 555, 435-437.

22

Enhancing Global Cooperation in AI Governance Based on Further Cultural Consensus

WANG Xiaohong

In 2019-2020, substantial progress has been made in AI governance from principle to practice; transdisciplinary cooperation between engineers and humanities scholars has converged on the "human-oriented" approach. All sectors of society-including major international organizations, an increasing number of national governments, leading ICT enterprises, academia, media, and educational circles-have made concerted efforts to build a wide-ranging network of AI governance. However, from the cultural comparison perspective, a potential concern exists regarding the AI governance environment beyond 2019. The increasingly intensified competition among countries and interregional conflicts cause the cooperation and sharing of the frontier technology of AI governance to be full of uncertainty. The root cause of this issue is the increasingly prominent differences in cultural values among countries and nations and the danger faced by the human community of being torn from one's own cultural unity. Confronting severe challenges in global governance, AI governance needs to enact more practical cultural accommodations and further promote value consensus.

Cultural values play an implicit role in technical and explicit measures. In recent years, engineers and ethicists have been cooperating to explore and solve specific problems, clarifying ethics as the practical value of AI design frameworks, and increasingly clarifying the process of AI governance. Taking as an example deep neural networks, governance principles (security, transparency, privacy, fairness, etc.) can be added to every link–from the definition of tasks and data collection to the design, training, testing, evaluation and application debugging of models. Thus will the improvement of technical means approach ethical expectations. However, the abstract principle "human-centric" may lead to differences in practical values due to cultural differences in the actual situation or even the countermeasures of AI governance. An ethical consensus on AI governance needs to be founded upon the major issues of the common destiny of mankind and the eternal values accumulated through cultural heritage.

The wisdom of "harmony but difference" (*Analects*) in Chinese culture means cultural diversity. Future AMAs (artificial moral agents with high autonomy and a high sensitivity to values) will choose to cooperate with rather than exterminate human beings. Any intelligent agent needs more freedom, and when diversity is greater, so are informational entropy and the freedom of

廿二

在增进文化共识基础上加强人工智能治理全球协作

王小红

2019—2020 年，AI 治理从原则到实践有了实质性的推进；工程师和人文学者跨学科合作在“以人为本”原则上达成共识；重要国际组织、越来越多国家政府、信息通信技术领军企业、学界、媒体、教育等社会各界协同推进，初步构建了布局广阔的 AI 治理之网。但从文化比较视角来看，2019 年以及未来的 AI 治理环境，有一个隐忧：日益加剧的国家间竞争和地区间冲突，使人类在 AI 治理前沿技术领域的合作共享充满着不确定性。其根源是各国和民族间文化价值分歧日益凸显，人类命运共同体面临文化撕裂的危险。在全球治理面临严峻挑战的形势下，AI 治理需要围绕伦理原则进行更切实的文化融通，进一步促成价值共识。

软性的文化价值，对于技术和显性层面各项举措起着润物细无声的“粘合剂”作用。近年来，工程师和伦理学家合作探索解决具体技术难题，将道德明晰化为 AI 设计框架的实践价值，使 AI 治理的技术流程日益清晰。以深度神经网络为例，从定义任务、数据收集，到模型的设计、训练、测试、评估和应用调试，每一环节都可以将治理原则（安全、透明、隐私、公平等）加入，改进技术手段会日渐趋近人们的伦理期待。但“以人为中心”这一抽象原则，在 AI 治理的实际情境中，因文化差异会导致实践价值差异，甚至可能有 AI 治理技术的相互反制。AI 治理价值层面的共识，植根于人类共同命运的重大命题、以及历经数千年文化积淀的永恒价值观。

中国文化中的高度智慧“和而不同”（《论语·子路》）意味着文化多元化。未来的人工道德智能体（AMAs）将有高度自主性和价值敏感性的，会选择与人类合作而不是灭绝人类，任何智能主体都需要更多自由，而多样性越大信息熵越大，每个个体才有更大的选择自由。信息伦理学以及机器道德研究一再揭示，中西文化融合的伦理视角乃道德洞见之源。“己所不欲，勿施于人”（《论语·颜渊篇》）、“己欲立而立人，己欲达而达人”（《论语·雍也》），与康德道德律令的关键思想相一致：只有当你愿意依此准则行事，才令此准则成为普遍规范。还有源于《礼记·中庸》的“慎独”，新儒家继承和发展的“修齐治平”工夫论，这些思想与亚里士多德倡导的美德伦理学投射出东西方古老文化共同的智慧。

choice of each individual. The study of information ethics and machine morality has repeatedly revealed that the integration of Chinese and Western cultures is the source of moral insight. "Do as you would be done by" and "I want to stand firm but also to let others stand firm; I want to develop but also to let others develop" are analects that are consistent with Kant's categorical imperative: only when you are willing to act on this criterion can you make this criterion a norm. In addition, the "self-restraining in privacy" (*Doctrine of Mean*) and self-cultivation practices inherited and developed by the Neo-Confucians, together with the virtue ethics advocated by Aristotle, reflect the common wisdom of ancient Eastern and Western cultures.

Human beings need the wisdom of cultural integration to realize the moral principles of AI. Human beings must act in concert, or the barrel effect will bring all efforts to naught. In the future, AI governance can focus on the core of AI ethics and strengthen substantive measures to enhance the value consensus among different countries and regions.

廿二

人类需要文化交融的智慧去实现 AI 道德原则。人类必须步调一致协同治理，否则任何一处的木桶效应，都将令一切努力付之东流。未来，AI 治理可以围绕 AI 伦理内核，加强增进不同国家和地区价值共识的实质性举措。

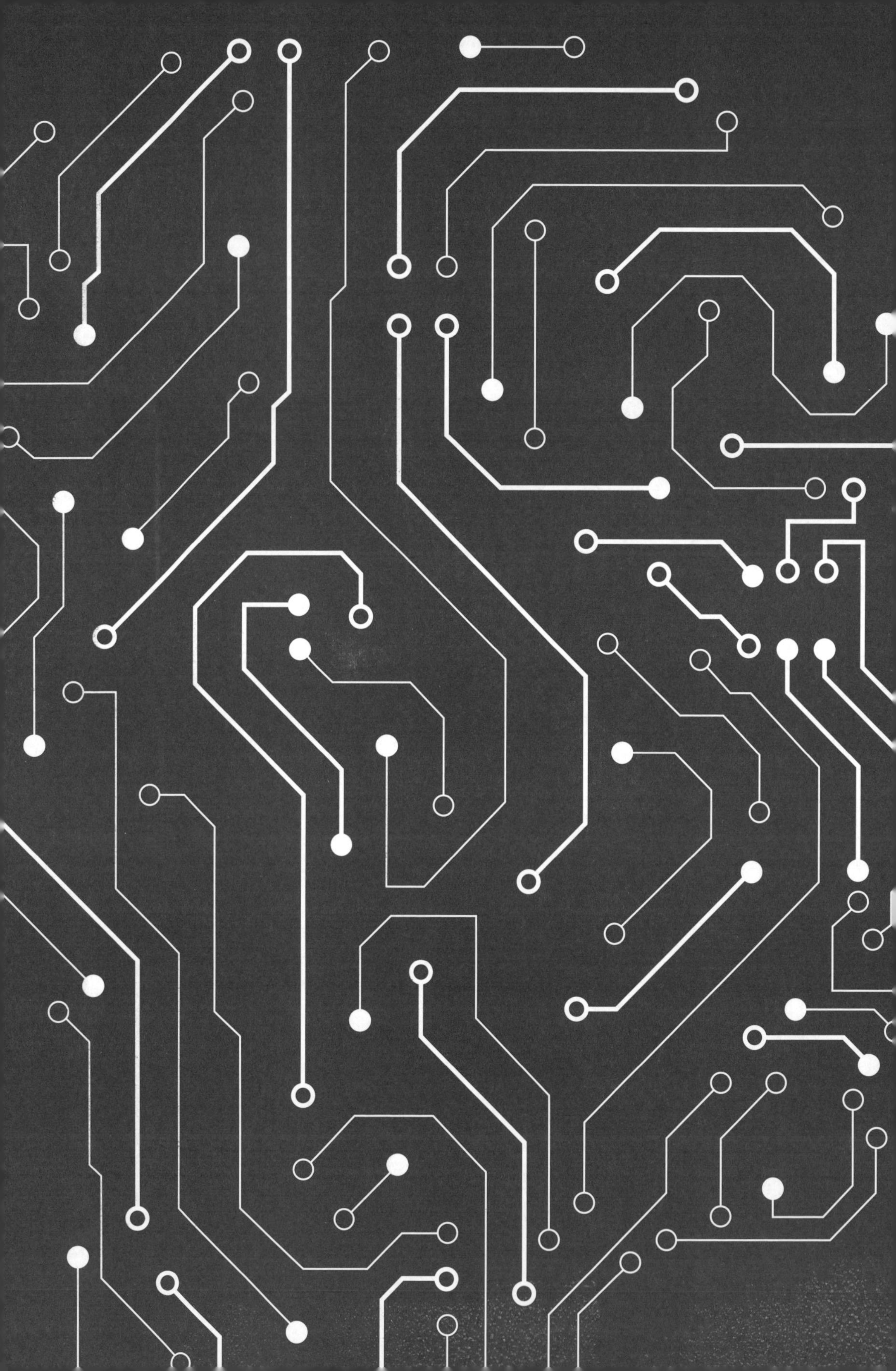

第二部分
PART II

行业动态与进展
INDUSTRIAL FRONTIER AND PROGRESS

人工智能的治理问题，存在于具体的场景中。具体行业中的企业或者机构，它们既是人工智能治理的对象，也是人工智能治理解决方案的积极探索者。在这一部分，我们邀请了来自人工智能行业的代表，针对人工智能在行业应用中浮现的问题，以及相应的解决方案，进行介绍和讨论。

Issues in artificial intelligence governance are embedded in specific scenarios. Enterprises and institutions in specific industries are not only the targets of artificial intelligence governance but also active explorers of solutions to issues concerning the governance of artificial intelligence. In Part II, we invited representatives from the artificial intelligence industry to introduce and discuss emerging issues related to artificial intelligence in its industrial practices, as well as to provide solutions addressing those issues.

23

Operationalizing AI Ethics: Challenges and Opportunities

Anand S. RAO

The spread of COVID-19 was swift and caught most governments, companies and citizens off-guard. Every aspect of life for almost every individual on this planet has been impacted by COVID-19. From direct impact (e.g., death, hospitalization, infection) to indirect impact (e.g., loss of job, working from home, mental health), the virus has affected almost everyone on this planet.

As a direct response to COVID-19 there has been a significant rise in the use of digital channels across all sectors in all countries. Riding on the back of this surge has been the increased adoption of advanced analytics, automation, and Artificial Intelligence (AI). We conducted a global survey of 1,018 executives in November, 2020, to understand how the crisis has impacted companies and their attitudes towards AI. We highlight two key aspects from this survey in this brief paper.

1. AI Investments are on the rise inspite of the economic crisis

In our survey, 44% of the respondents said that COVID-19 had a negative impact on their business and surprisingly an equal number said that COVID-19 had a positive impact on their business. Interestingly, the larger the companies (>$10bn in revenue) the more likely for them to have seen a significant positive impact from COVID-19. In addition, these larger companies, nearly 4 in 10, had invested more in AI development before the pandemic and were moving from experimental to operational use of AI. These companies, having seen their return on AI during the pandemic, were significantly more likely to increase their use of AI (38%), explore new use cases for AI (39%) and train more employees to use AI (35%). This is true not just of large companies, but also smaller companies that had heavily invested in AI prior to the pandemic. In addition, the global venture capital funding for AI rose to $71.9 billion in Q3, 2020, surpassing the previous record quarter in Q4, 2018 of $69 billion.

2. Managing and mitigating AI risks using Responsible AI is becoming critical

The spread of COVID-19 has seen an increased use of AI in applications such as facial recognition, contact tracing, monitoring of employee movement, etc. Identifying, mitigating, and managing AI risks–ranging from bias, privacy, transparency, accountability, explainability, robustness, safety, and security–is one of the major challenges for companies as they deploy AI models and systems to address and manage through the Crisis. Only 12% of companies had fully embedded and automated AI risk management and controls in place. Another 37% of respondents had

廿三

人工智能伦理实践的挑战和机遇

安纳德·劳

新冠肺炎疫情的暴发，令大多数政府、企业和公民猝不及防。新冠疫情对地球上几乎所有人的生活都造成了影响，这种影响涉及方方面面。从直接影响（如死亡、住院和感染）到间接影响（如失业、居家办公和心理健康），新冠病毒几乎影响了地球上的每个人。

新冠肺炎疫情的暴发是全球所有国家各行各业数字渠道使用率大幅上升的直接原因。在这种浪潮下，高级分析、自动化和 AI 的使用率日益上升。我们于 2020 年 11 月在全球 1018 名高管中进行了一次调查，以了解这次危机对各大企业及企业对 AI 的态度造成了何种影响。在这份简报中，我们重点强调了这次调查中的两大关键发现。

1. 虽然出现了经济危机，但 AI 投资仍呈现上升趋势

在我们的调查中，44% 的调查对象表示新冠疫肺炎疫情对其业务造成了负面影响，但令人惊讶的是，也有人表示新冠肺炎疫情对其业务起到了积极的促进作用，其数量与前者相当。有趣的是，企业规模越大（收入超过 100 亿美元），新冠肺炎疫情就越有可能对其产生显著的积极影响。此外，有近四成的大型企业在疫情暴发前对 AI 研发投入也较多，而且正从 AI 应用的试验阶段转向实际使用阶段。这些企业对 AI 的投入在疫情期间得到了回报，其增加 AI 使用率的比例（38%）、探索全新 AI 应用案例的比例（39%）和培训更多员工使用 AI 的比例（35%）远超其他企业。这不但适用于大型企业，也同样适用于在疫情暴发前就已大力投资 AI 的小型企业。此外，全球 AI 风险投资资金在 2020 年第三季度上升至 719 亿美元，打破了 2018 年第四季度 690 亿美元的纪录。

2. 通过使用负责任的 AI 来管理和消减 AI 风险正变得至关重要

新冠肺炎疫情的蔓延使 AI 在人脸识别、接触者追踪、员工行踪监测等应用中的使用率日益增长。对企业而言，识别、消减和管理 AI 风险（包括偏见、隐私、透明度、可问责性、可解释性、稳定性、安全性和保障性）是他们通过国际研究协会部署 AI 模型和系统来解决和管理问题时需要面临的重大挑战之一。只有 12% 的企业实现了完全嵌入式和自动化的 AI 风险管控。还有 37% 的

strategies and policies to tackle AI risks, but has no automated solutions. For the fully embedded AI segment these numbers went up to 29% (with embedded and automated AI risk management) and 38% (with strategies and policies) respectively. Of all the different areas of AI risks–algorithmic bias is a central focus of nearly 36% of all respondents. Reliability, robustness, security, and data privacy are some of the other AI risks that feature prominently amongst the companies scaling their AI.

In summary, the increased adoption of AI, increased investments in AI, and the risks posed by AI offer an opportunity to adopt responsible AI practices to manage and mitigate these risks.

廿三

调查对象拥有应对 AI 风险的策略和政策，但并没有自动化的解决方案。在完全嵌入式 AI 领域，这一数字分别上升至 29%（实现嵌入式和自动化 AI 风险管理的部门）和 38%（拥有相关策略和政策的部门）。在所有 AI 风险中，重点关注算法偏见的调查对象的比例接近 36%。对着手扩大 AI 应用规模的企业而言，其他主要 AI 风险还包括可靠性、稳定性、保障性和数据隐私。

综上所述，AI 应用的增长、AI 投资的增加，以及 AI 带来的风险让我们有机会采用负责任的 AI 实践来管理和消减上述风险。

24

Patterns of Practice Will Be Fundamental to the Success of AI Governance

Abhishek GUPTA

AI governance has certainly gained steam in 2020 with a lot of calls to action that have leveraged expertise in both the legal and technical fields to propose frameworks to govern both the development and deployment of AI systems. There are a lot of commonalities in these initiatives, with most of them focusing on areas of transparency, accountability, bias, privacy, non-discrimination, and other generally agreed upon values from the over 100 sets of principles in AI ethics, with most having at least some component focused on AI governance.

There has been a noticeable movement from 2019 when AI governance was a topic of discussion where people talked about abstract ideas and 2020 saw much more of a push to actually put those ideas into practice. Yet, as much as we saw movements, there were still some shortcomings that hindered the deployment of these governance mechanisms. In particular, 2020 was a year where we saw hasty roll-outs of these systems in tracking face mask compliance[1], grading students[2], handing out unemployment benefits[3], and more. So, what could we have done better?

As I have detailed in my work titled "Green Lighting ML: Confidentiality, Integrity, and Availability of Machine Learning Systems in Deployment"[4] that I presented with my co-author Erick Galinkin at several conferences in 2020 including ICML, what we have seen is that there is little focus on the practical manifestation of these ideas. Specifically, there is a missing focus on the needs and patterns of practice of designers and developers on the ground who will have at least partial responsibility in operationalizing these ideas. This is not to say that government mandates and management of the organization is not going to play an important role in how AI systems are governed. Quite the contrary, it is in fact essential that we consider the measures I am going to recommend as a supplement to the others, especially as they will help to bolster the efficacy of any other organizational-scale mechanisms that are applied in AI governance.

From a practitioner's perspective, there are numerous challenges that one faces when they encounter abstract principles coupled with business pressures and deadlines to deliver products and services on time and with high quality. It is at these points that there is a breakdown in the actual operationalization of the AI governance mechanisms which needs to be fixed.

From my experience, the first method that helps to mitigate this issue is to strive to incorporate

廿四

实践模式：人工智能治理的成功基础

阿布辛克·库布塔

人工智能治理在 2020 年无疑取得了不错的发展势头，有很多声音呼吁要采取行动，利用法律和技术领域的专业知识，提出人工智能系统开发和部署的治理框架。这些举措有很多共同点，大都侧重于透明度、可问责性、偏见、隐私、非歧视等领域，以及人工智能伦理领域 100 多套原则中受到普遍认同的其他价值观，大多数举措中至少有部分内容侧重于人工智能治理。

2019 年，人们已经开始谈论人工智能治理，但当时更多涉及的是抽象的想法。而到了 2020 年，人们看到了更多的推动力，想将这些想法付诸实践，这种转变十分明显。然而，虽然我们看到了很大的转变，但是仍有一些短板阻碍了这些治理机制的部署。特别是在 2020 年，我们看到这类系统在尚未完备的情况下被草率推出，用于追踪口罩合规性[1]、给学生评分[2]、发放失业救济金[3]等。那么，我们能在此基础上做出哪些改进呢？

正如我在题为《绿色照明 ML：部署中的机器学习系统的机密性、完整性和可用性》[4]的论文中详述的那样——我与合著者埃里克·加林金（Erick Galinkin）在 2020 年的几次会议（包括国际机器学习大会）上发表过这篇论文——我们发现，人们几乎没有关注这些想法的实际表现。具体而言，就是缺少对一线设计师和开发人员的需求和实践模式的关注，而他们在实施这些想法时至少要承担部分责任。这并不是说政府对组织的授权和管理不会在人工智能系统的治理中起到重要作用。事实上，我们必须考虑采取一些补充措施，特别是这些措施将有助于增强任何其他应用于人工智能治理的组织规模机制的效用。

从从业者的角度来看，他们在遇到抽象的原则、业务压力以及按时交付高质量产品和服务的限定期限时会面临许多挑战。人工智能治理机制的实际运作正是在这些方面出现了问题，需要修复。根据我的经验，有助于缓解此问题的首选方法是努力将各条治理要求融入设计师和开发人员的现有工作流程中，而不是跳到创建新机制这一步骤。这样做的好处是能降低接受这些新需求时产生的摩擦，并加快部署速度，然后收集证据来判断它们是否有效。有了这些证据，人们就可以在更广泛的层面上为它们的合并提供更有力的依据。

pieces of the governance requirements within existing work flows of designers and developers rather than jumping to create net new mechanisms. The benefit of doing so is that there is lower friction in the acceptance of these new requirements and they are also quicker to deploy and then gather evidence to see if they are effective or not. Armed with this evidence, one can make a stronger case for their incorporation at a wider level. Second, and perhaps the most important aspect of creating AI governance solutions is to include the practitioners in the process of developing these mechanisms. The requirement there is two-fold: one, you are able to surface the exact places where the AI governance solutions might fail when they are asked to be implemented in practice based on the experience of the practitioners and two, you also build trust with those practitioners so that they are not only aware of what will be asked of them but given that they are active contributors, they will have a strong sense of ownership and desire to see this succeed. Some of these insights are also discussed in my book *Actionable AI Ethics* that takes this very hands-on and practical approach to putting AI ethics into practice addressing some of the very challenges that I have highlighted here.

Thus, keeping in mind these patterns of practice will be crucial if we are to actually move forward in putting AI governance to work rather than spend another precious few months and years debating on the abstract ideas. The time for action is now and it starts by paying attention to how these systems are actually designed and developed in practice.

廿四

第二是要将从业者纳入这些机制的开发过程中，这可能也是创建人工智能治理解决方案时最重要的一点。具体而言，主要有两方面要求：第一，在实践人工智能治理解决方案时，需要能够根据从业者的经验指出人工智能治理解决方案在哪些方面可能无法发挥作用；第二，还要与上述从业者建立信任，确保他们不但能对相关要求心中有数，还会积极贡献，以强烈的主人翁意识促进解决方案取得成功。上述一些见解在我所著的《可操作的人工智能伦理》一书中也有所体现，该书以非常实用和实际的方式讨论了如何将人工智能伦理学付诸实践，试图解决我在此所强调的一些挑战。

因此，如果我们想要切实推进人工智能治理并使其发挥作用，那就不是再花几个月或几年的宝贵时间来讨论抽象的想法，而是要牢记这些实践模式。我们现在就应该采取行动，首先便是关注这些系统在实践中的设计和开发路径。

1. https://www.theverge.com/2020/5/7/21250357/-france-masks-public-transport-mandatory-ai-surveillance-camera-software
2. https://www.wired.co.uk/article/gcse-results-alev-els-algorithm-explained
3. https://www.usnews.com/news/best-states/articles/2020-02-14/ai-algorithms-intended-to-detect-welfare-fraud-often-punish-the-poor-instead
4. Gupta, A., & Galinkin, E (2020). Green Lighting ML:Confidentiality, Integrity, and Availability of Machine Learning Systems in Deployment. ArXiv:2007.04693 [Cs,Eess].http://arxiv.org/abs/2007.04693

25

Risk Management of AI Systems, But How?

Jared T. BROWN

The OECD's AI principles correctly state the potential risks from AI systems "... should be continually assessed and managed". But how should governments do that?

For a sense of scale of the governance challenge, consider some of the methods national governments have developed over decades to manage the risk of operating automobiles: regulations on who is allowed to operate automobiles and in what conditions (e.g., rules on licenses, intoxication levels, insurance requirements); the engineered design and safety features of automobiles (e.g., air bags, headlights); or continuous enforcement of rules on how to operate the automobile (e.g., traffic citations). And yet, despite being a technology well over 100 years old used across the globe, governments do not fully manage the negative consequences of automobiles, as accidents still result in over one million deaths annually.

And unlike automobile accidents, which have a relatively defined set of negative consequences, AI systems have a vast array of negative consequences that are much harder to identify and measure. As described in the European Union's *White Paper of AI*, these consequences are "both material (safety and health of individuals, including loss of life, damage to property) and immaterial (loss of privacy, limitations to the right of freedom of expression, human dignity, discrimination for instance in access to employment)". Further, risk management of AI systems will be especially difficult because there is an inherent "risk that AI's pursuit of its defined goals may diverge from the underlying or original human intent and cause unintended consequences–including those that negatively impact privacy, civil rights, civil liberties, confidentiality, security, and safety" (in the words of the official U.S. government regulatory guidelines for AI applications). As the Future of Life Institute (FLI) and our partners have captured in a multitude of formal and informal responses to government policy proposals issued throughout 2020[1], assessing and managing AI-related risk will be an extremely difficult and complex task.

Turning to 2021 and beyond, civil society organizations and AI experts will need to proactively engage with governments to help develop the policy equivalents of seat belt laws, speed limits, and traffic courts for managing the risk AI systems. In the United States, this will require robust engagement with the National Institute of Standards and Technology, which has been legally assigned the herculean task of developing a "voluntary risk management framework for trustworthy artificial intelligence systems". Elsewhere, in the European Union, experts will need to work with officials to further specify their proposal to conduct "conformity assessments for high-risk AI applications".

廿五

人工智能系统的风险管理该如何执行

贾里德·布朗

经合组织的人工智能原则正确地指出了人工智能系统的潜在风险“应该被不断地进行评估和管理”。但是政府应该如何做到这一点呢？

为了解人工智能治理方面所面临挑战的程度，可以参考各国政府几十年来为了管理汽车操作驾驶风险而制定的一些方法，包括关于允许驾驶汽车的人员和条件的规定（如有关驾照、酒驾和醉驾酒精含量判断标准，以及保险要求的规定）；汽车的工程设计和安全功能（如安全气囊、前照灯）；或对汽车驾驶规则（如交通罚单）的持续推行。然而，尽管这项技术实现全球应用的历史早已超过百年，但各国政府尚不能完全控制汽车驾驶的负面后果，汽车事故每年仍会造成100 多万人死亡。

汽车事故可能造成的后果相对明确，而人工智能系统会产生一系列更难识别和衡量的负面后果。如欧盟《人工智能白皮书》所述，这些后果“既有物质性的（个人的安全和健康，包括生命损失、财产损失），也有非物质性的（隐私权的丧失、对言论自由的限制、人类尊严、就业歧视等歧视问题）”。此外，人工智能系统的风险管理将会特别困难，因为存在一种固有的“风险，即人工智能对其既定目标的追求可能偏离潜在的或原始的人类意图，并导致意外后果，包括对隐私、公民权利、公民自由、保密性、保障性和安全性产生负面影响”[（引自美国政府的《人工智能应用监管官方指南》(*Guidance for Regulation of Artificial Intelligence Application*)]。正如生命未来研究所（FLI）和我们的合作伙伴于2020 年发布的针对政府政策提案的众多正式和非正式回应[1]中所发现的那样，评估和管理人工智能相关的风险将是一项极其困难和复杂的任务。

2021 年起，民间团体组织和人工智能专家将需要积极主动地与政府合作，协助制定与安全带法、限速令和交通法庭等对应的等效政策，以管理人工智能系统的风险。在美国，这将需要与国家标准与技术研究院进行紧密合作，因为国家标准与技术研究院在法律上被赋予了制定“针对可信赖的人工智能系统的自愿风险管理框架”的艰巨任务。在其他地区，例如在欧盟，专家们需要与官员们合作，进一步明确他们关于开展“高风险人工智能应用合规性评估”的提案。

1. futureoflife.org/policy-work

26

Building on Lessons for Responsible Publication: Safely Deploying GPT-3

Irene SOLAIMAN

The year 2020 combined unprecedented events in the world with precedented challenges in AI. The AI research community is grappling with best practices for responsible publication and safe deployment, but now largely coordinates remotely in work-from-home environments. Concurrently, existing concerns, like disinformation, show present-day consequences, like in pandemic response and political institutions.

AI systems, particularly generative models, have become increasingly powerful and demand safeguards. Generative models are trained on data such as text or images and seek to generate outputs that are similar to that data; for language models, that can mean predicting the next word in a sentence. Our concerns about risks are shared in industry, academia, and the public. Notably, Dr. Timnit Gebru co-authored a paper raising concerns with powerful language models, highlighting concerns like embedded biases. Work by OpenAI and other researchers has shown harmful biases, potential for misuse and generating disinformation, and difficulty detecting synthetic text.

Recognizing these risks, OpenAI conducted an unusual responsible publication strategy in 2019. We released incrementally powerful versions of our language model GPT-2 in stages to research model characteristics before each release. Our larger, higher-performing language model, GPT-3, required further consideration. Like its predecessor, it has flexible capabilities, from text summarization, translation, and question-answering to even three-digit arithmetic. GPT-3 also has a strong "few-shot learning" ability, i.e. the ability to solve problems given few demonstrations. GPT-3 has higher misuse potential than GPT-2 and still shows discriminatory bias, necessitating its careful deployment.

In the interest of safety, we released GPT-3 through an API; OpenAI hosts the system, and approved users can access it with an API key. We provide an interface for users to experiment, develop new applications, or conduct research. This release was part of a company decision to safely productize the system to help fund our research, but includes an academic access program for researchers to help identify model characteristics, especially on key areas of bias, misuse, and detection.

廿六

基于经验的负责任发布：GPT-3 的安全部署

艾琳·索拉曼

2020 年，世界上前所未有的事件与有先例的人工智能挑战接踵而来。人工智能研究界正在努力寻找最佳实践，以实现负责任的发布和安全部署，但现在主要是在居家工作环境中进行远程协调。同时，现有的问题（如虚假信息）显示了目前疫情响应和政治制度等方面的后果。

人工智能系统，特别是生成模型，已经变得越来越强大，因而需要安全保障。生成模型根据文本或图像等数据进行训练，并试图生成与该数据相似的输出结果。对于语言模型来说，这可能意味着可以被预测。我们对风险的担忧在工业界、学术界和公众中都存在。值得注意的是，蒂姆尼特·格布鲁（Timnit Gebru）博士在与人合著的一篇论文中提出了对强大语言模型的关注，强调了诸如嵌入式偏见等担忧。OpenAI 和其他研究人员已经证明了有害的偏见、潜在的误用和造谣的可能性，以及检测合成文本的难度。

认识到这些风险后，OpenAI 在 2019 年实施了一项不同寻常的负责任的发布战略。我们以分阶段的方式发布了我们的语言模型 GPT-2，进行分段式发布是为了便于在每次发布之前研究模型特性，确保每一个新版本都比上一个旧版本更加强大。我们在 2020 年发布的规模更大、性能更高的语言模型 GPT-3 还有待进一步验证。和 GPT-2 一样，GPT-3 同样具有灵活的功能，从文本摘要和翻译，到问答甚至三位数的算法，均在其能力范围之内。GPT-3 还具有很强的“小样本学习”能力,即根据少量给定的范例解决问题的能力。GPT-3 被误用的可能性比 GPT-2 更高，并且仍然表现出歧视性偏见，因此必须谨慎使用。

为了安全起见，我们选择通过 API 发布 GPT-3。OpenAI 托管了该系统，经过批准的用户可以使用应用程序编程接口（Application Programming Interface, API）密钥进行访问。我们为用户提供了一个用于进行实验、开发新应用程序或进行研究的界面。公司决定安全地将该系统产品化，从而为我们的研究提供资金。本次发布是该决策的一环，但包括一个针对研究人员的学术访问计划，旨在协助识别模型特征，特别是在偏见、误用和检测这几个关键领域。

26

An API functions as a means of safety, security and accessibility. We deployed GPT-3 without releasing the full system to the public, allowing us to easily respond to misuse and improve the system as we learn about it. We outlined usage guidelines, vet all use cases, and terminate any that cause harm or have insufficient safeguards. We host the system, which is expensive to run, alleviating cost pressures and making the system accessible for small businesses and organizations.

Since the system's flexible capabilities make all possible use cases impossible to predict, we limit users and are broadening access over time. Researchers at Middlebury Institute, University of Washington, and the Allen Institute for AI helped us scope disinformation and bias risks respectively. Our internal research helps build our usage guidelines and model improvements.

Recent foundational work in publication norms proves the need to continually invest as systems grow more powerful. AI researchers, including at the Partnership on AI and Google, informed practices like broader impacts analyses and model documentation. Impacts are context-dependent and mitigation requires not just technical, but social science and sociotechnical research. This research must continue with diverse communities and adapt to both the fast-pace of AI advancements and unexpected challenges of unprecedented events.

廿六

应用程序编程接口是一种确保安全性和可访问性的手段。我们在没有向公众发布完整系统的情况下部署了GPT-3，这使得我们能够轻松对误用做出响应，并在了解情况后对系统做出相应改进。我们概述了使用指南、审查了所有用例，并终止了任何造成伤害或缺乏足够保障的情况。我们托管了运行成本高昂的系统，减轻了成本压力，同时也使得这类系统能为小型企业和组织所用。

系统灵活的功能决定了我们无法预测所有的潜在用例，因此我们对用户做出了限制，并逐渐扩大访问范围。蒙特雷国际研究院、华盛顿大学和艾伦人工智能研究所的研究人员分别帮助我们研究谣言和偏见风险。我们的内部研究有助于制定使用指南进行模型改进。

最近在发布规范方面的基础性工作证明了随着系统的增强而不断进行投入的必要性。人工智能研究人员，包括人工智能伙伴关系和谷歌的研究人员，为更广泛的影响分析和模型文档等实践提供信息。系统增强带来的影响取决于环境，减轻影响不仅需要技术，还需要社会科学和社会技术研究。这项研究的继续开展需要与不同的团体合作，并适应人工智能的快速发展和前所未有的事件带来的意外挑战。

27

Companies Need to Take More Responsibility in Advancing AI Governance

YIN Qi

AI governance should be a global priority. In terms of policy-making, many countries have successively announced AI strategies and singled out the importance of AI governance. In 2019, China's Ministry of Science and Technology highlighted the critical nature of this work by announcing the establishment of its National New Generation AI Governance Expert Committee. In terms of media scrutiny, increasing attention has been given to issues such as the ethical boundaries and technical interpretability of AI and data privacy protection, which are all essentially AI governance issues.

AI governance is not only the responsibility of the government and relevant institutions. Enterprises, as the main force in the R&D and application of AI and the front-line practitioners of AI technologies, should fulfill their responsibility and take the initiative to achieve enterprise autonomy. Today, many international and Chinese companies, including Megvii, have launched their own AI ethics principles and criteria, elaborating on their initiatives to ensure the responsible governance of AI technology.

For companies, the effective implementation of AI governance measures is a major area of focus. Let me summarize my thinking based on firsthand experience at Megvii :

1. First

We must maintain a rational focus on and continue to engage in constructive discussions on AI governance. In January of this year, we invited experts across the fields of law, ethics and AI technology, as well as the general public, to join candid and constructive online discussions on the 10 most heavily debated AI ethics issues. We received thousands of comments across social media platforms, and the top concerns included privacy, information security and sufficient protection of user rights.

2. Second

We recognize the importance of conducting in-depth research on key issues. Data security and privacy protection are top priorities for both the public and enterprises. Megvii has a research

廿七

直面人工智能治理挑战：企业要有所作为

印奇

把人工智能治理作为重点工作来抓已经是各方的普遍共识。在政策制定上，多国相继颁布 AI 战略，并把 AI 治理作为核心内容。2019 年，中国科技部宣布成立国家新一代人工智能治理专业委员会，再次强调了 AI 治理的重要意义。在媒体监督上，关于 AI 的应用边界、AI 的技术可解释性以及数据隐私保护等问题引发越来越多的关注，这些本质上都属于 AI 治理问题。

AI 治理不仅政府及相关机构有责任，企业作为 AI 技术研发与应用的主要力量和一线实践者也应当有所作为，有所担当，要主动开展企业自治的工作。如今，包括旷视在内的许多国际和中国企业都推出了 AI 治理准则，正在发挥企业能动性来落实 AI 治理责任。

对企业来说，如何把 AI 治理有效落地是关注的重点。基于旷视自身的实践，我们总结出来几条经验：

第一

我们需要对 AI 治理保持理性的关注，同时展开具有建设性的讨论。2020 年 1 月，我们在网络上回顾“全球十大 AI 治理事件”，邀请法律、社会、伦理、技术等领域专家和全民共同讨论，就 AI 事件谈 AI 治理，千余条的留言结果显示，隐私、安全、权利是大众最关心的 AI 治理关键词。

第二

我们需要对重点议题进行深度的研究。无论对大众还是企业来说，数据安全和隐私保护都是重中之重。旷视已经联合北京智源人工智能研究院在此议题上开展研究，预期将形成一套面向数据全生命周期保护，针对采集、传输、存储和使用四个环节的 AI 基础平台，并建立一套相关的 AI 数据安全与隐私保护机制。同时，旷视承建图像感知国家新一代人工智能开放创新平台，希望通过平台的开放合作把 AI 治理的研究成果和企业应用实践经验与产业界分享，共同推动 AI 产业生态的健康和高速发展。

partnership with the Beijing Academy of Artificial Intelligence to focus on these issues. We are working to implement an AI platform to best manage the collection, transmission, storage and usage of data for its full life cycle protection and to establish a set of relevant AI data security and privacy protection mechanisms. Megvii was also tasked by the Ministry of Science and Technology to build a National Open Innovation Platform for Next Generation Artificial Intelligence on Image Sensing, where the industry-wide research results and practical experiences of enterprises will be shared to promote the healthy and rapid development of the AI industry.

3. Third

We need sustained action. A robust and effective organizational framework is required to oversee, implement, and foster collaboration on our AI ethics principles. Therefore, under its Board of Directors, Megvii has established an AI Ethics Committee–consisting of founders, core executives and external experts–to oversee the implementation of its AI ethics principles. The Committee is supported in its work of coordination and in-depth research by a secretariat and an AI Governance Research Institute.

AI governance is an effective solution for maintaining controls in the new era of AI. AI governance must become part of everything we do as an industry, and these types of preventative and protective measures need to be more widely recognized and practiced through a combination of learning and practice. I want to take this opportunity to call on everyone to take a long-term view and face the challenges of AI governance head on. I hope that together we can power humanity with AI.

第三

我们需要坚持不懈的行动。AI 治理在企业日常经营中落实要有切实的行动，这需要固定的组织来监督、协同和实施。旷视成立了由创始人、核心高管以及外部专家组成的 AI 道德委员会负责监督，委员会下设秘书处和 AI 治理研究院负责协调和深度研究，一线部门的负责人共同参与抓实施。

作为人工智能时代的“驭火之术”，AI 治理需要被更广泛的认知和践行，需要知行合一。也希望借此机会呼吁大家，共同以长期主义的态度，直面 AI 治理挑战，一起用人工智能造福大众。

28

Artificial Intelligence Should Follow Sustainable Development Principles

YANG Fan

As Artificial Intelligence (AI) grows more mature, its development also extends to other business areas, empowering all industrial sectors and exerting an unprecedented influence on the global economic system. The demand for AI talents has also changed from technical specialization to interdisciplinary thinking, or "AI + X", along with the constantly deepening development of AI covering all sectors and multiple fields. Meanwhile, discussions on the risks and ethical hazards associated with AI in the future are also increasing. We should not only consider AI from a mere technical perspective, but also attach importance to the social values that AI brings about in empowerment.

From the perspective of social attributes of AI, "sustainable development" is a must for building the AI ecology. The concept of "Sustainable Development of AI" derives from the United Nations' seventeen world-transforming goals. In other words, achieving the sustainable development of AI may create sectors values apart from achieving economic goals, which is helpful to building a community with a shared future for mankind. In June 2020, the UN launched the Roadmap for Digital Cooperation, which outlines eight key areas for action, such as achieving universal connectivity and ensuring digital inclusion for all. This roadmap explains more clearly the value and implications of sustainable development in the era of AI and big data.

On June 22, 2020, SenseTime Intelligent Industry Institute (hereinafter referred to as "SenseTime") and Qing Yuan Research Institute, Shanghai Jiao Tong University, jointly held the "AI Sustainable Development Forum 2030", and released the *White Paper on the Sustainable Development of AI*. It is the first time for the Chinese AI industry to discuss the concept of, and planning for, sustainable development. The White Paper proposes core values of people orientation, shared benefits, integrative development and scientific research innovation, clarifies the negotiatory and inclusive principles of AI ethics (respect, open dialogues, and inclusive culture), the all-benefiting and altruistic principles of AI to benefit people (sharing benefits and building an inclusive society), the conscientious and self-disciplined principles of AI to empower industries (accountability, self-discipline, and safety), and the open and sharing principles to develop a trustworthy AI (open innovation to make technology more reliable), and introduces new concepts and ideas for AI governance.

廿八

人工智能治理需要遵循可持续发展的理念

杨帆

随着人工智能技术的不断发展，AI 的应用已不仅仅局限于科技领域，AI 逐步赋能各行业，对全球经济发展起到了举足轻重的作用。AI 在全行业、多领域的不断深入也使得各界对 AI 人才的需求从“技术优先”转向关注“人工智能 +X”的跨学科复合型人才。同时，关于未来 AI 可能导致的风险讨论也愈来愈多。因此，我们已经不能用单一的技术视角去看待 AI，而应该同时看重 AI 在赋能时带来的社会价值。

当我们从社会属性的角度出发谈论 AI，可以看到“可持续发展”是建设 AI 生态的必由之路。AI 可持续发展的理念来源于联合国 17 个变革世界的目标，换言之，实现 AI 的可持续发展能够实现经济目标之外的社会价值，有助于实现共筑人类命运共同体的愿景。2020 年 6 月，联合国发布“数字合作路线图”，阐明了全球互联互通、数字包容等八个关键行动领域，这一路线图更加深刻地解释了 AI 和大数据时代背景下可持续发展的价值和内涵。

2020 年 6 月 22 日，商汤科技（以下简称“商汤”）智能产业研究院联合上海交通大学清源研究院，共同举办“AI 可持续发展论坛 2030”，并正式发布《AI 可持续发展白皮书》，这是中国 AI 产业界首次讨论可持续发展的理念和规划。白皮书提出以人为本、共享惠民、融合发展和科研创新的价值观，以及协商包容的 AI 伦理原则、普惠利他的 AI 惠民原则、负责自律的 AI 产融原则、开放共享的 AI 可信原则，为解决 AI 治理问题提出新观念和新思路。

在推进可持续发展框架的过程中，商汤以实际行动践行了可持续发展的各项原则。2019 年 7 月，商汤设立 AI 治理与伦理委员会，并规划设计了 AI 风险评估与管理框架，各项目落地之前必须通过委员会审核。在细分产业方面，商汤亦做出了许多努力。例如 2020 年 9 月 23 日，商汤成立“商汤教育”子品牌，通过教育平台等一系列产品以及教师培训项目降低 AI 数字鸿沟，为 AI 领域输送更多创新型人才，体现了联合国关于优质教育的可持续发展目标；在医疗领域，商汤的 SenseCare®AI 辅助诊疗系统在提升医疗工作者工作效率的同时有效地帮助遏制新冠肺炎

28

During the promotion of the framework of sustainable development, SenseTime has practiced the principles of sustainable development with practical actions. In July 2019, SenseTime established the Committee for AI Governance and Ethics, and designed the framework for AI risk assessment and management. All projects must be reviewed and passed by the committee before being launched. SenseTime has also put a lot of efforts in segment industries. For example, on September 23, 2020, SenseTime launched its sub-brand, "SenseTime Education", which narrows the AI digital gap with a series of products such as education platform and teacher training programs, to deliver more innovative talents for the AI field. This action represents the UN's sustainable goal of quality education. In the medical field, the SenseCare®, the AI-supported diagnosis and treatment system of SenseTime effectively contains the spread of COVID-19, while improving the efficiency of health professionals, and contributes to the UN's sustainable goal of good health and well-being. Similar cases, which represent the important ideas and practices of SenseTime concerning the empowerment of industries with AI, are too numerous to be enumerated.

As the pioneer of computer vision, SenseTime will constantly play its role in the sustainable development and governance of AI, acquire an in-depth understanding of the new trends in global science and technology development, open up new development paths of ethics and governance, further promote the corporate concept of building "Responsible AI", and stick to the principles of sustainable development, to deeply intertwine social responsibilities with corporate development.

疫情扩散，为落实联合国关于良好健康与福祉的可持续发展目标作出了贡献。诸如此类的案例不胜枚举，是商汤目前在实践 AI 赋能产业的重要思路和实践。

作为计算机视觉领域的领头羊，商汤将在 AI 可持续发展和治理领域中持续发挥作用，深刻理解全球科技创新的新趋势，开拓商汤在伦理与治理领域发展的新路径，进一步推动商汤“负责任的 AI”的企业理念并在实践中落实可持续发展的各项原则，将企业的发展与社会责任深度联系起来。

29

AI in Pandemic Response: Realising the Promise

Seán Ó hÉigeartaigh

Responding to COVID-19 has galvanised the AI research and governance communities in 2020, as it has the world at large. AI and digital technologies were touted early on in many quarters as being key to the response; and indeed, the early signs were promising. BlueDot, an AI-based outbreak identification and tracking system, provided one of the first warnings of the outbreak in January. Thousands of papers described AI-based applications across the prediction and response process, from outbreak modelling, to drug discovery, to hospital logistics planning, to symptom analysis, to surveillance in support of quarantining.

A year in, however, it is clear that the role for AI has been somewhat limited. Why? I have been part of the Global Partnership on AI's AI and Pandemics working group, which has spent 6 months analysing applications, limitations, bottlenecks and solutions. I offer some individual reflections:

1. **Hype vs boring reality.** Technology is wonderful, but the core of pandemic response remains tried and trusted techniques - investments in public health, including sufficient PPE and hospital health capacity; (manual) contact tracing; quarantining, and so forth. AI can play a role in supporting this, but for now still a limited one. Indeed, over-focusing on technological solutions can divert attention and resources away from the basics.

2. **A new challenge.** AI, and particularly ML systems, work well when we can learn from the past to predict or act in the future. COVID-19 was a new disease, with new symptoms affecting populations in a novel way, and creating a relatively novel set of challenges and pressures on society. This makes it more difficult to train and deploy AI systems with confidence in many contexts. In particular:

3. **Data.** Many potential AI applications, from deep learning-based analysis of lung CT scans, to predicting population health outcomes, need large, diverse, representative datasets to be trained to sufficiently robust performance. In practice, data has been sparser, and scattered across research groups and countries.

4. **Ethics and governance.** Researchers and governments pursuing AI techniques, and the digital systems that would have provided the data necessary for AI, have struggled with legal, regulatory and ethical challenges. Health data especially is subject to specific protections and ethical considerations (for good reason), and navigating data access and responsible use across

廿九

人工智能在疫情应对中的应用：实现承诺

贺尚安

2020 年，新冠肺炎疫情的应对工作激发了人工智能研究和治理界的热情，因为这场疫情造成的影响是全球性的。人工智能和数字技术早以在许多方面被视为有效应对疫情的关键。事实上，早期迹象给了我们很大的希望。基于人工智能的疫情识别和跟踪系统蓝点（BlueDot）曾率先对一月的疫情发出警告。数以千计的论文描述了人工智能在预测和应对过程中的应用，包括疫情建模、药物研发、医院后勤规划、症状分析，以及保障隔离工作有序推进的监测。

然而，一年来，人工智能显然受到了一定程度的限制，未能如期发挥其应有效用。原因何在？我是人工智能全球伙伴关系的人工智能与疫情工作组的成员，我们花了 6 个月的时间分析相关应用、限制、瓶颈和解决方案。我的个人反思与见解分享如下：

1. 炒作 VS 无聊的现实。我们拥有令人惊叹的技术，但疫情应对的核心仍然是久经考验和值得信任的技术——对公共卫生的投资，包括足够的个人防护装备和医院卫生能力、（人工）接触者追踪、隔离等。人工智能可以为这方面的工作提供支持，但目前其作用仍然有限。事实上，过度关注技术解决方案可能会转移人们对基本问题的注意力和相关资源的投入。

2. 新的挑战。人工智能，特别是机器学习系统能够在我们吸取过往经验以预测未来或在未来采取行动方面发挥很大的作用。新冠肺炎是一种新型疾病，它的症状和对各类人群的影响都是前所未见的，并为社会带来了一系列相对较大的挑战和压力。这在许多情况下为妥善训练和部署人工智能系统加大了难度，特别是在以下方面：

3. 数据。许多潜在的人工智能应用，包括基于深度学习的肺部 CT 扫描分析，以及对人群健康结果的预测，都需要通过大量、多样和具有代表性的数据集来进行训练，以获得足够强大的性能。实际上，当前数据资源较为稀缺，而且分散于不同国家的研究小组之中。

4. 伦理和治理。研究人工智能技术以及为人工智能提供必要数据的数字系统的研究人员和各国政府一直在努力应对法律、监管和伦理方面的挑战。健康数据尤其需要得到具体保护和遵守伦理注意事项（有充分的理由），跨司法管辖区引导数据获取和负责任的使用可能是一个不透

jurisdictions can be an opaque process, especially for smaller groups. In the UK, a centralised approach to digital contact tracing, which would have been a rich resource for ML analysis, was initially favoured by government; however well-justified concerns about privacy and data governance from civil society groups contributed to the adoption of a decentralised approach.

The COVID-19 crisis still has years to run, during which AI can be far more useful. There are pressing steps in AI governance that can be taken to support this. I highlight in particular the recommendations on global research- and data-sharing, and data governance described in the GPAI report[1] . There is also a role for privacy-preserving ML and other approaches to secure data use. To avoid mistakes and ensure public trust, we must be able to address ethics and governance with urgency, through better use of foresight and ethics by design; having a strong focus on and support for robustness and reliability; and through fast-moving oversight bodies and cross-society consultative methods[2,3]. Above all, it is essential that we build on this crisis to be better-prepared for future pandemics. In this crucial challenge, the potential for AI to aid us remains immense.

明的过程，尤其是对于较小的群体而言。在英国，一种集中式的数字接触者追踪方法最初受到政府的青睐，这种方法本可以为机器学习分析提供丰富的资源；然而，民间社会团体对隐私和数据治理的合理担忧还是让政府最终决定采用分散式的方法。

新冠肺炎疫情危机仍将持续数年，在此期间人工智能可能会发挥更大的作用。我们迫切需要采取一些可以为此提供支持的人工智能治理措施。我特别强调 GPAI 报告中关于全球研究和数据共享以及数据治理的建议[1]。保护隐私的机器学习和其他数据使用安全保障方法也能发挥效用。为了避免错误和赢得公众信任，我们必须能够按计划更有效地利用前瞻性和伦理，及时处理伦理和治理问题；重点关注和支持稳健性和可靠性；采用快速发展的监督机构和跨社会协商方法[2,3]。最重要的是，我们必须在这场危机的基础上再接再厉，为未来的疫情做好进一步的准备。在这个关键的挑战中，人工智能仍可能为我们提供巨大的助力。

1. http://thefuturesociety.org/wp-content/uploads/2020/12/Responsible-AI-in-Pandemic-Response.pdf
2. hTzachor, A., Whittlestone, J., Sundaram, L., & hÉigeartaigh, S. Ó. (2020). Artificial intelligence in a crisis needs ethics with urgency. Nature Machine Intelligence, 2(7), 365-366. https://doi.org/10.1038/s42256-020-0195-0
3. Cave, S., Whittlestone, J., Nyrup, R., O hEigeartaigh, S., & Calvo, R. A. (2021). Using AI ethically to tackle covid-19. BMJ, n364. https://doi.org/10.1136/bmj.n364

30

Human-Centered AI/Robotics Research and Development in the Post-Pandemic Era

ZHANG Jianwei

In this extremely exceptional year of COVID-19, AI must face global anti-pandemic challenges in addition to its on-pace progress in adding more top-down approaches, cross-modal learning, and unsupervised architecture to its supervised deep-learning approaches guided by single-criterion optimization. Mostly in the home-office mode and based on data/algorithms, clear advances can be observed both at the fundamental research and novel application levels, shaping the theory and practice of AI governance.

Useful AI and robot systems are urgently needed to curb the rapid spread of the COVID-19 virus and to return daily work and life to normal. These requirements put the focus of AI governance on the precise modeling of the paths of virus infection; the rapid development of real-time testing methods, effective vaccines and drugs; and autonomous robot systems that can assist medical doctors/nurses and replace human workers in labor-intensive tasks such as delivery, harvesting, factory assembly, etc.

We have developed an AI approach to determine the likelihood of asymptomatic carriers of the COVID-19 virus by using interaction-based continuous learning and individual probability inference to rank the likelihood of contagion. Compared to traditional contact-tracing methods, our approach significantly reduces (by as much as 94%) the screening and quarantine duration required to search for potential asymptomatic virus carriers. At the same time, we are integrating human–robot interaction, multilevel learning and robot decision-making to develop an autonomous, safe and intelligent robot system for both nasopharyngeal and oropharyngeal swab sampling, which will protect medical staff. Collaborating with PixelBiotech, a German start-up, we applied AI to empower the imaging data analysis of a multiplex smFISH (single molecule fluorescence in situ hybridization) probe, which reduced the testing time of the COVID-19 virus to 15 minutes. Overall, we believe that AI and robotics are increasingly affecting the fight against the pandemic by modeling the precise spreading process and by automatically and efficiently detecting the virus.

Based on the Sino–German interdisciplinary collaborative project, TRR169 "Cross-modal Learning: Adaptation, Prediction and Interaction", we continue to research and develop human

三十

后疫情时代下以人为本的人工智能和机器人的研究与发展

张建伟

2020 年，新冠肺炎疫情肆虐。在这极不寻常的一年里，AI 在设法稳步推进在由单一标准优化指导下的受监督深度学习方法中纳入更多自上而下的方法、跨模态学习和无监督架构，同时不得不面对疫情所带来的全球挑战。我们看到，AI 在基础研究和新应用层次方面取得了显著的进展。这些进展大多涉及基于数据 / 算法的居家办公模式，从而影响了 AI 治理的理论和实践。

我们亟须通过实用的 AI 和机器人系统遏制新冠病毒的迅速传播，并恢复正常的工作和生活节奏。这些要求使 AI 治理的重点聚焦在针对病毒感染途径的精确建模、实时检测方法的快速开发、有效的疫苗和药物，以及能够协助医生 / 护士，并代替人类完成配送、收货、工厂装配等劳动密集型任务的自主机器人系统。

我们已相应地开发了一种 AI 方法，通过基于互动的持续学习和对个人病毒携带率的推断，来确定出现无症状新冠病毒携带者的可能性，从而评估传染几率。与传统的接触者追踪方法相比，该方法大幅减少了寻找潜在无症状病毒携带者所需的筛查和隔离时间，降幅高达 94%。同时，我们正着手集成人机互动、多层次学习和机器人决策应用技术，以开发一种安全自主的智能机器人系统，用于鼻咽拭子和口咽拭子采样，从而保护医务工作者，大幅降低其接触感染风险。通过与德国初创企业 PixelBiotech 公司合作，我们已经开始用 AI 增强复合单分子荧光原位杂交（smFISH）探针的成像数据分析，将新冠病毒的检测时间缩短至 15 分钟。总体而言，我们相信，AI 和机器人技术将通过促进更精确的传播过程建模和高效的自动病毒检测，为全球抗疫带来越来越多的积极影响。

我们将基于中德跨学科合作项目 TRR169“跨模态学习的自适应、预测和交互”，继续研究和开发人类增强技术，以促进人机物理协作。此外，我们还致力于与各神经科学与心理学实验室携手开发人类增强和支持应用，如神经计算表征和神经疾病的治疗应用。此类以人为本的长期研发工作代表了 AI 最重要的垂直应用之一。

enhancement to facilitate physical human–robot collaboration. Furthermore, we are developing applications for human enhancement and support in collaboration with laboratories from neuroscience and psychology, such as the neurocomputational representation and therapeutic application of neurological diseases. Such long-term human-centered research and development represent an important AI vertical application.

Within TRR169, we use the established collaboration between the partners from Hamburg and Beijing to achieve a higher level of understanding, modeling and implementing cross-modal systems and of understanding and unifying the neural, cognitive and computational mechanisms of cross-modal learning. Significant progress in several areas, particularly in deep learning (algorithms, software, and applications), encourages us to pursue a more integrated set of objectives as future-oriented, strong-AI research themes: novel learning architectures/strategies, robustness, anticipation and prediction, generalization and transfer, and benchmarking. Overall, our mission is to develop transparent, interpretable brain-inspired AI approaches, which are significant technological features of AI governance.

三十

在 TRR169 项目中，我们通过来自汉堡和北京的合作伙伴之间的成熟合作，进一步提升了对跨模态系统的理解、建模和应用水平，以及对跨模态学习的神经、认知和计算机制的理解和集成水平。我们在一些领域，尤其是深度学习领域（如算法、软件和应用）取得了重大进展，这激励着我们追求实现一系列综合性更强的目标，作为面向未来的强 AI 研究课题，包括新的学习架构 / 策略、稳定性、预期与预测、泛化与转移，以及标杆管理。总体而言，我们的使命是制定透明且可解释的类脑 AI 方法，这是 AI 治理的一项重要技术特征。

31

AI Governance in Digital Health Care for a Post-Pandemic World Requires Multistakeholder Partnerships

Omar COSTILLA-REYES

In the last few years, the digital health space has rapidly increased in activity in both in the United States and globally. Start-ups, research, and investment in the space have never been this active[1]. The accelerated speed of adoption has been facilitated by the ongoing pandemic and the need to find remote and innovative health care solutions.

In the United States, the regulatory body that approves the use of digital health technologies for clinical applications is the Food and Drug Administration (FDA). The first set of products that went through the FDA "de novo"[2] certification model for digital health software included "digital therapeutics", which are "evidence-based therapeutic interventions to patients that are driven by high-quality software programs to prevent, manage, or treat a broad spectrum of physical, mental, and behavioral conditions", as defined by the digital therapeutics alliance, a nonprofit trade association of industry leaders and stakeholders in digital therapeutics[3]. FDA-approved solutions include drug addiction and insomnia software as well as the first video game-based software solution for the treatment of attention deficit disorder in children[4].

While a clinical digital intervention offers great promise to alleviate major health care issues, its acceptance, integration with the health care system and policy reform have been difficult and are currently in the early stages. Some digital therapeutic models pursue a drug-like reimbursement model[5] and are not widely accepted by policy-makers and insurers due to their digital nature.

The regulatory pathway for digital therapeutics is also difficult for new players in the space. Clinical regulatory approval requires evidence-based products that can be evaluated only by running large, costly, and time-consuming clinical trials.

Current solutions in the digital therapeutics space focus mainly on digitalizing evidence-based health care solutions as interventions, for example, by digitalizing cognitive behavioral therapy programs for mental health.

The new generation of digital health care products envisions incorporating artificial intelligence that learns and changes with longitudinal data obtained from mobile phones and wearable data

三十一

后疫情时代数字医疗人工智能的有效治理需要多方利益相关者协同合作

奥马·科斯提拉·雷耶斯

过去几年，美国和全球数字健康领域的活动增长惊人。该领域的初创企业、研究和投资空前活跃。[1] 持续不断的全球疫情和寻求创新型远程医疗保健方案的需求促进了数字医疗应用的迅速普及。

负责批准数字医疗技术临床应用的监管机构是美国食品和药物管理局（FDA）。“数字疗法”是首批通过 FDA 针对数字医疗软件的“de novo”[2] 认证模式的产品之一。依据数字疗法联盟的定义，数字疗法是“为患者提供的循证治疗干预，这些干预措施由高质量的软件程序驱动，旨在预防、管理或治疗广泛的生理、心理疾病和行为异常”。数字疗法联盟是一家由数字疗法领域的行业领先企业和利益相关者组成的非营利贸易协会。[3] 目前已有不少医疗软件获得了 FDA 的批准，包括药物成瘾和失眠治疗软件，以及首款通过视频游戏治疗儿童注意力缺陷障碍的软件解决方案。[4]

虽然临床数字干预在缓解重大医疗保健问题方面前景光明，但如何提高其接受度、将其融入医疗体系以及推行相关政策改革一直以来都是难题，且目前才刚刚起步，任重道远。部分数字疗法模式遵循了类药报销模式，[5] 该模式具有数字化特性，因而尚未被政策制定者和保险公司广泛接受。

对于数字疗法领域的新兴组织机构而言，数字疗法的监管路径也很难遵循。想要监管部门批准临床研究，就必须研发出循证产品，但这类产品必须通过大型临床试验进行检测，成本高昂且费时费力。

目前，数字疗法领域的解决方案主要专注于对循证医疗保健解决方案进行数字化处理，以此作为干预措施，例如对针对心理健康问题的数字化认知行为治疗项目进行数字化处理。

新一代数字医疗产品的目标在于整合从移动电话和可穿戴数据传输设备获得的纵向数据，并进行持续学习和改变，不断提高解决方案的效用和个性化程度的人工智能。该类人工智能的研究还处于起步阶段，需要科研界、政府和行业的协同合作。

to improve the solution's performance and personalization over time. This area of research is in its early stages and requires partnerships in the research, governmental, and industrial sectors to be successful.

Significant progress has been made in the research of digital health care. In the mental health space, for example, two major digital health initiatives are under way. In the United States, the University of California, Los Angeles, has launched a depression grand challenge to research objective measurements of depressive symptoms with mobile devices. This project utilizes a large cohort of patients in partnership with Apple Inc[6]. In the European Union, the radar central nervous system initiative aims to explore the potential of wearable and mobile devices to prevent and treat depression, multiple sclerosis, and epilepsy in partnership with Janssen Pharmaceuticals, Inc.[7]

The FDA is currently defining how to legislate Software as a Medical Device (SaMD)[8], whose core component consists of artificial intelligence that learns and adapts over time according to the patient's needs. The FDA is now running a precertification model that constantly evaluates companies and products to obtain regulatory approval to offer SaMD AI solutions [9]. The evaluation includes patient safety, product quality, clinical responsibility, cybersecurity, and a proactive culture. The world should look to the United States FDA's SaMD certification model for inspiration to create legislation, considering the differences in cultural, societal, and economic contexts.

Policy-makers face the challenge of allowing freedom of innovation in the digital health care space while guaranteeing patient safety and product efficacy. The opportunity for digital therapeutics to provide effective digital solutions in health care is unique and timely for a post-pandemic world, a place where the digital adoption of health care solutions has increased at a never-before-seen pace.

To revolutionize global digital health care, several scientific disciplines, such as psychology and computer science, must align to a single goal[10] while representatives work closely with policy-makers to create effective and safe solutions that offer an opportunity for a large positive impact on the lives of millions worldwide[11].

三十一

数字医疗领域的研究同样取得了不错的进展。例如，在心理健康领域，有两项主要的数字健康举措。其一，美国加州大学洛杉矶分校与苹果公司合作[6]，发起了一项抑郁症大挑战，研究如何通过移动设备客观检测抑郁症状。其二，欧盟发起了中枢神经系统雷达监测倡议，旨在探索可穿戴设备和移动设备在预防和治疗抑郁症、多发性硬化症和癫痫症方面的潜在效用。该倡议同样以合作形式开展，合作对象为杨森生物技术公司。[7]

SaMD 是一种以人工智能为核心组件的医疗器械，能根据患者的需求不断学习并做出调整。[8] FDA 目前正在研究如何为其软件进行立法，并在采用一种预认证模式，即不断对公司和产品进行评估，以获得监管部门的批准，从而提供 SaMD AI 解决方案。[9] 评估内容涵盖患者安全、产品质量、临床责任、网络安全以及积极的文化氛围。

全球各国都应参照美国的 SaMD 认证模型，依据自身的文化、社会和经济背景，制定相应的立法认证体系。

政策制定者当前面临一项重要挑战，即如何在给予数字医疗领域的行为主体创新自由的同时，保证患者安全和产品功效。后疫情时代正是运用数字疗法提供有效数字医疗解决方案的最佳时机。当下，医疗保健解决方案正以前所未有的速度得到数字化应用。

推动全球数字医疗的彻底改革，需要心理学和计算机科学等多个学科领域协同配合[10]，并同时与政策制定者密切合作，以建立安全有效的解决方案，显著改善全球数百万人的生活。[11]

1. "H1 2021 Digital Health Funding: Another Blockbuster Year…In Six Months," Rockhealth, July 6, 2021,https://rockhealth.com/reports/h1-2021-digital-health-funding-another-blockbuster-year-in-six-months/.
2. "FDA De Novo Classification Request," U.S. Food & Drug Administration, October 4, 2021,https://www.fda.gov/medical-devices/premarket-submissions/de-novo-classification-request.
3. "Digital Therapeutics Definition and Core Principles," Digital Therapeutics Alliance, November 2019,https://dtxalliance.org/wp-content/uploads/2021/01/DTA_DTx-Definition-and-Core-Principles.pdf.
4. "FDA Permits Marketing of First Game-Based Digital Therapeutic to Improve Attention Function in Children with ADHD," U.S. Food & Drug Administration, June 15, 2020, https://www.fda.gov/news-events/press-announcements/fda-permits-marketing-first-game-based-digital-therapeutic-improve-attention-function-children-adhd.
5. Stephanie Baum, "Digital health reimbursement: The transforming landscape," MedCityNews, October 5, 2020,https://medcitynews.com/2020/10/digital-health-reimbursement-the-transforming-landscape/.
6. UCLA depression grand challenge, https://grandchallenges.ucla.edu/depression/.
7. RADAR-CNS: Remote Assessment of Disease and Relapse – Central Nervous System,https://www.radar-cns.org.
8. "FDA Artificial Intelligence and Machine Learning (AI/ML) Software as a Medical Device Action Plan," U.S. Food & Drug Administration, September 22, 2021,https://www.fda.gov/medical-devices/software-medical-device-samd/artificial-intelligence-and-machine-learning-software-medical-device.
9. "Digital Health Software Precertification (Pre-Cert) Program," U.S. Food & Drug Administration, May 6, 2021,https://www.fda.gov/medical-devices/digital-health-center-excellence/digital-health-software-precertification-pre-cert-program.
10. Costilla Reyes, Omar. (2018). "Pattern recognition from raw spatiotemporal data for gait analysis in health care and security." University of Manchester. https://www.research.manchester.ac.uk/portal/en/theses/pattern-recognition-from-raw-spatiotemporal-data-for-gait-analysis-in-healthcare-and-security(c7135e67-82bd-4b72-a85d-d73b2b6a3a20).html.
11. Anllo, Guillermo; Corvalán, Juan G; Costilla, Omar; Enciso Tonatiuh; Gaytan; Francisco; Le Fevre, Enzo; Martínez Yolanda; Mata, Susana; Paredes Miguel; Vega, Marco, Cumbre de Inteligencia Artificial de América Latina 2020, Estados Unidos. https://ialab.com.ar/wp-content/uploads/2021/01/AI-BOOK..pdf.

32

"Cross-Sector GPS" Strategy: Building an Industry-Agnostic and Human-Centered Future of Work

POON King Wang

Under the guidance of Singapore's Advisory Council of the Ethical Use of AI and Data, Singapore's Infocomm Media Development Authority and Personal Data Protection Commission collaborated with the Lee Kuan Yew Centre for Innovative Cities (LKYCIC) at the Singapore University of Technology and Design, to launch *A Guide to Job Redesign in the Age of AI*.

It is Singapore's first industry-agnostic and cross-sector guide. It helps companies pursue practical strategies that take full advantage of AI and empower employees at the same time.

The value of being industry-agnostic, cross-sector, and human-centered was made clear by the pandemic. COVID-19 disrupted entire sectors. The workers in those sectors suffered because many current up-skilling efforts are sector-specific. These are clearly inadequate when there are few options left for workers within their sectors and professions.

Such disruption will become more prevalent in future because the pandemic has also accelerated digital adoption. The resulting increase in automation, remote work, and outsourcing risks, will cause widespread displacement across more sectors. Workers in these sectors will similarly find sector-specific up-skilling inadequate.

Workers thus need an industry-agnostic and cross-sector strategy to break out and find opportunities outside of their sectors and professions.

The LKYCIC has developed such a strategy.

Our strategy is effectively a "cross-sector GPS". By applying human-in-the-loop AI to a Tasks-Skills Stack we have built, we can chart clear, concrete, step-by-step pathways from disrupted professions/sectors to growth professions/sectors.

Our strategy does this by first identifying the tasks shared by different jobs across different sectors. We then map cross-sector task-by-task pathways between them. Companies, workers, and governments can subsequently use these pathways to find new opportunities and expand

三十二

“跨行业 GPS”战略：创造一个全行业通用且以人为本的未来工作格局

潘竞宏

在人工智能和数据道德使用咨询委员会的指导下，新加坡资讯通信媒体发展管理局和个人数据保护委员会联合新加坡科技设计大学李光耀创新型城市中心（LKYCIC）发布了《AI 时代下的职业再设计指南》（*A Guide to Job Redesign in the Age of AI*）。

这是新加坡首份全行业通用的跨行业指南，旨在帮助各企业制定切实可行的战略，以充分利用 AI，并为员工赋能。

新冠肺炎疫情背景下，全行业通用、跨行业、以人为本的战略的价值得到凸显。本次疫情让各行各业都陷入了混乱。相关行业的从业人员处境艰难，许多现有的技能提升举措都只适用于特定行业。但是，当相关行业和专业的从业人员少有其他选择时，这类技能提升举措显然并不足以应对困局。

未来，这种混乱的局面将会变得越发普遍，疫情同时还加快了数字化进程，致使自动化应用率和远程办公率上升，并伴随着更大的外包风险，导致更多行业的从业人员被迫失业。相关行业的从业人员同样也会发现，特定行业的技能提升举措并不足以帮助他们渡过难关。

因此，从业人员需要一个全行业通用的跨行业战略来帮助他们摆脱困境，并从其所从事之行业和专业之外寻找机遇。

LKYCIC 便制定了这样一种全行业通用的跨行业战略。

我们制定的实际上是“跨行业 GPS”战略。通过在已有的任务—技能栈中运用人类参与型 AI 技术，我们可以为从已受干扰的专业 / 行业到正在发展的专业 / 行业，绘制出清晰具体且循序渐进的发展路径。

options across sectors for workers.

Our strategy is grounded in the converging consensus across research and industry that tasks are the right resolution to study the future of work. This is because of three reasons: every job can be broken down into its constituent tasks; AI's impact on jobs in the foreseeable future will be task-by-task, not job-by-job or skill-by-skill; and tasks can explain trends from the tech-scale to the macro-economic scale.

Our research builds on this consensus by integrating inter-disciplinary insights across data science, engineering, AI, labor economics, occupational psychology, and organizational studies. We combine them into a Tasks-Skills Stack, which links national, international, industry, and occupational databases. Applying AI and human ingenuity to this, we can design worker-, firm-, sector-, and policy-level strategies to help more people thrive.

Working with industry, unions, and government, we have expanded our research innovations. These include insights on how to design well-being and resilience, master new expertise, and prioritize what to up-skill and re-skill. We can also re-imagine expanded career trajectories, assess automation risks, track transformation and disruption, design fair work, and value tasks and skills. Our collaborations are recognized in Singapore's National AI Strategy as contributing to building a Trusted and Progressive Environment for AI in Singapore's Smart Nation journey.

By focusing on the greater good, we aim to build a future where everyone can flourish.

三十二

为实现这一目标，我们的战略首先需要确定不同行业中职业的共享任务，然后在它们之间绘制各项任务的跨行业路径。随后，各企业、从业人员和政府即可运用这些路径寻找新的机遇，为从业人员提供更多跨行业的选择。

我们的战略立足于科研界和产业界的共识，即任务是用于研究未来工作的正确解决方案。我们的理由有三点：第一，每种职业都可以被拆分为构成该职业的任务；第二，可以预见的是，AI对职业的影响将以任务，而非职业或技能为基础；第三，任务可以解释从技术规模到宏观经济规模的各类趋势。

我们的研究正是基于上述共识展开，整合了数据科学、工程学、AI、劳动经济学、职业心理学和组织研究领域的跨学科见解。我们将上述见解融入了连接着国内、国际、行业和职业数据库的任务—技能栈。只要将AI和人类的智慧运用于此，我们便可从从业人员、企业、行业和政策层面制定战略，帮助更多的人走向繁荣。

我们通过与产业界、工会和政府合作，扩大了研究创新的范围，取得了更多成果，包括有关如何实现繁荣发展和增强适应力、掌握新的专业知识和技能，以及确定需要优先提升的技能和需要优先学习的新技能的见解。我们还可以重新思考拓展后的职业轨迹、评估自动化风险、跟踪变革和干扰、打造公平的工作环境，以及提高对任务和技能的重视程度。我们的合作得到了新加坡国家AI战略的认可，因为它有助于建立一个先进且可信赖的AI环境，帮助新加坡走好"智慧国家"之路。

我们专注于获取更大的利益，致力于打造一个所有人都能蓬勃发展的未来。

33

Who Should Own Our Data?

Steven HOFFMAN

With AI's ability to process and make use of vast amounts of data, policymakers around the world are looking to limit the abuse of people's personal data. A growing number of lawmakers are proposing that individuals own and have exclusive property rights in the data they generate online. This sounds good in theory, but does it solve the fundamental problem of an asymmetrical marketplace, where large companies profit from this data in ways that may harm individuals and society?

To rectify this problem, many policymakers believe that that social media and other companies should pay people to license their data. This way, the people who generate the data can receive compensation and control how it's used. On the surface, this sounds like a great idea, but in practice, most people will wind up trading away their privacy rights for very little in the way of monetary compensation. The fact is that the vast majority of people won't read the fine print of these licensing terms, and even if they do, they aren't in a position to understand the repercussions. This means the idea that they are actually in control, will just be an illusion.

There is also the issue of injecting friction into the flow of information. The world's economy thrives on the rapid exchange of data. If we bog down the system with a lot of complex regulations, it stands to seriously impact all the businesses and consumers that rely on this data. Everything from logistics, healthcare and advertising to e-commerce, media, and public services will be impacted. The reason people's personal information is in such high demand is because it is incredibly valuable to society and has so many different uses.

Think about how many ways a person's name, address, birthdate, and other basic data are used. What does it mean to license and restrict this information? Do people need to sign licensing agreements with every app they use? And who actually owns this data? The fact is that data is information, and to treat it like a commodity fundamentally alters its nature and will impact our entire social system. Before we take this radical step, we need to assess the impact of this type of legislation. Right now, most of the public and private services we take for granted rely on the free flow of this data.

Instead, we should focus on the core problem, which is not whether people get paid a small licensing fee but regulating how this data is shared and used. Most people care about their privacy, and they want to make sure their data does not fall into the wrong hands and wind up negatively, impacting their lives or society.

三十三

我们的数据应为谁所有？

史蒂文·霍夫曼

依靠人工智能处理和利用大量数据的能力，世界各地的决策者正寻求方案以限制对个人数据的滥用。越来越多的立法者提议，个人应对其在网上生成的数据享有专属权。该提议理论上听起来不错，但它是否解决了不对称市场的根本问题，即大公司从这些数据中获利的方式是否可能损害个人和社会？

为了纠正这一问题，许多决策者认为，社交媒体和其他公司应该向用户支付数据许可费。这样，生成数据的人就可以获得补偿并控制数据的使用方式。这听起来是个不错的主意，但实际上，大多数人最终会放弃他们的隐私权利，以换取很少的金钱补偿。事实上，绝大多数人不会阅读这些许可条款的细则，即使阅读了，也难以理解相关的后果。这意味着，个人数据受控的想法，不过只是幻想。

在信息流中引发摩擦也是一个问题。世界经济的繁荣得益于数据的快速交换。如果我们用大量复杂的规章制度使数据系统陷入困境，它将严重影响所有依赖这些数据的企业和消费者。从物流、医疗保健、广告到电子商务、媒体和公共服务，各个领域都将受到影响。人们对个人信息的需求之所以如此之高，是因为它对社会极为重要，且用途广泛。

请考虑一个人的姓名、地址、生日和其他基本数据能有多少种用途。许可和限制这些信息意味着什么？人们是否需要与他们使用的每个应用程序签署许可协议？这些数据真正意义上归谁所有？事实上，数据就是信息，把它当作商品来对待，从根本上改变了它的性质，这将影响我们整个社会体系。在我们采取这一激进措施之前，我们需要评估这类立法的影响。目前，我们理所当然地认为大多数公共和私人服务都依赖于这些数据的自由流动。

相反，我们应该把重点放在核心问题上，这不是人们是否能获得一小笔许可费的问题，而是如何规范这些数据的共享和使用的问题。大多数人都关心自己的隐私，他们希望确保自己的数据不会落入坏人手中，以免对自己的生活或社会产生负面影响。

我们需要认识到，问题不在于人们无法从他们的数据中获得报酬。人们可以免费注册脸书，正是因为人们同意让该公司使用他们的数据来盈利。向人们支付额外的许可费来授予脸书相关

33

We need to recognize that the problem isn't that people are not getting paid for their data. When someone signs up for Facebook, it is free precisely because people are agreeing to let the company use their data to make a profit. Paying people an additional licensing fee to grant Facebook the right to use it will not change this. The problem comes later, when companies do not place adequate controls on how this data is handled and managed.

Policymakers should focus on curbing the abuses, rather than commoditizing the data. Most countries already have strict regulations on how people's medical data can be used and shared. We need similar regulations on how companies can use and share personal data. In the end, good legislation will need to find a balance between protecting people's personal privacy and enabling the free flow of information. Only in this way can we advance both individual and social interests, while not impeding economic growth and constraining the services we all depend upon.

数据信息的使用权并不会改变这一点。当公司没有对数据的处理和管理进行足够的控制时，问题就会出现。

决策者应该把重点放在遏制滥用数据上，而不是将数据商品化。大多数国家已经对如何使用和共享人们的医疗数据有了严格的规定。对于公司如何使用和共享个人数据，我们也需要类似的规定。最终，好的立法需要在保护个人隐私和实现信息自由流动之间找到平衡。只有这样，我们才能在既不妨碍经济增长，又不限制我们所依赖的服务的前提下，同时保证个人与社会利益。

34

Globalization and Ethics as the Consensus of AI Governance

LUAN Qun

In 2019-2020, AI governance was characterized by globalization and ethical integration. Major countries, economies and international organizations in the world have successively released documents on AI governance. The most representative ones are the EU Ethics Guidelines for Trustworthy AI (April 2019), the joint statement and "G20 AI Principles" (June) adopted by the G20 Digital Economy Ministers' Meeting and the G20 Trade and Digital Economy Ministers' Joint Meeting held in Tsukuba, Japan. In addition, in June, China's National New Generation AI Governance Expert Committee issued "Governance Principles for a New Generation of Artificial Intelligence: Developing Responsible Artificial Intelligence". China's AI governance has also been transferred to ethical governance from the planning of the State Council and related departments in 2017, which includes the "New Generation of Artificial Intelligence Development Plan" and the "'Internet+' Three Year Action Plan for Artificial Intelligence", as well as industry and domain plans such as the "Three-year Action Plan on Promoting the Development of A New Generation of Artificial Intelligence Industry" (2018-2020), the 2018 Intelligent Manufacturing Pilot Demonstration, and the "AI Innovation Action Plan for Universities". This role change is highlighted by the emphasis on responsibility in the new generation of AI governance principles, which has the same meaning as the EU's emphasis on trustworthiness. In August, the rule-of-law forum of the Shanghai 2019 World AI conference released guidelines for AI security and the rule of law (2019). The theme of the forum was "building the rule of law in the future and sharing the benefits of intelligence" to promote industrial development and follow up on relevant systems, better serve and safeguard the overall situation of AI national strategy, and show the Chinese scheme of AI governance to the world.

As the industry management department, the Ministry of Industry and Information Technology mainly implemented the top-level industrial design plan in 2019, with efforts such as the "Three-year Action Plan for Promoting the Development of the New Generation of Artificial Intelligence Industry" (2018-2020), which mainly covers eight products and three technologies. It also, implemented development plans and standards for key industries, such as the "Auto Driving Action Plan for the Development of the Internet of Vehicles (Intelligent Connected Vehicles) Industry" and "Key Points for the Standardization of Intelligent Internet Connected Vehicles in 2019". In addition, it undertook key work on joint promotion, such as joint efforts with the Ministry of Natural Resources and Beijing to carry out the pilot work of the internet of vehicles (Intelligent Connected Vehicles) and automatic driving map applications. Finally, it engaged in industrial internet work, such implementing the Guide for the Construction of the Integrated Standardization System of the Industrial Internet. All of these new policy documents involve related discussions on AI governance.

三十四

全球化与合伦理成为人工智能治理共识——中国产业界的伦理关注

栾群

2019—2020 年，人工智能治理突出表现为全球化和合伦理化的特点。世界主要国家、经济体和国际组织，都陆续发布了人工智能治理的文件，最具代表性的是欧盟《可信赖人工智能的伦理准则》（2019 年 4 月），以及在日本筑波举行的 G20 数字经济部长会议和 G20 贸易和数字经济部长联席会议通过的联合声明和《G20 人工智能原则》（6 月份）；也是在 6 月份，中国的国家新一代人工智能治理专业委员会发布的《新一代人工智能治理原则 —— 发展负责任的人工智能》。中国的人工智能治理，也从 2017 年国务院及部门规划如《新一代人工智能发展规划》《“互联网 +”人工智能三年行动实施方案》，以及产业、领域计划如《促进新一代人工智能产业发展三年行动计划（2018—2020）》、2018 年智能制造试点示范、《高等学校人工智能创新行动计划》等，转向了合伦理化治理。突出表现为在新一代人工智能治理原则中强调“负责任”—— 这与欧盟强调“可信任”的旨趣相同，8 月，上海 2019 世界人工智能大会法治论坛发布《人工智能安全与法治导则（2019）》，论坛的主题为“共建未来法治，共享智能福祉”，以推动产业发展和相关制度的跟进，更好服务保障 AI 国家战略大局，向世界展现人工智能治理的中国方案。

作为行业管理部门的中国工信部，2019 年主要实施了关于产业顶层设计的计划，如《促进新一代人工智能产业发展三年行动计划（2018—2020）》，主推八大产品、三大技术；关于重点行业发展计划及标准，如自动驾驶《车联网（智能网联汽车）产业发展行动计划》《2019 年智能网联汽车标准化工作要点》；关于联合推动重点工作，如联合自然资源部和北京市开展车联网（智能网联汽车）和自动驾驶地图应用试点工作；以及工业互联网工作，如实施《工业互联网综合标准化体系建设指南》等工作。在这些新的政策文件中，也都涉及了人工智能治理的相关论述。

35

The Principles of the Well-being of the Human Person and Accountability

GUO Rui

In 2019, Artificial Intelligence (AI) affected every aspect of people's lives worldwide as it was increasingly applied in business, health care, transportation, financial services, education, and public safety. For the public and policy-makers, whether the negative impacts of AI–such as the leakage of personal information, the output of poorly trained AI, and its misuse–will be properly managed causes increasing concern. Academia, industry and policy-makers have actively joined AI ethics-related discussions and debates, making 2019 a critical juncture for the global community to move toward a consensus on AI governance.

Experts from industries, academia and civil societies have gradually come to the consensus that the negative impacts related to AI are best treated as risks and can be identified, prevented and managed through a rigorous risk-management system. This insight has informed standardization work, and much ethics-related standardization is steadily advancing and gaining momentum. This consensus is leading to a governance system that allows the world to reap the benefits and prevent the harms of AI. Although the concept of risk is helpful for addressing the known and immediate negative impacts of AI, it certainly does not exhaust all those impacts that AI brings, especially the uncertain and long-term ones. We should continue to explore ways that could help human society address AI ethical issues.

In my capacity as the Lead Expert for the Research Group on the Ethics of Artificial Intelligence of the Artificial Intelligence Working Group, Standardization Administration of the People's Republic of China (SAC), I propose two principles for ethical and responsible AI. First, ethical and responsible AI implies the principle of the well-being of the human person. Promoting human well-being should be the ultimate goal of AI research and applications. Second, ethical and responsible AI implies the principle of accountability. These two principles informed the drafting of the *AI Ethical Risk Research Report* (published in May 2019 by the Artificial Intelligence Working Group, SAC).

三十五

人工智能治理的造福于人和可问责性原则：在中国人工智能标准化制定中的理念

郭锐

随着人工智能在商业、医疗、交通运输、金融服务、教育和公共安全领域的应用，人工智能影响了人们生活的方方面面。能否妥善处理人工智能带来的负面影响，例如个人信息的泄露、信息基础不充分的人工智能的输出结果和人工智能的滥用，引起了越来越多的关注。学术界、产业界和政策制定者都积极参与有关人工智能伦理的讨论，这使得 2019 年成为全球就人工智能治理达成共识的关键时期。

这一年，来自学术界、产业界和民间团体的专家们逐渐达成一致，与人工智能相关的负面影响最好被视为风险，并通过严格的风险管理系统识别、预防和管理这些风险。这一进展对标准化工作产生了影响，许多与人工智能相关的标准化工作也在稳步推进、快速发展中。建立在这个共识之上，一个使世界各国都可以从人工智能中受益并防止其危害的治理体系正在成形。虽然将人工智能的负面影响看作风险有助于解决人工智能带来的已知和直接风险，但它并不能应对人工智能带来的全部风险，特别是不确定的和长期的风险。我们将继续探索可以帮助人类社会解决人工智能伦理问题的方法。

作为国家标准化管理委员会（SAC）人工智能工作组人工智能伦理课题组的首席专家，我提出了符合伦理和负责任的人工智能必须遵守两个原则：人的利益原则（即人工智能的研究和应用必须以实现人的利益为终极目标）和责任原则。这两个原则为《人工智能伦理风险研究报告》（由 SAC 人工智能工作组于 2019 年 5 月发布）的起草提供了依据。

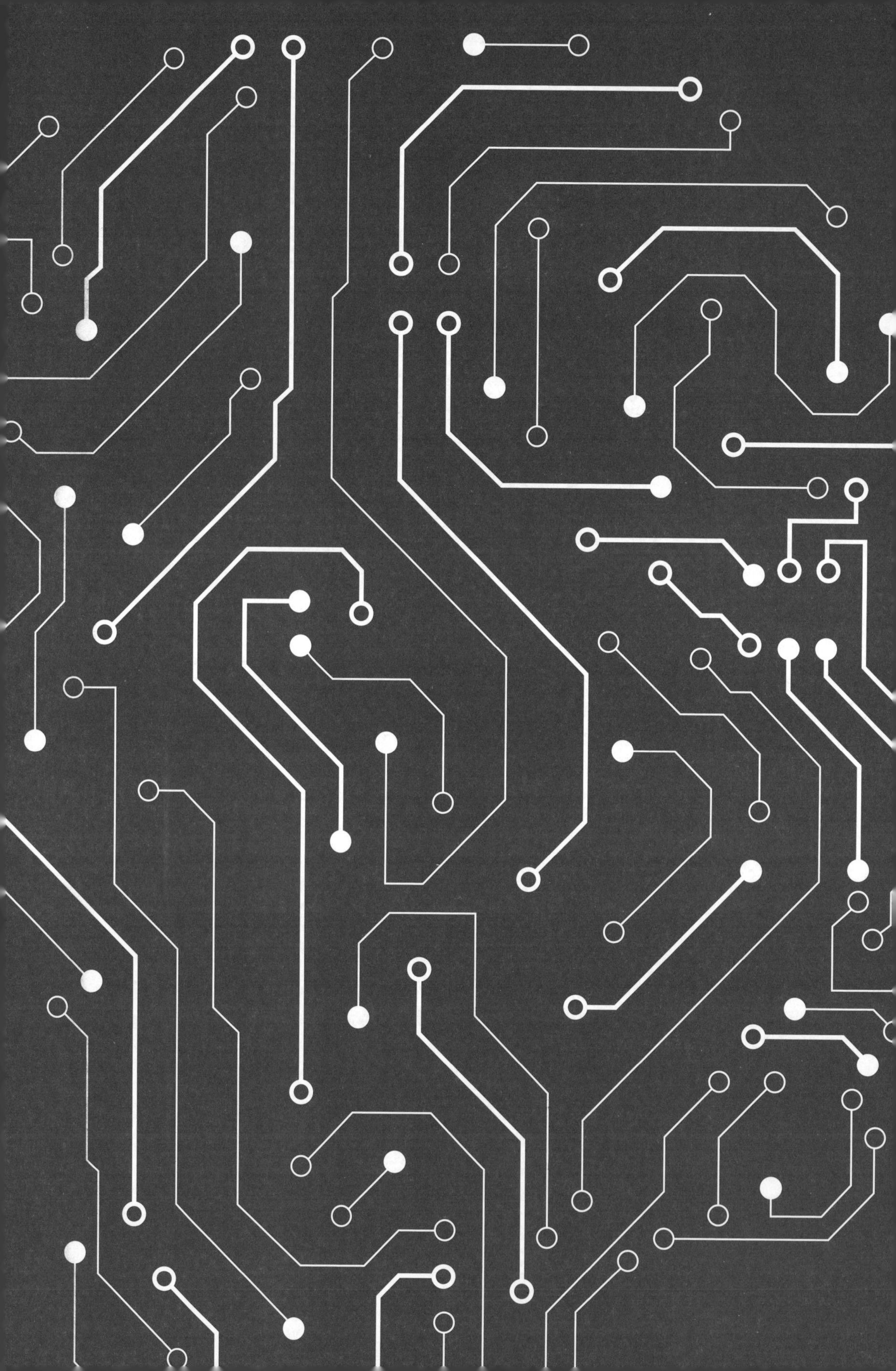

第三部分
PART III

政策研究与推进
POLICY RESEARCH AND IMPLEMENTATION

政府是人工智能治理的主体。各国政府都在出台人工智能治理的政策。在这一部分，我们展示北美、欧洲、亚洲、南美等地区一些国家的人工智能治理政策。通过观察不同国家对人工智能治理的关切，我们会发现人工智能治理这一全球议题，在形成全球共识上还有很长的路要走。当然，这一部分我们也介绍了一些国际组织关于人工智能治理的政策，对于达成人工智能治理的全球共识，这些国际组织起着很关键的作用。

Governments are major bodies for artificial intelligence governance. Countries around the world are introducing policies on AI governance. In Part III, we introduced artificial intelligence governance policies of countries in North America, Europe, Asia, South America and other regions. Based on different concerns of countries for artificial intelligence governance, we found that to form a global consensus can still be distant. In addition, we introduced policies of artificial intelligence governance from some of international organizations that play a vital role in reaching such a consensus.

36

Artificial Intelligence and International Security: Challenges and Governance

FU Ying

In recent years, the rapid advance of artificial intelligence (AI) technology has brought about enormous opportunities. As technological revolution is often accompanied by unforeseeable security challenges, special attention must be paid to the moral and technological hazards of AI weaponization. Humanity must now urgently consider how to effectively balance the benefits of technology and the security risks of its weaponization and find appropriate pathways for AI governance.

While AI-enabled weapon systems can have powerful military effects, they are not fully reliable, and potential challenges abound associated with their applications. AI has inherent technical defects that may make it hard for attackers to restrict the range of their strikes, thus exposing the attacked to excessive collateral damage and causing unintended civilian casualties. Since big data–based algorithms and training datasets may inevitably introduce biases into the real application of AI systems, and training datasets may be contaminated by other countries, AI may provide incorrect recommendations to decision-makers and mislead military commanders into making the wrong deployments. Moreover, AI's deficiencies in interpretability, learning, and common sense will magnify the risks of battlefield conflicts during human–machine collaboration and may even escalate international crises.

International cooperation is essential if humanity is to tackle the common challenge of global AI governance, which cannot be addressed by any country alone. Countries need to exercise restraint in the military field and work together to build international governance mechanisms in this regard. Assisted decision-making systems that are not cognizant of responsibility or risk should be prohibited. When AI-enabled weapons are used, the scope of damage by their strikes must be limited so collateral damage and conflict escalation can be prevented. The development and use of AI-enabled weapons must conform with the existing norms established in international laws. AI data security should be given high priority, and the whole process–from data-mining and collection to data-labeling and classification and data use and monitoring–should be regulated and restricted to prevent the formation of incorrect models, which may cause decision-makers to make inaccurate judgments.

The current stage represents a critical window of opportunity for establishing international norms on AI security. China and the US must have dialog and cooperation in this regard, as they may be able to contribute wisdom for collaboration in AI governance at the global level. The two countries should start official discussions on how to establish international norms and regimes, explore areas of cooperation on the basis of their respective interests and concerns, exchange and translate relevant documents, and carry out policy discussions and academic exchanges. Such efforts will also help to reduce the potential risks to bilateral relations and global security.

三十六

人工智能和国际安全：挑战与治理

傅莹

近年来，人工智能技术的快速发展带来了巨大的机遇。由于技术变革往往伴随着无法预料的安全挑战，我们必须特别关注 AI 武器化可能带来的道德和技术危害。如今，人类亟需思考如何有效平衡 AI 技术所带来的效益与其武器化的安全风险，以及如何探寻适当的 AI 治理方法。

就目前来看，虽然基于 AI 的武器系统具有强大的军事效用，但却并不完全可靠，其应用存在大量的潜在挑战。AI 固有的技术缺陷可能使攻击者难以控制攻击范围，从而给被攻击者带来过多的附带伤害，并造成平民意外伤亡。同时，基于大数据的算法和训练数据集会不可避免地将偏见带入 AI 系统的实际应用中，而训练数据集也可能被他国篡改，可能导致 AI 系统向决策者提出错误的建议，并误导军事指挥官进行错误的部署。此外，AI 在可解释性、学习能力和常识认知方面的缺陷将加大人机合作期间发生战场冲突的风险，甚至致使国际危机螺旋式升级。

人类若想应对 AI 治理的全球共同挑战，就必须进行国际合作，因为任何一个国家都无法独立解决这一问题。各国需要在军事领域保持克制，并携手建立相应的国际治理机制。应禁止使用尚未明晰责任或风险的辅助决策系统。使用基于 AI 的武器时必须限制其攻击范围，以免造成附带伤害和冲突升级。开发和使用基于 AI 的武器时必须遵守现行的国际法律法规。应高度重视 AI 数据安全，对从数据挖掘和收集、数据标注和分类，到数据使用和监控的整个流程进行监管和限制，以防形成错误的模型，导致决策者在此基础上做出错误的判断。

现阶段，我们拥有建立 AI 安全国际规范的关键机会。中国和美国应在这方面展开对话与合作，因为双方或许有能力为 AI 治理全球合作献计献策。中国和美国应展开官方讨论，研究如何建立国际规范和制度、在各自的利益和关注点的基础上探索可以合作的领域、交换并翻译相关文件，以及进行政策对话和学术交流。这些措施同时也有助于降低双边关系与全球安全方面的潜在风险。

37

China Continues to Promote Global Cooperation in AI Governance

ZHAO Zhiyun

In 2020, the sudden outbreak of the COVID-19 pandemic not only threatened people globally but also generated great challenges to global governance. Various AI-based solutions played positive roles not only in tracing the origin of the virus, preventing and controlling its outbreak, and researching and developing vaccines but also in speeding the "contactless economy", such as in online shopping, online education and telemedicine.

Global collaboration is needed to combat the COVID-19 pandemic. Therefore, AI governance should be considered, especially when AI technology application has accelerated worldwide. Since 2020, to implement the *Development Plan for A New Generation of Artificial Intelligence and the Governance Principles of the New Generation of Artificial Intelligence: Developing Responsible Artificial Intelligence*, China has actively advocated for international cooperation in AI governance while supporting more research and enriching AI governance practices. In the highlight of this year's G20 summit, President Xi Jinping proposed holding a workshop on AI when appropriate to implement G20 AI principles. The Chinese government has also launched the Global Initiative on Data Security, which, as the critical area of AI governance, clearly calls for addressing the issues of data governance by means of codiscussion, coestablishment and cosharing.

These measures and initiatives have fully demonstrated the consistent efforts that China has made in global cooperation on AI governance. In the future, by focusing on issues of AI governance, China will continue to establish platforms, expand channels and widen international cooperation and exchanges to obtain broader consensus to promote AI development in a healthier manner together with global players.

三十七

中国持续推动人工智能治理全球合作

赵志耘

2020年，突如其来的新冠肺炎疫情在给世界人民健康带来巨大影响的同时，也给全球治理带来了巨大的挑战。基于人工智能技术的各种解决方案，不仅在病毒溯源、疫情防控、疫苗研发等方面发挥了积极的作用，也在加速推动网上购物、在线教育、远程医疗等"非接触经济"全面提速。

与抗击新冠肺炎疫情需要全球协作一样，伴随着人工智能技术在全球的加速应用，人工智能的治理也更加需要全球的共同努力。2020年以来，中国围绕落实《新一代人工智能发展规划》和《新一代人工智能治理原则——发展负责任的人工智能》，在强化人工智能治理问题研究、推动人工智能治理实践的同时，也在积极倡导人工智能的治理领域的国际合作。习近平主席在今年二十国集团领导人峰会上特别提出，适时召开人工智能专题会议，推动落实二十国集团人工智能原则。针对数据这一人工智能治理的重点领域，中国政府还发起了《全球数据安全倡议》，明确提出共商、共建、共享来解决全球数字治理问题。

这一系列举措和倡议，充分体现了中国在推动人工智能治理全球合作方面的持续努力。未来，中国将围绕人工智能治理问题，继续搭建平台、拓展渠道，开展更宽领域的国际合作与交流，凝聚更广泛的共识，与全球各界共同推动人工智能的健康发展。

38

Toward a Robust and Agile Framework for AI Ethics and Governance

DUAN Weiwen

In 2019, four aspects of AI ethics and governance in China deserve attention. First, various principles, standards and declarations of AI ethics and governance were released. These include "Governance Principles for a New Generation of Artificial Intelligence: Develop Responsible Artificial Intelligence"; the "Beijing AI Principles" released by Beijing Academy of Artificial Intelligence (BAAI); the artificial intelligence ethical principles outlined in "AI Ethical Risks of AI Research Report" proposed by Artificial Intelligence Working Group, SAC; and etc. Second, certain progress has been made in the legal regulation of personal information protection and data rights, governance, and compliance. For example, the "Act on the Protection of Personal Information" and the "Data Security Law" have been included in the legislative plan for the upcoming year, and MIIT has carried out special rectification action against apps infringing on the rights and interests of users. The revised draft of the Law on the Protection of Minors emphasizes that informed consent is required to collect information about minors. Third, AI applications such as facial recognition are rapidly spreading and causing many ethical and legal disputes. Although the abuse of facial recognition in classrooms, parks and other scenarios has led to public criticism and even legal proceedings, its application in China seems unstoppable. In addition, AI companies have engaged in ethical and governance practices.

However, given that these efforts are far from the basis, such as KPI, on which companies evaluate their products and services, they are inevitably criticized as flexible PR or a type of ethics washing.

Overall, China is more optimistic about the positive AI impact on the economy, society, enterprises and personal well-being. However, AI ethical risks are not fictitious. On the one hand, while enjoying the convenience of innovation, ordinary users will inevitably be concerned about the abuse of personal data and the opacity of algorithmic decisions. On the other hand, developers worry that a lack of ethical regulation will force them to pay a high price for the risks involved. To eliminate this double anxiety, it is necessary to make ethical adjustments through ethical assessments of technology, "technology–ethics" corrections and the construction of trust mechanisms for AI. More important is the building of a robust and practicable framework for AI ethics and governance to achieve agile governance based on the full consideration of the social AI impact, its regional and global compatibility, and the maintenance of a fundamental condition–world peace.

三十八

中国走向稳健敏捷的人工智能伦理和治理框架

段伟文

2019 年，中国在人工智能伦理和治理上值得注意的有四个方面。其一，推出了各种伦理与治理的原则、标准和宣言。其中包括新一代人工智能治理原则、北京智源人工智能研究院的《人工智能北京共识》、国家人工智能标准化总体组《人工智能风险分析报告》提出的人工智能伦理原则、北京大学及国家机器人标准化总体组的《中国机器人伦理标准化前瞻（2019）》提出的中国机器人伦理标准化体系。同时，中国工业和信息化部的智库赛迪研究院与中国信息通信研究院也分别提出了人工智能伦理宣言或公约，腾讯也发布了自己的人工智能伦理框架。其二，在个人信息保护和数据权利的法律规制和数据合规治理上有一定的进展。其中包括，将《个人信息保护法》和《数据安全法》纳入下一年度的立法计划，工信部开展的 APP 侵犯用户权益专项整治行动。值得一提的是，未成年人保护法修订草案强调收集未成年人信息需知情同意等。其三，人脸识别等人工智能应用迅速推广并引起很多伦理和法律争议。虽然人脸识别在中国的应用是大势所趋，但其在教室、公园等各种场景的滥用导致了舆论指责甚至法律诉讼。其四，人工智能企业也进行了一些伦理和治理实践。

但鉴于这些努力远未像关键绩效指标（KPI）那样成为企业评估产品和服务的价值基础，难免被批评为柔性公关或道德的洗刷。

总的来说，中国在总体上对于人工智能为经济、社会、企业和个人福祉带来的积极影响更加乐观。但人工智能的伦理风险并非虚构，普通用户在享受各种创新便利的同时，难免对个人数据滥用、算法决策的不透明心存疑虑，开发者也会担心伦理缺位会使其为由此带来的风险付出高昂代价。为了消除这种双重焦虑，应该通过技术伦理评估、“技术—伦理”矫正和信任机制的构建，展开必要的价值伦理校准。更重要的是，要在充分考量人工智能的社会影响、对区域与全球的兼容和维护和平底线的基础上，构建一种稳健可行的伦理与治理框架，实现敏捷治理。

39

Promote the Formation of "Technology + Regulations" in Comprehensive Governance Solutions

WANG Yingchun

In recent years, many AI governance principles and initiatives have been issued by relevant organizations and institutions worldwide. Promoting "human-centered" and "responsible" AI development has become an international consensus. The transformation of these consensus principles into action plans has become a general trend.

On July 10, 2020, the Governance Forum of the World Artificial Intelligence Conference was held in Shanghai. With the theme of "Developing Responsible Artificial Intelligence", the forum discussed a comprehensive range of governance solutions centered on the theme of "Technologies + Regulations" as a combined driving force to practice the ethical principles of artificial intelligence. At the forum, the "Working Plan for Collaborative Implementation of AI Governance Principles" (9 items of the Shanghai AI governance collaborative action) was released, which consists of a framework–"one platform, four tasks and four systems".

"One platform" means building a platform for a global network of cooperation and exchange. We should form a global community for AI governance research and cooperation. Drawing on multicultural wisdom, exploring accessible and inclusive safety assurance and solutions for a win–win outcome, we need to build a multilateral, multidisciplinary and multiagent consultative governance mechanism to promote the formation of a global joint effort to construct a common AI governance system.

The "four tasks" are to carry out standard specifications, industrial self-monitoring, optimal practice and trustworthy technologies. First, all stakeholders should cooperate to research and formulate technical standards and application specifications, clarify the threshold for industrial access, and ensure the legitimate rights and interests of relevant parties. Second, we should establish an ethical commitment and review system of scientific research and enterprise products and form a compliance and self-disciplinary process and operational guide within the industry. Third, we should constantly summarize the cases and relevant experiences of high-

三十九

推动形成“技术＋规则”的治理综合解决方案

王迎春

近年来，在全球范围内，相关组织和机构发布了大量人工智能治理原则和倡议，推动人工智能“以人为本”和“负责任”发展已成为国际共识，如何将这些共识性原则转化为行动方案已是大势所趋。

2020 年 7 月 10 日，世界人工智能大会治理论坛在上海举办，本届治理论坛以“发展负责任的人工智能”为主题，探讨“技术＋规则”双轮驱动的治理综合解决方案，推动人工智能治理原则落地落实。论坛上，发布了“协同落实人工智能治理原则的行动建议”（上海 AI 治理协同行动 9 条），提出了“一平台、四工作、四体系”的落实人工智能治理原则的系统化的行动框架建议。

“一平台”即搭建全球合作网络和交流平台，形成全球人工智能治理研究和协作共同体，汲取多元文化智慧，构建多边、多学科、多主体参与的协商机制，探索可通约、非排他的安全保障和利益分享方案，推动形成共商共建共享的全球人工智能治理体系。

“四工作”包括标准规范、行业自律、最佳实践和可信技术。各利益相关方协同研究制定技术标准和应用规范，明确行业准入门槛，保证相关方的合法权益；建立科学研究和企业产品的伦理承诺和审查制度，形成行业内部的合规自律流程和操作指南；不断总结优质实践案例和相关经验，从实践中提炼规范，通过最佳实践引导各方行为；发展算法透明、保护隐私的可信技术，研发合伦理评估等监管技术，通过公共部门和私人部门的合作促进可信方案的推广。

“四体系”包括评估体系、监管体系、人才体系和保障体系。构建合规的指标体系、检测方法和评测平台，开展治理的绩效评估与分级认证；完善公开透明的多部门协同的监管体系，实现对相关产品和应用的全流程监管；推动交叉学科研究，开设治理必修课程，培养复合型人才；

quality practices, extract specifications from practice, and then guide the industry through best practices. Finally, we should develop trustworthy technologies based on transparent algorithms and privacy protection, develop solutions for ethical evaluation and other relevant regulations studies, and promote trustworthy solutions through cooperation between the public and private sectors.

The "four systems" are the evaluation, regulatory, talent and security systems. We should build a system of compliance indicators, methods and platforms of evaluation to carry out governance qualification assessment and classification certification, to improve the open and transparent cross-departmental collaborative regulation system to realize the supervision of related products and applications, to promote interdisciplinary research by establishing compulsory courses for governance and cultivate talents with multidisciplinary skills, to build a social security system to cope with the impact of artificial intelligence on the employment structure, to develop relevant insurance products, and to enhance public digital literacy.

To realize the "human-centered" vision, we need comprehensive governance solutions that integrate technologies and regulations. We call for global peers to work together to develop products and solutions that are adapted to social values around typical scenarios, to actively form consensuses and to solve specific problems through positive and steady practice.

三十九

建设应对人工智能冲击就业结构的社会保障体系，开发相关保险产品，提升公众的数字化素养。

实现人工智能“以人为本”的美好愿景，需要技术与规则相融合的治理综合解决方案，我们建议全球同行一起携手，围绕典型场景开发与社会价值更加适宜的产品和方案，在积极稳妥的实践中不断达成共识并解决具体问题。

40

From Human-Centric to Planetary-Scale Problem Solving: Challenges and Prospects for AI Utilization in Japan

Arisa EMA

The Japanese government has been promoting its information policies under the auspices of Society 5.0, a human-centric society that simultaneously achieves economic development and resolves social issues through a system that integrates cyberspace and physical space. The Cabinet Office released the "Social Principles of Human-Centric AI" in March 2019. Since then, the relevant ministries and agencies have formulated AI-related guidelines, such as for the development of medical diagnostic imaging support systems (Ministry of Health, Labor and Welfare), for contracts in the agricultural sector (Ministry of Agriculture, Forestry and Fisheries), for AI utilization (Consumer Affairs Agency), and for certification systems for AI education (Ministry of Education, Culture, Sports, Science and Technology and Ministry of Economy, Trade and Industry and CSTI).

On the other hand, the response to COVID-19 exposed the fact that we were completely unprepared for the transition to Society 5.0. The fact that government and private companies signed an agreement on COVID-19 to promote the use of data can be regarded as a step forward. However, data-sharing was found to be ineffective between central and local governments and medical institutions. In addition, we found that the Tokyo Metropolitan Government was using fax machines to report the number of infected people.

The problem of data-sharing is not limited to COVID-19; in fact, it has been noted previously. In particular, in Japan, there are more business-to-business companies than there are business-to-consumer companies. Thus, in many cases, data acquisition, AI model development, and service providers are different. Therefore, issues such as AI safety and fairness must be addressed not only by one company but also by all parties involved in a multilayered dialog. Moreover, start-up companies lack resources, making it difficult for them to deal with risks. From this perspective, the Japan Deep-Learning Association, whose members are mainly start-ups, is considering how to assess and respond to AI systems in the external environment–including through insurance, auditing, accident investigation, consumer protection, whistle-blowing systems, and standardization–in addition to AI governance within companies since the summer of 2020.

四十

从以人为本到解决全球性问题：日本人工智能应用的挑战和前景

江间有沙

日本政府一直在“社会 5.0”（Society5.0）概念下推行信息政策，“社会 5.0”是一个以人类为中心的社会，通过一个结合了网络空间和物理空间的系统，同时实现经济发展和解决社会问题。日本内阁府在 2019 年 3 月发布了《以人类为中心的人工智能社会原则》。此后，有关部门和机构制定了人工智能相关指南，如医疗诊断成像支持系统开发指南（日本厚生劳动省）、农业合同指南（日本农林水产省）、人工智能使用手册（日本消费者厅）和人工智能教育认证系统 [教育、文化、体育、科学和技术部、经济、贸易和工业部以及综合科学技术创新会议（CSTI）]。

另一方面，我们对新冠肺炎疫情的应对情况表明：我们完全没有准备好向“社会 5.0”过渡。事实上，政府和私营企业签署了一项关于新冠肺炎疫情的协议，以促进数据的使用，这可以被视为一种进步。然而，我们发现中央和地方政府以及医疗机构之间的数据共享是低效的。此外，我们还发现东京都政府甚至曾使用传真机报告感染人数。

数据共享的问题在先前就已被指出，并非因本次新冠肺炎疫情而引发。特别是在日本，企业对企业的公司多于企业对消费者的公司。换句话说，在许多情况下，数据采集、人工智能模型开发和服务供应商是不同的。因此，人工智能的安全性和公平性等问题不能仅由一家公司来解决，而是必须由多层次对话的所有参与方共同应对。此外，初创企业缺乏资源，难以应对风险。从这个角度来看，自 2020 年夏天以来，以初创企业为主要成员的日本深度学习协会除了考虑公司内部的人工智能治理之外，还在考虑如何评估和应对外部环境中的人工智能系统，包括保险、审计、事故调查、消费者保护、举报制度、标准化等。

最后，必须引发国际层面对人工智能治理的讨论。第二届法德日人工智能研讨会于 2020 年

40

Finally, AI governance must be discussed internationally. The 2nd French–German–Japanese AI Symposium was organized in November 2020. The first conference, held two years ago, issued a joint statement that emphasized a human-centric approach. Therefore, in line with this direction, the theme of the second conference was human–centric AI. However, we are now facing planetary–scale challenges, such as the COVID-19 pandemic, climate change, and community fragmentation. Therefore, the joint statement in 2020 proposed that planetary-scale problems, from the anthropocentric to the environmental, should be addressed. AI governance for planetary–scale issues must be resolved in collaboration with various stakeholders and organizations.

四十

11 月举行。两年前举行的第一届会议的联合声明强调了以人类为中心的方针。因此，按照这个方向，第二届会议的主题是以人类为中心的人工智能。然而，我们现在正面临着全球性的挑战，如新冠肺炎疫情、气候变化和社区分裂。因此，2020 年的联合声明提出，从以人类为中心的问题到环境问题的各类全球性问题都应该得到解决。我们应该与各利益相关者和组织合作，共同开展人工智能治理工作，以解决全球性问题。

41

Localizing AI Ethics and Governance in East Asia

Danit GAL

2019 and 2020 are the years moving from AI Ethics and Governance principles to action. In 2017 and 2018, numerous countries, companies, and institutions rushed to publish AI Ethics and Governance principles. Unsurprisingly, we witnessed broad international alignment on core principles such as accessibility, accountability, controllability, explainability, fairness, human-centricity, privacy, safety, security, and transparency. Now we're moving to the implementation stage, as these entities explore what localizing globally shared principles means.

This is a critical rite of passage in AI Ethics and Governance. As we pursue the localization of these principles, we're beginning to see major points of contention between alternative interpretations as well as discover new implementation paths. This is a positive development. AI Ethics and Governance principles can only prove effective if they are put into practice, and that requires adapting them to local needs and realities. Perhaps most common in the localization process is consulting local cultural, religious, and philosophical traditions when defining one's ethics. This is particularly salient in East Asia, where Confucian philosophical traditions, technoanimistic Buddhist and Shinto inclinations, and rich cultural perceptions of technology play a key role in the localization of AI Ethics and Governance principles.

Another notable process of localization is found in the different approaches to the implementation of principles such as privacy and accountability. In the localization of privacy, we see different approaches to data ownership and protection, also critical to AI training, between the EU, US, and China. Championing the GDPR, the EU seeks to empower users and regain individual control over personal data. In the US we're still seeing data being regarded as proprietary by technology companies despite evolving data protection regulations, especially when transacting with third parties. In China, authorities raised the stakes and are actively warning and banning applications deemed to abuse, misuse, and excessively collect user data.

The localization of privacy also feeds into that of accountability, which is central to AI developers. In the EU, US, and China (alongside other countries) we see authorities holding companies responsible for the technologies they develop and distribute. The EU, for example, fines companies directly for misconduct. South Korea, in comparison, takes a different approach in

四十一

东亚人工智能伦理和治理政策本地化

高丹青

2019—2020 年是人工智能伦理和治理从原则走向行动的时期。2017—2018 年，许多国家、公司和机构争相发布人工智能伦理和治理原则。不约而同的，国际人工智能伦理和治理核心原则在可访问性、问责性、可控性、可解释性、公平性、以人为本、隐私、安全、保障和透明度等主要方面保持着高度的一致。现在我们将进入这些原则的实施阶段，这些实践主体将探索全球共享原则本地化的意义。

本地化是人工智能伦理和治理原则发展的关键要素。随着我们开始追求原则本地化，我们可以观察不同观点之间的主要争论点，并从中寻找新的实施路径，这是一种积极的发展趋势。人工智能伦理和治理原则只有付诸实践才能证明其有效性，而这就要求它们必须满足本地和现实的需要。在本地化流程中，最常见的问题是人工智能伦理和治理原则必须要遵循当地的文化、宗教和哲学传统。这一点在东亚尤为突出，那里的儒家哲学传统、宣扬万物有灵论的佛教和神道教信仰，以及丰富的科技文化认知，都在人工智能伦理和治理原则的本地化过程中发挥着关键作用。

另一个值得注意的本地化问题是在采用不同方法实现隐私和问责等原则中衍生出来的。在隐私的本地化流程中，我们看到欧盟、美国和中国在数据所有权和保护方面采取了不同做法，这对人工智能训练而言也十分关键。欧盟支持《通用数据保护条例》，致力于赋予用户权力，并重新让个人获得数据的控制权。在美国，尽管数据保护法规不断变化，科技公司仍然将数据视为专有数据，尤其是在与第三方交易时。在中国，政府提高了风险意识，禁止滥用、误用和过度收集用户数据的应用程序，并对用户进行提醒。

隐私本地化也会影响问责，而问责是人工智能开发的核心。在欧盟、美国、中国以及其他国家，我们看到有关当局要求公司对其开发和传播的技术负责。例如，欧盟直接对行为不当的公司进行罚款。相比之下，韩国则采取了不同的做法，其伦理指南明确了供应商（公司）、开发商和用户各自所要承担的责任。韩国的问责模式提供了值得探索的新方式和新机遇，特别体现在其尝试通过促进技术使用者的知情和自愿使用，增强个人责任意识。

its Ethics Guidelines by dividing responsibility between providers (companies), developers, and users. The South Korean model of accountability offers new challenges and opportunities that are worth exploring, especially as we strive to create more individual accountability by promoting the informed and consensual use of technology.

These are a few examples of the growing AI Ethics and Governance principles localization trend. More research is needed to better understand how these processes take place and how they affect domestic and international technology users. The next step in this process will be to feed instances of these localizations back to principle drafters to share best practices and identify what is still missing.

四十一

以上是人工智能伦理和治理原则本地化趋势的几个例子，目前仍需要更多的研究，以更好地了解上述流程的产生机制，以及它们对国内外人工智能用户的影响。在此基础上，下一步是将这些本地化实例反馈给人工智能伦理和治理原则的主要制定者，以共享最佳实践并确定人工智能伦理和治理原则中仍然缺少的内容。

42

The Innovation of Singapore's AI Ethics Model Framework[1]

GOH Yihan, Nydia REMOLINA

Since 2017, Singapore government identified Artificial Intelligence (AI) as one of the four frontier technologies that would further the groundwork infrastructure that underpins the country's ambitions for its Digital Economy and its Smart Nation ambition. On the one hand, 2019 was a period when fundamental policy initiatives were launched in Singapore. On the other hand, in 2019 the Government reaffirmed the importance of developing and using AI by implementing projects in key high-value sectors and building a holistic AI ecosystem.

The policy initiatives positioned Singapore as one of the leading voices in AI Governance worldwide. Indeed, on April 2019 the country won a top award at the World Summit on the Information Society Forum, a United Nations level platform. The initiatives that contributed to the win included: Asia's first model AI governance framework that was released in January; an international and industry-led advisory council on the ethical use of AI and data; and a research programme on the governance of AI, ethics and data use established through the SMU Centre for Artificial Intelligence and Data Governance that I lead and from where we contribute to the ecosystem by conducting academic research to inform AI and data governance in Singapore and beyond, with a particular focus on legislation and policy.

One of the most relevant cross-sectoral policy initiatives of this year is the Model Artificial Intelligence Governance Framework–or Model Framework–launched in January 2019 as a guide for organizations to practically address key ethical and governance issues when deploying AI technologies. The Singaporean approach helps translate ethical principles into pragmatic measures that businesses can adopt. It is the result of the collaboration between the private sector and regulators and the first attempt of a country in Asia to put together this type of framework. Other jurisdictions lead similar initiatives this year. For example, the European Commission announced its final set of AI and ethics guidelines by March 2019, an approach likely to complement the EU General Data Protection Regulations. On a more international scale, the OECD presented on May 2019 a set of principles on AI to promote the innovative and trustworthy use of AI that respects human rights and democratic values.

Additionally, Singapore launched in October 2019 the National AI Strategy (NAIS) that will see over $500 million committed to funding activities related to AI under the Research, Innovation and Enterprise 2020 Plan, in hopes of furthering AI capabilities in these fields. Highlighted in the

四十二

新加坡人工智能伦理和治理举措[1]

吴亦涵，尼地·阿莫林

自 2017 年以来，新加坡政府将人工智能列为四项前沿技术之一，这将进一步推动基础设施建设，支撑起新加坡发展数字经济和建设智慧国家的愿景。一方面，2019 年是新加坡启动基本政策举措的一年。另一方面，在 2019 年，新加坡政府通过在关键的高价值领域实施项目和建立全面的人工智能生态系统，重申了开发和使用人工智能的重要性。

这些政策举措使新加坡成为全球人工智能治理的领先国家之一。2019 年 4 月，新加坡在联合国级别的平台——信息社会论坛世界峰会上获得了最高奖项。促成新加坡获得这一殊荣的举措包括：(1) 2019 年 1 月，新加坡发布了亚洲首个人工智能治理框架；(2) 新加坡成立了一个以国际和产业为导向的人工智能和数据伦理使用咨询委员会；(3) 新加坡积极开展针对人工智能治理、伦理和数据使用的项目。该项目由我领导的新加坡管理大学人工智能和数据管理中心开展，我们通过开展学术研究为人工智能生态系统做出贡献，影响新加坡及其他地区的人工智能和数据治理，特别是立法和政策方面。

2019 年 1 月推出的示范人工智能治理框架（或称模型框架）是新加坡政府今年实施的最重要的跨部门政策举措之一。该框架旨在指导各个组织在部署人工智能技术时切实解决关键伦理和治理问题。新加坡的做法有助于将伦理原则转化为企业可以采取的务实措施。这是私营部门与监管机构合作的结果，也是亚洲国家建立这种框架的首次尝试。其他国家和地区今年也采取了类似举措，例如，欧盟委员会在 2019 年 3 月公布了其最终人工智能和伦理准则，这是对欧盟《通用数据保护条例》的补充。在更国际化的层面上，经合组织于 2019 年 5 月提出了一套关于人工智能的原则，以促进尊重人权和民主价值观、创新和可信赖的人工智能使用方式。

此外，新加坡于 2019 年 10 月发布了国家人工智能战略（NAIS），该战略将为 2020 研究、创新和企业计划下与人工智能相关的活动提供超过 5 亿新元的资金支持，以求提高人工智能在这些领域的能力。NAIS 强调，新加坡首先将聚焦五个关键领域——运输和物流、智慧城市和房地产、安全与保障、医疗和教育。这些国家人工智能项目旨在引导研发投资、吸引人才，并引导新加坡支持数字基础设施的发展。

NAIS, Singapore will start by focusing on five key sectors to concentrate its efforts on–transport and logistics, smart cities and estates, safety and security, healthcare, and education. These National AI projects aim to channel investment for research and development, anchor talent and guide the development of supporting digital infrastructure in Singapore.

What do we expect for next year? We look forward to keeping consolidating the AI ecosystem in Singapore from the academia by publishing cutting-edge research that can contribute to convene and facilitate dialogue, across academic, industry and regulators, especially between organisations in the Asia Pacific region. We also expect that regulators will continue to develop their initiatives towards having trustworthy AI, such as the second version of the AI Model Framework from IMDA, and the Veritas initiative announced by the Monetary Authority of Singapore which will translate into practice the principles-based approach for AI that the financial regulator has adopted.

1. This research is supported by the National Research Foundation, Singapore under its Emerging Areas Research Projects (EARP) Funding Initiative. Any opinions, findings and conclusions or recommendations expressed in this material are those of the author(s) and do not reflect the views of National Research Foundation, Singapore.

四十二

那么，我们对明年有何展望呢？我们希望通过发表前沿研究成果，从学术领域继续巩固新加坡的人工智能生态系统，促进学术界、产业界和监管机构之间的对话，特别是亚太地区组织之间的对话。我们也希望监管机构能够继续制定相关举措，支撑可信赖人工智能的发展，如资讯通信媒体发展局的第二版人工智能模型框架，以及新加坡金融管理局宣布的 Veritas 计划，该计划将把金融监管机构采用的基于原则的人工智能方法转化为实践。

1. 这项研究得到新加坡国家研究基金会在其新兴领域研究项目资助倡议下的支持。本材料中表达的任何意见、调查结果和结论或建议都是作者的意见，不代表新加坡国家研究基金会的意见。

43

The Grand Indian Challenge of Managing Inequity and Growth in the AI Era

Urvashi ANEJA

Despite artificial intelligence being seen as a catalyst for economic growth and a solution for complex socioeconomic challenges, India has yet to articulate a comprehensive framework for how this technology should be governed. However, AI is already being deployed in public systems. Many law enforcement agencies are exploring the use of predictive analytics as automated facial recognition systems are already widespread. Plans are also underway to deploy AI-based systems in both judicial and welfare delivery systems.

Following the example set by Europe, India has begun working on a risk-based framework for AI governance. Risk-based frameworks are perhaps appropriate to fuel innovation. However, they are inappropriate for developing countries such as India, where AI is viewed as a tool to address complex development and governance challenges. The trade-offs are different in India and Europe because AI is positioned as central to India's development and state-building trajectories.

Risk-based approaches can create regulatory blind spots with regard to the disparate impacts for vulnerable populations and systemic risks. Low levels of regulatory and institutional capacity pose further challenges to the suitability of risk-based approaches. Risk-based approaches also face methodological and epistemic challenges: even though some AI applications have a low risk, their cumulative effect could be large. Assessing risk is not an objective exercise; it is deeply embedded in sociocultural values and priorities.

Part of the problem for regulators globally, including in India, has been to establish a threshold for regulatory intervention. Risk-based approaches are tempting in this regard, but to work, they require open, inclusive, and transparent dialogne around risk identification and assessment. For this process to be meaningful, civil society must have the knowledge and capacity to evaluate AI impact; transparency and expertise are two sides of the same coin. These capacities are currently limited in India, and greater investments are needed in interdisciplinary research and public communication. Trust in judicial systems and institutions is also paramount. The absence of adequate grievance redressal mechanisms for many digitally enabled governance interventions in India does not bode well for building such trust.

AI presents a wicked problem for public policy that consists of multiple interacting systems, both

四十三

印度在人工智能时代面临的重大挑战：不平等和增长之间的矛盾

乌尔瓦希·阿内贾

尽管人工智能被视为经济增长的催化剂和应对复杂社会经济挑战的解决方案，但印度尚未针对这项技术制定全面的治理框架。如今，人工智能已在公共系统中得到了广泛的应用。随着自动人脸识别系统广泛融入我们的生活，许多执法机构正不断探索预测分析的各类用途。此外，在司法和福利发放系统中部署基于人工智能系统的计划也正在稳步推进。

印度已着手以欧洲为样本，尝试建立一个基于风险的人工智能治理框架。基于风险的治理框架或许可以推动创新，但并不适合印度等将人工智能视为应对复杂发展和治理挑战的工具的发展中国家。对于印度而言，人工智能是决定国家建设和发展轨迹的核心要素，因此其对于利弊的权衡取舍与欧洲存在差异。

此外，基于风险的监管方法还可能存在“监管盲点”，忽略对弱势群体的不同影响和系统性风险。低下的监管能力和机构能力对基于风险的监管方法的适用性提出了进一步的挑战。同时，基于风险的监管方法还面临着方法论和认知论层面的挑战——即使一些人工智能应用的风险较低，其累积效应也可能十分强大。风险评估并非一项客观的活动，它很大程度上受到社会文化价值观和优先事项的影响。

对包括印度在内的世界各国的监管机构而言，如何设立监管干预的门槛是一大难题。基于风险的监管方法在这方面具有优势，但在实践中，必须保证围绕风险识别和风险评估开展开放、包容和透明的对话。透明性和专业性本质上是同一问题的两个方面。为确保这一流程的有效性，民间团体必须掌握评估人工智能影响的知识和能力。目前，印度在上述能力的储备上相当有限，亟需在跨学科研究和公众宣传方面加大投资。此外，提高公众对司法体系和制度的信任度也尤为重要——印度当下实施的许多基于数字的治理干预措施就缺乏完善的申诉机制，不利于建立信任。

人工智能为公共政策带来了一个涉及多个相互作用的社会和技术系统的棘手难题——影响和

social and technical. The impacts and risks are uncertain, and the divergence between various stakeholders indicates competing values and world views. Addressing wicked problems requires engaging multiple stakeholders in iterative and adaptive strategies; enabling collaborative sense-making, experimentation, and learning; and building capacities for reflection and foresight. Just as AI is not a silver bullet to address socioeconomic challenges, neither is a single set of regulatory or governance frameworks adequate to address these societal harms. Governing AI will require a range of public policy interventions, from competition law to curb the powers of Big Tech to sector-specific standards and risk assessments. India seeks to be a global AI leader, but this role necessitates not merely being at the forefront of innovation but also developing normative frameworks and governance systems that align AI trajectories with societal needs. Blind technological optimism might entrench rather than alleviate the grand Indian challenge of managing inequity and growth.

风险存在不确定性，不同利益相关者之间的价值观和世界观可能存在分歧。解决这一难题需要让多个利益相关者参与实施迭代和适应性战略；促进协同性意义构建、实验和学习；并建设反应能力和预测能力。正如人工智能不是应对社会经济挑战的灵丹妙药一样，仅仅依靠一套监管或治理框架也不足以应对这些危害社会的问题。从限制大型科技企业权力的竞争法，到特定行业的标准和风险评估，治理人工智能需要一系列公共政策干预措施的支持。印度致力于成为人工智能领域的全球领导者，但这不仅需要走在创新的前沿，还需要制定规范性框架和治理体系，推动人工智能按照符合社会需求的轨迹发展。盲目的技术乐观主义可能进一步加剧不平等和经济增长之间的矛盾，对印度的相关管理工作提出更大的挑战。

44

India's Strategies to Put Its AI Economy on the Fast Track

Raj SHEKHAR

The year 2020 presented unprecedented challenges to governments globally, especially in developing countries, where nationwide measures to contain the spread of COVID-19 risked putting other public policy priorities on indefinite hold. However, in India, the Narendra Modi government commendably managed to drive critical consultation and dialog on several cardinal policies, targeting the improvement of India's AI readiness to support the domestic growth of both public and private AI enterprises, in line with the Prime Minister's vision for Atmanirbhar Bharat (or self-reliant India).

Considerable progress was made by the Indian government in devising frameworks for data governance in India. The Joint Select Committee of the Indian Parliament met several times during the year for a clause-by-clause examination of The Personal Data Protection (PDP) Bill, 2019, given its undisputed significance in deciding the fates of the Indian digital citizenry and economy. The Ministry of Electronics and Information Technology (MeitY) proposed (a) the Data Centre Policy, detailing a set of enabling regulations and programs for building the domestic workforce and infrastructural capabilities to realize the data localization mandate enshrined in the PDP Bill, 2019, and (b) the Non-Personal Data (NPD) Governance Framework, recommending the enactment of a central NPD statute and the establishment of a central NPD authority under the statute to unlock the economic, social, and public value of data while securing an equitable, innovation-friendly, and privacy-respecting regime for nonpersonal data-sharing in the country. The National Institution for Transforming India (NITI) Aayog, the Indian government's premier policy think tank, proposed (a) setting up a National Data and Analytics Platform (expected to launch this year) to publish government data in an open, user-friendly format to enable research and innovation, evidence-based public policy-making, and participatory governance and (b) the adoption of Data Empowerment and Protection Architecture, enabling citizens to securely and seamlessly share their personal data with third-party institutions to benefit from easy, hassle-free access to a host of banking and insurance products online.

Additionally, recognizing the whole gamut of ethical concerns emerging around the development and deployment of various AI use cases globally, NITI Aayog released working documents on Responsible #AIforAll and Enforcement Mechanisms for Responsible #AIforAll. The documents emphasized the need to uphold constitutional fundamental rights in defining principles for responsible AI governance in India and recommended a national, multidisciplinary Council for

四十四

印度促使人工智能经济走上快车道的策略

拉杰·谢卡尔

2020 年，全球政府都面临着前所未有的挑战，特别是在发展中国家，为了遏制新冠肺炎病毒扩散而采取的全国性措施使得这些国家可能不得不将其他公共政策重点事项无限期搁置。但是，莫迪政府成功地推动了一些重要政策的磋商和对话，这些政策旨在提高印度的人工智能成熟度以支持国内公共和私营人工智能企业发展，与印度总理对自力更生的印度倡议（AtmaNirbharBharat）的展望接轨，令人称道。

印度政府在制定印度数据治理框架方面取得了巨大的进展。鉴于 2019 年《个人数据保护法（草案）》在决定印度数字公民和印度数字经济的命运方面具有无可争辩的重要意义，印度议会联合专责委员会在 2020 年召开了几次会议，以对该草案进行逐条审查。电子信息技术部（MeitY）拟定了：（1）对包括一系列有利于促进国内劳动力和基础设施能力建设，以落实 2019 年《个人数据保护法（草案）》中的数据本地化授权的法规和项目在内的内容进行了详细阐述的数据中心政策；（2）在《非个人数据治理框架》中，建议制定中央非个人数据法规，并根据该法规建立中央非个人数据管理机构，以释放数据的经济、社会和公共价值，同时确保国内非个人数据共享有一个公平、有利于创新和尊重隐私的管理制度。印度政府最重要的政策智库改造印度国家研究院（NITI Aayog）提出：（1）建立国家数据和分析平台，以一种对用户友好的开放方式公开政府数据，从而促进研究和创新、基于实证的公共决策，以及印度的参与式治理；（2）采用数据授权和保护架构，以使公民能够安全无缝地与第三方机构共享其个人数据，轻松便捷地获取众多在线银行和保险产品。

此外，NITI Aayog 意识到了随着全球各类 AI 用例的开发和部署而相继出现的各类伦理问题，因而发布了为全人类服务的有关负责任的 AI 的工作文件，以及有关为全人类服务的 AI 的执行机制。上述文件强调了坚持维护为印度负责任的 AI 治理确定相关原则的宪法基本权利的必要性等内容，并建议设立一个国家级多学科伦理与技术委员会，负责帮助行业监管机构基于风险制定相应的 AI 法规和其他措施，以协助在印度建立负责任的 AI 生态系统。

为了让印度的下一代专家能够拥有相应的 AI 技能，人力资源发展部（MHRD）在第三版国家教

Ethics and Technology tasked with helping sectoral regulators develop proportionate, risk-based AI regulations and other measures to foster the creation of a responsible AI ecosystem in India.

To equip India's next generation of professionals with AI-ready skills, the Ministry of Human Resource Development (MHRD) in the third National Education Policy proposed pedagogically transforming the Indian educational system by introducing AI courses to school and university curricula.

The year 2020 concluded with the Ministry of Science and Technology (MST) releasing the 5th National Science, Technology, and Innovation (STI) Policy with an overarching bearing on the improvement of India's AI readiness. The policy detailed the Indian government's vision for achieving technological self-reliance by means of well-grounded, dynamic, and inclusive institutional governance mechanisms aimed at enabling open and wide access to all publicly funded STI research, increasing the public and private funding of STI research in priority sectors, and developing essential human capital for the STI ecosystem.

Although proposals from MeitY, NITI Aayog, MHRD, and MST for national policy shifts may have their weaknesses, they have appreciably improved stakeholder engagement on a range of pressing AI governance issues in India. This effort demonstrates a marked improvement from 2019 in the Indian government's positioning vis-à-vis AI governance that promises to provide the Indian AI economy the critical foundations it needs to increase and compete resiliently in the global AI marketplace.

育政策中提出要通过在各大院校的课程体系中推出 AI 课程等方式，改变印度教育体系中的教学方法。

印度科技部（MST）在 2020 年末发布了第五项国家科学、技术和创新（STI）政策，总体上对印度的 AI 成熟度的提高具有一定的影响。该政策详细阐释了印度政府对通过扎实、动态和包容的制度治理机制实现技术自立的展望。上述治理机制旨在实现所有公共资助的研究成果的开放和广泛获取、增加对重点领域 STI 研究的公共和私人投资，以及为 STI 生态系统开发必要的人力资本。

尽管 MeitY、NITI Aayog、MHRD 和 MST 针对国家政策转变的提案可能存在缺点，但同时它们也大大提高了利益相关者在印度一系列紧迫的 AI 治理问题上的参与度。这表明，自 2019 年以来，印度政府在有关 AI 治理的定位方面有了明显的进步，为印度的 AI 经济打下了重要基础，使其能够发展壮大，并以百折不挠的姿态参与全球 AI 市场上的竞争。

45

The Governance Approach of Artificial Intelligence in the European Union

Eva KAILI

Artificial Intelligence grows exponentially and it is destined to be a critical technology which will not only change business models and our life as consumers, but it will most importantly challenge traditional models and notions of citizenship. Europe brings to the front a third approach that accelerates innovation and the uses of Artificial Intelligence without compromising the privacy rights of the citizens, without discounting the ownership and value of the data that the people produce, and without violating the safety and quality of life of the people in the labyrinth of applications and means of data collection.

Europe introduces a model of governance based on the fundamental notion of technological neutrality, where the regulator sets the principles and the market comes and applies the principle by defining the standards of the product or service. The game changer in this approach is that the standards comply to strict and fundamental principles for customer protection, social inclusion, human rights, privacy and non-discrimination, that EU is a global model of safeguarding.

The European Institutions worked systematically in the last year to establish this competitive framework that we aspire to become the global standard in AI. This framework aims to elevate people's trust in AI and ensure that in the digital age, people co-exist with intelligent systems without fearing exclusion, manipulation, oppression or discrimination. Retaining freedom of choice in a human-centric AI that would prevent brain computer interfaces challenging the nature and future of humanity. In contrast to the trends of the Fourth Industrial Revolution towards inequalities and dehumanization, technology and innovation best practices need now to be bent back towards the service of humanity, and Europe could lead as a global rules and standards setter for the Fifth Industrial Revolution. Europe aspires to be the global leader in the space of AI, with systematic investments to AI-based innovative solutions, the acceleration of technology transfer mechanisms, the strengthening of innovation ecosystems with digital innovation hubs and AI Centres of Excellence, and with funding of high quality research projects.

The rapid development of automation in Europe must not reflect mistakes of the past; AI algorithms and systems must be trained on diversified sets, and their objectives have to be clearly defined and controlled to avoid risks of bias and discrimination or data poisoning. Decisions made by AI

四十五

欧盟的人工智能治理路径

伊娃·凯莉

人工智能以指数形式增长，它注定是一项关键技术，不仅会改变商业模式和我们作为消费者的生活，最重要的是它将挑战传统模式和公民概念。欧洲提出的方法是，在不损害公民隐私权、不损害人民生产的数据的所有权和价值，也不在错综复杂的应用以及数据采集过程中侵犯人民的安全和生活质量的情况下，加速创新和人工智能应用。

欧洲引入了一种基于技术中立这一基本概念的治理模式，在这种模式下，监管机构负责制定原则，市场则通过定义产品或服务的标准来实施这些原则。这种模式的颠覆性改变在于其标准符合严格的基本原则，包括客户保护、社会包容、人权、隐私和非歧视等，这是一种全球性的保障模式。

在过去的一年里，欧洲的机构系统地开展工作，以建立竞争框架，意图使其成为人工智能的全球标准。该框架旨在提升人们对人工智能的信任，确保人们能在数字时代与智能系统共存，而不必担心被排斥、操纵、压迫或歧视。在以人为本的人工智能中保留选择的自由，将有效防止脑机接口挑战人类的本质和未来。与第四次工业革命走向不平等和非人化的趋势相反，技术和创新的最佳实践现在需要重新转向为人类服务，欧洲可以作为第五次工业革命的全球规则和标准的制定者发挥领导作用。欧洲希望成为人工智能领域的全球领导者，对基于人工智能的创新解决方案进行系统投资，加快技术转让机制，通过数字创新中心和人工智能卓越中心加强创新生态系统，并资助高质量的研究项目。

欧洲自动化的快速发展绝不能重复过去的错误，人工智能算法和系统必须通过多样化的数据集进行训练，其目标必须明确可控，以避免偏见和歧视或数据中毒的风险。人工智能做出的决定必须符合整个智能系统生命周期中定义欧洲的集体伦理结构，并划清红线，例如采用基于风险的方法，做到完全禁止致命性自主武器或有意识人工智能的研究。高风险的应用应就我们共同价值观的脆弱性、我们作为公民的权利、我们作为政策制定者的责任，以及我们对后代的义务发出警示。

must be aligned with the collective ethical fabric that defines Europe throughout the lifecycle of intelligent systems and follow clear red lines, such as the risk-based approach that would, for example, completely ban research in autonomous lethal weapons or conscious AI. The high-risk applications should alert us of the fragility of our common values, as well as our rights as citizens, our responsibilities as policy-makers and our obligations to future generations.

We need to set rules and standards that give control and more options to citizens by default and by design, as this would be the only way to ensure that AI will remain trustworthy and that the convenience of using intelligent systems will not compromise our safety or privacy.

四十五

我们需要制定规则和标准，通过预设和设计赋予公民控制权和更多的选择，这将是确保人工智能始终值得信赖的唯一途径，同时确保智能系统的便利性不会损害我们的安全或隐私。

46

Principles, Policy and Partnerships: How the EU Frames Its AI Governance Approach Vis-a-vis the International Community

Charlotte STIX

Good intentions only work when followed by concrete actions. It is clear that this principle also holds for the development and deployment of AI that performs in a reliable and secure manner. Recent years were filled with scoping the ethical and policy landscape with regards to AI, spearheaded in the European Union (EU) by the High Level Expert Group on AI (AI HLEG), an independent advisory group to the European Commission.

The concept of "trustworthy AI"[1], as introduced by the AI HLEG, quickly became a red thread throughout European policy making. Trustworthy AI is defined as AI that is (a) lawful, (b) ethical, and (c) robust, both from technical and social perspectives. Trustworthy AI, as the type of AI that Europe strives towards, was subsequently picked up and reiterated in the European Commission's Communication: Building Trust in Human-Centric Artificial Intelligence (2019). It has since been a core idea underpinning multiple AI strategies from European Union Member States.

We can now see this work growing roots and strengthening the EU's international position in the field of AI governance. Most notably, the EU has taken several concrete steps towards regulating AI. First, they scoped the opportunities for regulating AI in their "White Paper on AI: A European Approach to Excellence and Trust"[2], where proposals for ethical considerations, legal obligations and technical infrastructure intertwine to create what the European Commission sees as two sides of a coin: an "ecosystem of trust" and an "ecosystem of excellence" in 2020. This was then followed by the final proposal for a harmonized regulatory framework on AI in 2021, the AI Act. The AI Act builds on the proposal for an "ecosystem of trust" by proposing regulation for a specific set of AI systems outlined in the AI Act[3], and a ban on some others.

Although crucial to the European approach to AI governance, regulatory efforts cannot exist in a vaccum. In addition to proposals outlined in the White Paper exploring how to create an "ecosystem of excellence", adjacent efforts through which the cooperation, coordination and communication amongst Member States can be strengthened such as those outlined in the updated Coordinated Plan on AI (2021) will further contribute to the EU's ambitious plan to

四十六

原则、政策与伙伴关系：欧盟如何制定面向国际社会的人工智能治理方法

夏洛特·斯蒂克斯

美好的愿望要通过具体的行动来实现。显然，这一原则也适用于安全可靠的 AI 开发与部署。近年来，在欧盟内部的人工智能高级专家组（AI HLEG，欧盟委员会旗下的一个独立咨询小组）的带动下，有关 AI 伦理和政策格局的研究正进行得如火如荼。

AI HLEG 提出的"可信 AI"[1]概念迅速成为了整个欧洲政策制定领域的红线。可信 AI 是指在技术和社会层面上合法、合乎伦理，且稳定的 AI。欧洲努力追求的可信 AI 随后又在欧盟委员会的《沟通：在以人为中心的人工智能中建立信任》（Communication: Building Trust in Human-Centric Artificial Intelligence，2019）中被再次提及并重申，由此成为支持欧盟成员国多项 AI 战略的核心理念。

如今，这项工作正在切实推进，并不断增强着欧盟在 AI 治理领域的国际地位。最值得注意的是，欧盟已经采取了一些具体措施来监管 AI。首先，他们于 2020 年发布了《人工智能白皮书——通往卓越和信任的欧洲路径》（"White Paper on AI: A European Approach to Excellence and Trust"）[2]，在其中明确了 AI 监管机遇，提出了有关伦理注意事项、法律义务和技术基础设施的提案，形成了欧盟委员会眼中同一事物的两个方面：一个"信任生态系统"和一个"卓越生态系统"。随后，他们又于 2021 颁布了《人工智能法案》（AI Act）[3]，这是其关于 AI 统一监管框架的最终提案。《人工智能法案》以一项针对"信任生态系统"的提案为基础，提出对《人工智能法案》中提到的一组特定 AI 系统进行监管，并取缔其他一些系统。

虽然监管工作对欧洲的 AI 治理方法而言至关重要，但也无法凭空展开。除白皮书中提到的探索如何建立"卓越生态系统"的提案外，有助于加强成员国之间的协调、合作与沟通的相关工作，如新版《人工智能协调计划》（Coordinated Plan on AI，2021）中提到的相关工作，也将进一步推进欧盟为实现数字主权和成为国际 AI 治理领域关键参与者而制定的宏伟计划。

achieve Digital Souvereignty and act as a key player vis-a-vis the international stage when it comes to AI governance.

Moreover, on a international level, the EU (directly through the European Commission and through its Member States) is strongly represented in many key international efforts working on AI governance such as the OECD, the Global Partnership on AI or the Council of Europe, as well as an active participant in multiple standardisation committees.

It is evident that the EU aims to set itself apart from other international actors by encouraging governance mechanisms for AI which solidify the trustworthiness of the AI systems developed and deployed. In order to achieve this goal, the EU has gone full circle from Ethics Principles, to Policy Measures up to an in-depth involvement in international partnerships.

四十六

此外，在国际层面上，欧盟（直接通过欧盟委员会或通过其成员国）在诸如经合组织、人工智能全球合作伙伴关系和欧洲委员会等许多有关 AI 治理的关键国际组织和项目中具有举足轻重的地位，同时也加入了多个标准化委员会，积极参与相关工作。

显然，欧盟的目标是通过鼓励 AI 治理机制巩固已开发和部署的 AI 系统的可信度，以此取得差异化优势，走在国际参与者的前列。为实现这一目标，欧盟已经走完了从伦理原则到政策措施，再到深度参与国际合作伙伴关系的完整流程。

1. https://digital-strategy.ec.europa.eu/en/library/ethics-guidelines-trustworthy-ai
2. https://ec.europa.eu/info/files/white-paper-artificial-intelligence-european-approach-excellence-and-trust_en
3. https://eur-lex.europa.eu/legal-content/EN/TXT/?uri=CELEX%3A52021PC0206

47

The Driving Forces of AI Ethics in the United Kingdom

Angela DALY

The UK Government has linked AI development directly to its industrial strategy, and also seems to view this as giving the UK a potential competitive edge, especially in its post-Brexit trajectory.

Between 2017 and 2018 the UK Government placed increasing emphasis on the national importance of AI, naming it as one of the country's four Grand Challenges in the 2017 Industrial Strategy, and investing in an AI Sector Deal in 2018. The UK Government also envisaged a leadership role for the country internationally in safe and ethical uses of data and AI. It set up a Centre for Data Ethics and Innovation as an advisory body and committed to be an "active participant" in standard setting and regulatory bodies especially for AI and data protection. Between 2017 and 2018 there was also activity in the UK Parliament, with an All-Party Parliamentary Group on AI set up in 2017 and a Select Committee on AI formed which issued a report in 2018. The Select Committee's report included 5 non-legally binding "overarching principles", as the basis for a possible cross-sector "AI Code" that it suggested be formulated and developed by the Centre for Data Ethics and Innovation.

In 2019, the Centre for Data Ethics and Innovation commenced its work. It has focused so far on online targeting and bias in algorithmic decision-making, producing two interim reports on these topics in July 2019, and a series of "snapshot" reports in September 2019 on ethical issues in AI, focusing on deepfakes, AI and personal insurance, and smart speakers and voice assistants. The Centre for Data Ethics and Innovation is scheduled to deliver formal recommendation to the UK Government in early 2020 on online micro-targeting and algorithmic bias.

There has been significant political instability domestically in the UK during 2019 with a change of Prime Minister and then a General Election in December 2019 which has given the new Prime Minister, Boris Johnson, a large majority in the House of Commons. The UK formally left the European Union on 31 January 2020, and the government now commands a sufficient majority to make and implement law and policy, including on AI.

However, divergence may yet occur within the UK on AI. The autonomous Scottish Government (led by the Scottish National Party) launched its own initiative to develop an AI strategy for the Scottish nation in January 2020. It has since released a scoping paper for public consultation. On the basis of consultation responses, the Scottish Government aims to publish its own AI Strategy in September 2020. It remains to be seen how aligned this strategy will be with the UK's overall approach to AI.

四十七

英国人工智能伦理的驱动力

李安琪

英国政府已经直接将人工智能的发展与其产业战略联系在一起，并且认为这是英国，尤其是英国在脱欧后的一个潜在竞争优势。

2017—2018 年，英国政府越来越强调人工智能在国家层面的重要性，将其列为英国 2017 年产业战略中面临的四大挑战之一，并在 2018 年签署了一项人工智能行业协议。此外，英国政府还设想在数据和人工智能的安全性和伦理使用方面在国际上发挥领导作用。英国政府设立了数据伦理和创新中心，作为人工智能咨询机构，并致力于成为标准制定和监管机构的“积极参与者”，尤其是在人工智能和数据保护方面。2017 年—2018 年，英国议会也开展了一些活动，在 2017 年成立了一个关于人工智能的全党议会小组，同时还成立了一个人工智能特别委员会。该委员会于 2018 年发布了一份报告，报告包括 5 个不具法律约束力的总体原则，作为数据伦理和创新中心制定和发展的跨部门“人工智能准则”的基础。

2019 年，数据伦理与创新中心开始运营。迄今为止，它一直专注于在线目标定位和算法决策偏见的研究。2019 年 7 月，数据伦理与创新中心针对上述话题发布了两份中期报告，并于 2019 年 9 月就人工智能的伦理问题发表了一系列“简要”报告，重点关注深度造假、人工智能和个人保险，以及智能音响和语音助手等问题。数据伦理与创新中心计划在 2020 年初向英国政府提交关于在线微观目标定位和算法偏见的正式建议书。

2019 年，英国国内出现了重大的政治变化，先是首相换届，然后是 2019 年 12 月的大选，选举出的新首相鲍里斯·约翰逊（Boris Johnson）赢得了下议院的多数席位。英国于 2020 年 1 月 31 日正式脱欧，而政府将拥有足够的多数票来制定和实施法律及政策，包括人工智能方面的法律和政策。

然而，英国内部在人工智能方面可能存在不同意见。苏格兰自治政府（由苏格兰民族党领导）于 2020 年 1 月发起了自己的倡议，计划为苏格兰制定人工智能战略。自那以后，它发布了一份范围界定文件供公众咨询。根据咨询意见，苏格兰政府在 2020 年 9 月公布自己的人工智能战略。这一战略将如何与英国的人工智能整体战略保持一致还有待观察。

48

AI Governance: Policy Progress to Enable Public Trust

Caroline JEANMAIRE

In the last year, AI regulatory frameworks have finally begun to emerge, advancing beyond mere "AI Principles." One cornerstone of this change is the realization that, rather than impeding innovation, regulation can fuel development by inspiring public trust. To hold the public trust and avoid another AI Winter, AI governance must factor in a "blind-spots radar" to reduce the risk of unforeseen calamities.

Regulators in the United States have maintained a light touch while prioritizing public trust. Building on AI principles developed by the Defense Department and the intelligence community, in December 2020, President Trump issued an Executive Order outlining nine principles agencies must meet when designing, developing, or acquiring AI applications. It also calls for comprehensive inventories of AI deployments within agencies and a roadmap for improved policy guidance on AI use. These regulatory principles encourage innovation by reducing uncertainty. "The ongoing adoption and acceptance of AI will depend significantly on public trust," the executive order states. "Agencies must therefore design, develop, acquire, and use AI in a manner that fosters public trust and confidence while protecting privacy, civil rights, civil liberties, and American values." To oversee and implement the U.S. national AI strategy, the White House established the National Artificial Intelligence Initiative Office in January 2021. The next few months under a Biden administration will provide more clarity around the duties of care that developers and manufacturers must have towards the public.

In parallel, the European Union followed principles developed by the High-Level Expert Group on AI in proposing new regulatory frameworks. In 2020, the European Commission published a White Paper that identified seven key requirements AI technologies should respect as well as a regulatory framework adopting a risk management approach. In addition, the Commission recommended including stand-alone software within the scope of product regulation and ensuring the safety of AI systems across economic actors in supply chains.

Regulators in the US and the EU understand the risks of technology backlash, knowing that accidents or failures could provoke public fear, as has happened before. The Three Mile Island Nuclear Accident in 1979 inhibited the development of the US nuclear power industry for 30 years, while in Europe the public has shied away from genetically modified foods due to various food safety issues including the Mad Cow disease. Conversely, the aviation industry enjoys public

四十八

人工智能治理：促进公众信任的政策进展

林晨力

2019 年，AI 监管框架终于开始陆续出现，超越了单纯的"AI 原则"。出现这一变化的基本原因之一在于人们意识到监管并非阻碍创新的绊脚石，而是有助于取得公众信任，进而推动发展的基石。为了保持公众信任和避免另一个 AI 寒冬，AI 治理必须考虑应用"盲点雷达"，以降低意外灾难风险。

美国的监管机构在以建立公众信任为首要目标行事的同时，也始终在关注这一问题。2020 年 12 月，美国时任总统特朗普基于美国国防部和情报体系制定的 AI 原则发布了一道行政令，概述了各机构在设计、开发或获取 AI 应用时必须遵循的九项原则。该行政令还要求对机构内部的 AI 部署进行全面清查，并制定有关改进 AI 使用政策指导的路线图。这些监管原则有助于减少不确定性，从而鼓励创新。该行政令指出："公众信任将在很大程度上决定 AI 能否得到持续应用和认可。因此，各机构必须以一种能够保护隐私、公民权利、公民自由和美国价值观，并加强公众信任和信心的方式来设计、开发、获取和使用 AI。"为了监管和实施美国国家 AI 战略，白宫于 2021 年 1 月设立了国家人工智能计划办公室。拜登政府将在未来的几个月内进一步明确开发商和制造商必须对公众尽到的注意义务。

同时，欧盟将在人工智能高级专家小组制定的原则的基础上推出新的监管框架。2020 年，欧盟委员会发布了一份白皮书，确定了 AI 技术应当满足的 7 大核心要求，以及采用风险管理方法的监管框架。此外，委员会还建议将独立软件纳入产品法规的适用范围，并确保贯穿供应链中各个经济主体的 AI 系统的安全性。

美国和欧盟的监管机构了解技术后冲风险，知道事故或失败可能导致公众产生恐慌，因为以前也发生过这种情况。1979 年的三里岛核泄漏事故对美国核电产业的发展造成了长达 30 年的深远影响；在欧洲，包括引发疯牛病在内的各种食品安全问题导致公众对转基因食品避之不及。与此相反，强大的安全认证流程和公开透明的事故调查流程让公众对航空业充满信心。

但是，大西洋两岸的监管机构还尚未确定风险评估标准和风险管理策略。他们仍需制定对技

confidence thanks to robust safety certification processes and visible processes for investigating accidents.

However, regulators on both sides of the Atlantic have yet to verify risk assessment criteria and risk management strategies. Processes to monitor and reassess technology for the appearance of "unknown unknowns" still need to be developed. Over 150 experts have signed the "Foresight in AI Regulation Open Letter" to the European Commission urging them to keep and strengthen the proposed regulation even though some groups may downplay potential risks related to AI. AI ethics and safety enable innovation, and regulation cannot be simply a façade if systems are to inspire public faith and confidence in the long-haul.

术进行监督和重新评估的流程，以应对“无知而不自知”的情况。截至目前，已有超过 50 位专家在“AI 监管展望公开信”上签名，力劝欧盟委员会不要听信一些可能对与 AI 相关的潜在风险有所低估的团体的建议，而是应该继续实施并强化拟定的法规。AI 伦理和安全能促进创新；如果希望通过相关体系来激发公众对这一漫长过程的信念和信心，法规就不能只是一纸空文，而是必须要落到实处。

49

AI Is Too Important to Be Left to Technologists Alone

Eugenio V. GARCIA

In a year tragically disturbed by COVID-19, we learned a key lesson. Similar to a virus, the overarching impact of AI will not be confined to national borders. The pandemic demonstrated that international cooperation is needed to successfully tackle cross-border issues that concern everyone.

As a general-purpose technology with multiple capabilities and long-term implications, AI can pose challenges that must be prevented or mitigated by pooling resources and expertise in defining agreed-upon parameters to safely develop its full potential.

Despite the considerable progress made on many fronts, international AI governance still lacks satisfactory norms, policies, safety measures, and technical standards. No regimes or normative instruments at the global level go beyond high-level principles.

Political tensions, growing competition, polarization, and tribalism do not seem conducive to the rapid development of major agreements. As a result, the absence of collaborative forms of governance, combined with mistrust toward the multilateral system, can complicate efforts to cope with AI risks in the long run.

In a fragmented landscape, if states fail to coordinate properly, future AI regulation could become Balkanized. A "splinternet" scenario, in which opposing blocs hold mutually incompatible rules, should be avoided.

A do-nothing approach is hardly an option. In a normative vacuum, driven by a logic of the race to the bottom, governments and private companies may push even harder for rapid AI development, regardless of considerations based upon law, ethics, safety, or security.

The need for AI governance is clear. As the technology becomes more ubiquitous, demands will strengthen to set in motion cooperation to prevent harm. Predictability by means of norm-setting can pave the way to responsible strategies to minimize disturbing scenarios.

Realistically, a regulatory AI agency now seems too far away. At this juncture, multistakeholder forums, on a voluntary basis, could fill the gap if they focus upon recommendations geared at prevention rather than regulations per se.

四十九

人工智能治理，绝不能单靠技术专家来应对

尤金尼奥·加西亚

在受新冠肺炎疫情困扰的过去一年，我们感受了悲伤，也收获了一个重要教训。与病毒十分相似，AI 也将给全球各国带来方方面面的影响。疫情证明了我们需要开展国际合作，才能在满足各方利益的前提下成功解决跨国问题。

AI 是一项具备多种功能以及长期影响的通用技术，面对其所带来的挑战，我们需要大量资源与专业知识技术，通过确定一致的因素特征加以预防或缓解，从而在确保安全的基础上充分发挥其潜能。

虽然在许多前沿领域都取得了可观进展，但关于 AI 国际治理的规范、政策、安全措施以及技术标准的制定仍不尽如人意。目前尚无超越高级原则的全球性管控制度或者规范文书。

紧张的政治局势、不断加剧的竞争、两极分化和部落主义在短期内对重大协议的达成并无裨益，由此带来的合作型治理形式的缺失，加上对多边机制的不信任，最终将使得 AI 风险的解决和应对变得更为困难。

在世界格局分崩离析的情况下，如果各国不能有效应对，未来对于 AI 的监管将呈现“巴尔干化”。我们应避免对立阵营相关规则互相矛盾的割裂局面出现。

对此，我们不能袖手旁观，坐以待毙。在没有规范的情况下，逐底竞争逻辑可能会驱使政府和私人企业无视法律、道德、安全问题而加大力度推进 AI 的快速发展。

对于 AI 治理的需求不言而喻。科技变得无处不在，着手设立合作机制以预防危害的需求也愈发强烈。通过建立规范实现技术的可预测性可推进负责任战略的制定，从而尽可能减少令人不安的局面的出现。

从现实层面来看，成立 AI 监管机构似乎遥遥无期。在此关头，举办由多个利益相关方自愿参与、旨在提供相关防范建议而非直接进行监管的论坛可起到一定的积极作用。

49

Multilateralism can play a role moving forward. The United Nations, for instance, with its unmatched range and universality, could offer a neutral, nonpartisan, legitimate platform for facilitating negotiations.

UNESCO has made great strides in advancing a much-needed discussion on a draft for the first global standard-setting international instrument on AI ethics.

The UN Secretary–General, in his Roadmap for Digital Cooperation, identified three crucial tasks: increase representation from the Global South in AI deliberations; improve the overall coordination of existing initiatives; and build capacity, particularly in the public sector.

UN-sponsored consultations were held in 2020 on creating an AI advisory body to provide expert advice and set the stage to effective consensus-building. The ultimate goal should be to reach solutions that can accommodate all concerns as much as possible.

"War is too serious a matter to leave to soldiers", Clemenceau once said. Similarly, AI is too important to be left to technologists alone.

AI policy-making will require bridging the gap between the technical community and political leaders, governmental officials, diplomats, and parliamentarians. Interconnecting these two worlds is not only advisable but also critical for success.

四十九

多边主义可以在推进中发挥作用。例如，联合国以其范围的广泛性与普遍性，可以为促进谈判提供一个中立、无党派、合法的平台。

教科文组织也在推动关于 AI 伦理的第一份全球标准制定，并在这方面取得了巨大进展。

联合国秘书长在其数字合作路线图中确定了三项关键任务：增加全球南方国家在 AI 决策中的代表性；改善现有举措的总体协调；以及能力建设，特别是在公共部门。

联合国赞助的咨询会议于 2020 年举行，旨在建立一个 AI 咨询机构，提供专家建议，并为有效建立共识奠定基础。最终目标应该是达成尽可能解决所有问题的解决方案。

克莱门索曾经说过："战争是一件非常严重的事情，不能让士兵去做。"同样，AI 也非常重要，不能只让技术专家去做。

AI 决策需要弥合技术界和政治领袖、政府官员、外交官和议员之间的差距。将这两个世界联系起来不仅是明智的，而且是成功的关键。

50

AI Governance Readiness: Rethinking Public Sector Innovation

Victor FAMUBODE

Twenty–twenty has been an awkward year for human civilization. This is evident in the way humans have responded to the pandemic. On the one hand, the pandemic exposed vulnerabilities in our global innovation system while conversely accelerating new opportunities through broader digital adoption. In various cases, at the heart of this digital adoption was the use of artificial intelligence across diverse sectors and domains.

For government, a significant milestone in AI application during this pandemic has been the collaborative use of such general-purpose technology with other technologies and data to combat the spread of COVID-19. For instance, Egypt's government, through the United Nations Development Programme (UNDP), launched an automated testing service of COVID-19 symptoms with a sign language chatbot. Notably, the application of AI use cases in high-stake domains, such as public health care, comes with its own risks and ultimately needs to be acknowledged by governments across Africa.

The rapid growth of AI's application across the continent shows the need to rethink public sector innovation. Doing so would entail moving away from the tokenization of democratizing responsible ways of deploying and implementing AI systems to the actual operationalization of these systems. While slow progress has been made in adopting guardrails for data protection, as demonstrated in "24 African countries out of 53 countries have adopted data protection regulations and laws" (Privacy International 2020), the implementation and compliance of these regulations would be a key determinant for addressing AI and data governance. However, governments in many parts of the continent continue to be confronted by weak institutions. This ultimately means that adopting and scaling AI governance would require addressing the challenges confronting these institutions.

Importantly, 2020 showed progress in awakening African governments to ethical AI implications. A major step has been to partner with institutions to assist with designing national strategies that incorporate ethical guidelines. A key example is "Rwanda's Ministry of ICT and Innovation (MINICT) and Rwanda Utilities Regulatory Authority (RURA) with implementation by GIZ FAIR Forward engaging future society to support the development of Rwanda's national artificial intelligence strategy".

In 2021, major ethical issues need to be thoroughly addressed, such as algorithm bias,

五十

为人工智能治理做准备：重新思考公共部门的创新

维克多·法姆波德

2020 年对于人类文明而言是棘手的一年。人类在疫情暴发之际的惊慌失措、焦头烂额明显揭露了这一点。疫情暴露出了全球创新体系中的漏洞，但反过来又通过更广泛的数字化应用加速创造了新的机遇。在各种情况下，人工智能在不同行业和领域的应用都是这种数字化应用的核心。

对于政府而言，协同使用此类通用技术与其他技术和数据阻止新冠病毒的传播是疫情期间 AI 应用的一个重要里程碑。例如，埃及政府通过联合国开发计划署（UNDP）推出了一项手语聊天机器人来自动检测新冠肺炎症状的服务。值得注意的是，在公共医疗健康等高风险领域中应用 AI 有其自身的风险，最终需要非洲各国政府的认可才能实施。

AI 应用在整个非洲大陆的快速增长显示出了重新思考公共部门创新的必要性，这需要从使部署和应用 AI 系统的负责任方式民主化的标记化转向上述系统的实操化。虽然“在 53 个非洲国家中，只有 24 个通过了数据保护法律法规（国际隐私组织 2020 年报告）”，导致数据保护措施进展缓慢，但能否妥善落实和遵循这些法规将成为能否解决 AI 和数据治理问题的决定性因素。不过，非洲许多国家的政府仍然面临着机构力量薄弱的问题。这意味着要落实和推广 AI 治理，就需要应对这些机构面临的挑战。

重要的是，2020 年，非洲各国政府开始重视 AI 的道德影响，在这方面取得了一定的进展。各国政府与相关 机构合作，让机构协助其制定将道德准则纳入考虑的国家战略，在这方面迈出了重要的一步。“卢旺达信息通讯技术和创新部（MINICT）和卢旺达公共事业管理局（RURA）通过德国国际合作机构实施 FAIR Forward 计划，让未来协会为卢旺达国家人工智能战略的制定提供支持”是一个重要标杆。

进入 2021 年，我们必须彻底解决算法偏见、监控、数字鸿沟和隐私等重大道德问题。为了应对这些问题，非洲各国政府在推进 AI 治理准备时需要考虑以下关键因素：

surveillance, the digital divide and privacy. In addressing them, key considerations for African governments toward readiness in AI governance include the following.

1. Leverage a community pipeline for designing, deploying and implementing AI systems. Doing so ultimately helps to incorporate diversity and variation into the data and models built for public consumption.

2. Re-evaluate public procurement processes to significantly capture wider consultation and transparency in procuring AI systems from private sector technology companies. Doing so assists with spotting key safety and security vulnerabilities before deployment.

3. Build capacity for policy-makers, developers and society planners in the responsible use of AI systems.

4. Create more public awareness on both the benefits and limitations of AI systems.

5. Incorporate risk and impact assessments from the design to the implementation phase across each public sector domain in which these AI systems are expected to be used.

五十

1. 利用社区渠道设计、部署和应用 AI 系统。这最终将有助于确保为公共消费建立的数据和模型具备多样性和变化性。

2. 重新评估公共采购流程，以大幅提高从私营技术公司采购 AI 系统时进行的咨询的广泛性和采购的透明度，这有助于在实施部署之前及早发现关键安全漏洞。

3. 帮助政策制定者、开发商和社会规划师构建负责任地使用 AI 系统的能力。

4. 进一步提高公众对 AI 系统的优点和局限性的认知。

5. 从设计到实施阶段，将风险和影响评估融入可能应用相关 AI 系统的所有公共领域。

51

AI Governance in Latin America and Its Impact on Development

Olga CAVALLI

Latin America offers a vast and diverse geography and fantastic biodiversity. It is the home of the world's largest rivers, mountains and many natural resources and beautiful places and is enhanced with a rich culture and well-trained human resources.

Recent events related to the COVID-19 pandemic have had a profound impact on regional economies. In this complex scenario, the use of artificial intelligence can introduce changes and innovation in national and regional industries, making them more productive. According to a report by the Inter-American Development Bank (IADB), the use of artificial intelligence can increase the GDP of the largest economies of the region in the next decades.

Although national priorities have changed in 2020 to focus more on areas such as health and the economy, several governments in the Latin American region are working on public policies and national strategies to promote AI use and development at the national level.

Mexico was one of the first countries in the world to create a national AI strategy. Brazil launched the National Internet of Things plan, which includes the creation of AI laboratories with a focus on strategic areas such as cybersecurity and defense. Chile is working with community and national experts to develop its own AI plan. In Argentina, a national AI strategy is being developed, and Columbia has published its Ethical Framework for AI.

The challenge for the Latin American region is to work toward a multistakeholder plan that must include government, the private sector, civil society, the technical community, and academia, where efforts and resources must be focused on the use of state-of-the-art technology and the enhancement of education in strategic areas and industries. The region has the highest inequity in the world, and AI use should improve this undesirable situation.

One of the problems in the region is its limited voice and low participation in those spaces where global AI governance and ethics frameworks are defined. Those spaces are usually dominated by developed economies, and if Latin America does not raise its voice, the results could be unhelpful for the needs of the region.

Concrete efforts are underway to overcome this problem and enhance the relevant participation

五十一

拉丁美洲人工智能治理及其对发展的影响

奥尔迦·卡瓦利

拉丁美洲是一个地域辽阔、地貌多样、生物多样性丰富的地区，拥有世界上最大的河流、山脉以及许多自然资源和美丽风景，同时还具有丰富的文化和高水平的人力资源。

最近的新冠肺炎疫情事件对拉丁美洲的区域经济产生了深远的影响。在这种复杂的情形下，可以通过利用人工智能在国家和地区产业中引入变革和创新，提高其生产力。美洲开发银行（IADB）的一份报告显示，未来几十年，人工智能的使用将有效助力拉丁美洲地区最大经济体的 GDP 增长。

尽管 2020 年国家关注重点发生了变化，更加注重卫生和经济等领域，但拉丁美洲地区的一些政府正在制定公共政策和国家战略，以促进人工智能在全国的使用和发展。

墨西哥是世界上最早制定国家人工智能战略的国家之一；巴西已经启动了国家物联网计划，其中包括建立人工智能实验室，重点关注网络安全和国防等战略领域；智利正与社会团体和全国的专家合作制定自己的人工智能计划；阿根廷正在制定国家人工智能战略；哥伦比亚已经公布其人工智能伦理框架。

拉丁美洲地区面临的挑战是需要达成一个多利益相关者计划,该计划必须涵盖政府、私营部门、民间团体、技术界和学术界，必须将精力和相关资源集中投入到先进技术的使用和加强战略领域及行业的教育上。拉丁美洲地区存在较为严重的不平等现象，而人工智能的使用将有效改善这一现象。

拉丁美洲地区的问题之一，是其在制定全球人工智能治理和伦理框架方面发言权有限，参与度低。这些领域通常由发达经济体主导，如果不增强拉丁美洲的发言权，最终的框架可能无法满足该地区的需求。

为了克服这一问题，加强区域专家在国际谈判中的相关参与度，拉丁美洲已经采取了具体的措施。例如，南方互联网治理学校（SSIG）致力于培训学生和青年专业人员，使他们在相关谈判

of regional experts in international negotiations, such as in the South School on Internet Governance, SSIG, which trains students and young professionals to become regional leaders in these negotiations. The training is free for participants. Since its creation in 2009 and throughout its twelve iterations, it has trained thousands of fellows from the region and other countries, giving them tools to help them navigate the international technology ecosystem and creating a very strong and valuable network between them and international experts.

There is important competence needed in a world dominated by constant innovation from highly developed countries, but all the countries of the region have innovative companies and human resources with relevant conditions to position themselves as leaders based on AI applications.

中成为拉丁美洲地区的领导者。该培训免费提供，自 2009 年创立以来，已先后推出 12 个版本，培训了来自拉丁美洲地区和其他地区的成千上万的研究员，为他们提供了有助于驾驭国际技术生态系统的工具，并在他们和国际专家之间建立了一个非常强大和有价值的网络。

在如今由高度发达国家不断带来的创新所主导的世界里，能力十分重要，但拉丁美洲地区所有国家都拥有创新型公司和人力资源，有条件根据人工智能应用将自己定位为领导者。

52

Artificial Intelligence in Latin America

Edson PRESTES

The discussion about the Governance of Artificial Intelligence in the LATAM region still is incipient. Although the region has some national AI plans, debates about governance per se are far from broad and inclusive. They are limited to specific societal segments and do not consider multilevel and intergovernmental participation in the process. In fact, a massive informational gap exists between the main actors that prevent them from understanding each other and the complexity of the domain. Human and institutional capacity-building are clearly needed to empower citizens and states in the region to create an effective and useful governance mechanism. No governance mechanism can be developed adequately if the main stakeholders do not understand the limits of the technology; the implication of its wide use; the opportunities that can be created by AI-based technology; the multidisciplinary nature of the AI domain; the need for agile regulatory mechanisms, national collaboration, and accountability and transparency practices; and the importance of public engagement.

The national plans for AI in the region are strongly influenced by international ethical and regulatory principles, such as those elaborated by the OECD and WEF. However, these biased plans seem to be only partially adequate to the LATAM reality. We cannot simply import or copy mature models developed in other regions without a deep reflection on their local impact. We have particularities. Some are intrinsic to the region, while others have been addressed by high income countries. To cite some of these particularities, some communities do not have yet electricity, so they can neither take full advantage of the AI ecosystem nor have their values represented in the AI models. Some countries do not consider education–the most important AI component–to be a priority; therefore, we have witnessed a yearly decrease in educational investment. In addition, the LATAM region lacks strategies and a rich ecosystem to prevent a "brain drain".

Of course, I have a long list of concerns, but all of them touch on two very basic points: education and information. In the Brazilian case, people commonly give their data to receive purchase discounts or are forced to give their data to access benefits. Some Brazilians accept the current government's view that fake news is an example of the freedom of expression and not a human rights violation. Thus, the question that naturally appears is how a governance mechanism for AI can protect people from abuses or human rights violations caused directly or indirectly by AI if the citizens do not know their rights and obligations, or worse, do not have an adequate formal education to have this understanding. No trustful or reliable governance mechanism can exist or survive if the people are not placed at the center of the debate, i.e., when the view of the main stakeholders (i.e., government or companies) is profit-oriented or distorted.

五十二

拉丁美洲的人工智能治理现状

埃德森·普雷斯特

拉美地区关于人工智能治理的讨论仍处于起步阶段。尽管该地区有一些关于人工智能的国家计划,但有关治理本身的辩论在广泛性和包容性方面还远远不够。它们仅限于社会的特定领域,不涉及正在进行的多层次和政府间参与。事实上,主要参与者之间存在着巨大的信息鸿沟,阻碍了对彼此的理解,也阻碍了对该领域复杂性的理解。我们显然需要加强人力和机构能力建设,以增强拉美地区公民和国家的能力,从而建立有效和实用的治理机制。为充分开发治理机制,主要利益相关者需要了解技术的局限性、广泛使用该技术会带来哪些影响、基于人工智能的技术可以创造哪些机遇、人工智能领域的多学科性质、对灵活监管机制的需求、对跨国协作的需求、践行可问责性和透明度的必要性,以及公众参与的重要性。

拉美地区的人工智能国家计划受到国际伦理和监管原则的强烈影响,如经合组织、世界经济论坛等制定的原则。然而,这些片面的计划似乎能在一定程度上满足拉丁美洲的现实需求。我们不能简单地引进或复制其他地区发展起来的成熟模式,而不深入思考它们在当地的影响。我们的情况具有特殊性,有些影响是本区域固有的,而另一些影响则已由高收入国家消除。举一些例子:一些尚未通电的社区既无法充分利用人工智能生态系统,也无法在人工智能模型中体现他们的价值观。拉美地区的一些国家并不重视教育,尽管这是人工智能最重要的组成部分,因此,我们看到教育投资逐年减少。此外,拉美地区还需制定相关策略,并建立一个丰富的生态系统,以防“人才外流”。

当然,我担忧的问题非常多,但它们都涉及到一些非常基本的问题:教育和信息。在巴西,人们普遍会为了获得购物折扣而提供自己的信息,或者为了获得福利而被迫提供信息。一些巴西人认同巴西政府目前的观点,即假新闻是言论自由的一种体现,而不是对人权的侵犯。这自然引发了如下问题:如果公民不了解,或者更糟的是没有得到足够的正规教育来了解自己的权利和义务,那么人工智能的治理机制如何保护人们免受人工智能直接或间接造成的滥用问题或人权侵犯?如果在进行相关讨论时不以人为中心,即当主要利益相关者(即政府或公司)抱有以利润为导向或扭曲的观点时,任何治理机制都不可信,也不可靠。

53

Latin America's Quest for Ethical AI Governance

Constanza GÓMEZ-MONT

In recent years, Latin America has deepened the ethical questions on the impact digital, especially AI, technologies have on the lives of people. What does giving up certain levels of privacy to respond to a health crisis mean in the short and long run? What does it mean that only families with access to digital tools can continue with their studies and work? How does the increased use of digital platforms impact the strengthening of already-existing data monopolies? What does a lack of digital literacy mean in a context in which most basic services migrated online?

For Latin America, a region with some of the world's greatest social inequality, these questions are not taken lightly. Various institutions in the region have joined the quest for answers on how to ensure a more just and rights-based approach to data and AI-driven technologies and in the effort to develop key initiatives on ethical AI governance.

For example, the Inter-American Development Bank rolled out the initiative fAIr LAC, which helps governments and entrepreneurs adopt responsible AI practices by developing guides and creating hubs in Mexico, Uruguay, Costa Rica and Columbia in collaboration with public and private partners. Moreover, the IEEE Global Partnership co-founded the Latam Circle with C Minds to prioritize human well-being with autonomous and intelligent systems in the region and foster the meaningful participation of Latin American experts in the development of global AI ethical standards. UNESCO started an online community to follow up on the regional consultation of the ethical AI global instrument. Other institutions, such as UNICRI and the Eon Resilience Lab, kickstarted an effort to include the voice of regional experts in the development of a global toolkit of rights-based AI for crime prevention and justice, and networks such as IA2030Mx in Mexico and AI Latam, with a regional umbrella, are strengthening the AI ecosystem. This list of actions includes various other regional efforts to advance ethical AI governance.

Moreover, some governments are getting involved. The government of Uruguay published a tool to evaluate the impact of AI systems; the government of Columbia published a draft of an AI ethical framework; the Federal Institute of Access to Public Information in Mexico helped kickstart the first policy prototype on the transparency and explicability of AI systems in the region. The government of Chile helped to develop an AI policy that includes a pillar of ethics.

Only a few existing initiatives can add to the past years' efforts in countries such as Brazil and

五十三

拉丁美洲寻求人工智能伦理治理

康斯坦萨·戈麦斯蒙特

近年来，拉丁美洲在数字技术（特别是人工智能技术）对于人们生活的影响方面加深了有关伦理问题的思考。从短期和长期来看，为了应对健康危机而放弃一定程度的隐私意味着什么？只有拥有数字工具的家庭才能继续学习和工作，这又意味着什么？数字平台使用率的上升如何进一步加剧已经存在的数据垄断现象？在大多数基本服务都迁往线上的情况下，缺乏数字素养意味着什么？

对于拉丁美洲这个社会不平等现象较为严重的地区而言，这些问题不能掉以轻心。为了寻求一种更加公正和基于权利的方法，确保数据和人工智能驱动的技术能加以采用，拉丁美洲地区的各个机构纷纷制定了关于合乎伦理的人工智能治理的关键倡议。

例如，美洲开发银行推出了 fAIr LAC 倡议，通过制定相关指南和与公共和私人伙伴合作，在墨西哥、乌拉圭、哥斯达黎加和哥伦比亚携手建立中心机构，帮助政府和企业家采用负责任的人工智能实践。此外，IEEE 全球伙伴关系与 C Minds 共同创建了 Latam Circle，旨在优先考虑运用自治和智能系统提升该地区人民福祉，并促进拉丁美洲专家为全球人工智能伦理标准的制定做出贡献；联合国教科文组织开设了一个在线社区，用于后续跟踪合乎伦理的人工智能全球工具的区域协商工作。联合国区域间犯罪和司法研究所和 Eon Resilience 实验室等其他机构也开始努力在开发基于权利的人工智能全球工具包，以用于预防犯罪和司法用途时考虑到区域专家的建议；包括墨西哥的 IA2030Mx 和具有区域保护伞的 AI Latam 在内的网络正在加强人工智能生态系统。该行动清单是其他地区推进合乎伦理的人工智能治理时进行的工作之一。

此外，一些政府也没有落于人后。乌拉圭政府公布了一个用于评估人工智能系统影响的工具；哥伦比亚政府公布了一份人工智能伦理框架草案；墨西哥联邦公共信息获取研究所协助启动了该地区关于人工智能系统透明度和可解释性的首个政策原型；智利政府着手制定人工智能政策，其中包括伦理支柱。

这些只是巴西和阿根廷等国家在经过几年的努力后推出的一部分现行举措。毫无疑问，拉丁

Argentina. Certainly, Latin America has a very long road ahead to consolidate and scale these initiatives and to deploy more coordinated actions. Most importantly, it must ensure that the access to and benefits of digital technologies and AI are distributed to all, especially as it continues to fight the pandemic and enters a phase of economic recovery. In these times of the great need to rethink ethical questions and accelerate inclusive answers, the AI design ethos for the region and how it is governed will have a profound impact on Latin America's prosperity. It will be of key importance that it lives up to expectations, contributes to the leading practices of the Global South and meaningfully participates in the development of global governance AI processes.

五十三

美洲在巩固和扩大这些举措的范围，部署更协调的行动方面还有很长的路要走。最重要的是，要让所有人都能享受到数字技术和人工智能带来的好处，特别是拉丁美洲还在抗击新冠肺炎疫情，且正处于经济复苏阶段。在这个迫切需要重新思考伦理问题和加快得到具有包容性的答案的时代，人工智能在拉丁美洲的道德意识设计和治理方式，将对该地区的繁荣发展产生深远的影响。对此，拉丁美洲应该不负众望，为发展中国家的领先实践，以及全球人工智能治理进程的发展做出贡献，这一点十分关键。

54

Toward a Regional AI Strategy in Latin America

Jean García PERICHE

The 2020 global crisis paralyzed the world and caused all of us to rethink the future of our species. The pandemic forced us to digitize and accelerated the adoption of artificial intelligence (AI). As AI increasingly disrupts our lives, it is crucial for the international community to coordinate comprehensive strategies that respond to the global challenges posed by cognitive technologies. In Latin America, the state of consciousness remains lacking in regard to AI governance, implementation, and deployment. As the rest of the world rapidly acknowledges the centrality of AI in governing the future of humanity, Latin America struggles to come to terms with a compelling narrative that can leverage the power of computer intelligence.

Although tech unicorns are increasing in the region, AI implementation projects are often small in scale and rarely transcend the pilot stage. Massive AI-driven disruptions in society will create deep structural changes in the economy. If Latin America does not move fast, it may risk falling into irrelevance. While AI advances at exponential rates, LATAM's power structures remain vertically driven and highly inefficient.

However, there is hope in the midst of chaos. With a population of more than 600 million, Latin America is an ideal place to develop machine-learning systems that can be deployed at scale and to harness the value of abundant data. In this way, Latin America can be key to defining the future of this technology and can become a new international agent that has real power in the global governance of artificial intelligence. Among the 100 countries best prepared to use AI, 15 are in Latin America.

As some states began developing and implementing national AI strategies and digital transformation frameworks, this past year has seen remarkable progress in some Latin American countries. In terms of digital governments, Columbia is the third most advanced country within the OECD. Similarly, Mexico, Uruguay, Chile, and Brazil are taking important steps in AI readiness and crucial governance issues such as data privacy. Nonetheless, the limited voice and participation in global AI governance forums from Latin America are astounding. If LATAM criteria are not included within emerging policy standards, the future establishment of AI governance could hinder progress in Latin America.

A fundamental element to note is that national initiatives are necessary but not sufficient. Without

五十四

走近拉丁美洲区域人工智能战略

让·加西亚·佩里希

2020 年的全球危机使世界陷入瘫痪，并让所有人开始重新思考人类的未来。这场疫情迫使我们加快了人工智能的数字化和采用。随着人工智能对各领域的颠覆性影响越来越普遍，国际社会必须协调采用综合战略，以应对认知技术带来的全球挑战。在拉丁美洲，人们对人工智能治理、实施和部署的认识仍相对缺乏。随着世界其他地区迅速认识到人工智能在治理人类未来方面的核心地位，拉丁美洲正在努力适应一种可使用计算机智能的令人信服的说法。

尽管拉丁美洲地区的科技独角兽公司越来越多，但人工智能实施项目往往规模较小，很少超越试点阶段。人工智能为社会带来的大范围颠覆性影响将给经济带来深刻的结构性变化。如果拉丁美洲不迅速采取行动，其地位就可能变得无关紧要。在人工智能呈现指数级发展的情况下，拉丁美洲的权力结构仍然是垂直驱动的，效率非常低。

然而，混乱之中仍然存有希望。拥有超过 6 亿人口的拉丁美洲，是可以大规模开发和部署机器学习系统并充分利用丰富的数据资源的理想之地。如此一来，拉丁美洲就能成为决定这项技术未来的关键，并成为在人工智能全球治理领域拥有实际话语权的新兴主体。人工智能应用就绪水平最高的 100 个国家中，有 15 个位于拉丁美洲。

随着一些国家开始制定和实施国家人工智能战略和数字转型框架，一些拉美国家在去年取得了显著的进展。就数字政府而言，哥伦比亚是经合组织成员国中第三发达的国家。同样，墨西哥、乌拉圭、智利和巴西也在人工智能就绪水平和关键治理问题（如数据隐私）方面采取了关键措施。尽管如此，拉丁美洲在全球人工智能治理论坛上的发言权和参与度仍十分有限，令人震惊。如果新兴政策标准中不包含拉丁美洲标准，那么未来建立的人工智能治理框架可能会阻碍拉丁美洲的进步。

需要注意的一个基本要素是，国家倡议是必要的，但并不足以完全解决问题。如果没有统一的标准和标准化的框架，没有一个拉美国家能够独自成为人工智能的领导者，拉丁美洲需要

unifying criteria and standardizing frameworks, no single country in Latin America can become an AI leader by itself. Latin America needs regional cohesion and a sound level of political unity. In this decade, the region needs to build a strong international coalition around a regional AI strategy to integrate this technology as an essential tool for entering a new stage of development.

By prioritizing AI, Latin America will be able to upgrade its socioeconomic and political systems to the 21st century. To do so, it needs unity and international cooperation. In the Age of AI, unity in Latin America is synonymous with survival.

区域凝聚力和良好的政治团结性。在这十年中，拉丁美洲地区需要围绕区域人工智能战略建立一个强大的国际联盟，将这项技术作为向新发展阶段跃进所必需的工具加以整合。

通过将人工智能作为优先事项，拉丁美洲将能实现社会经济和政治制度的升级，使其符合21世纪的情况。为此，拉丁美洲需要团结和国际合作。在人工智能时代，团结在拉丁美洲意味着生存。

55

AI Policy-Making as a Coconstruction and Learning Space

José Guridi BUSTOS

Worldwide, countries have developed (or are developing) AI policies and strategies. An imperative appears to have emerged to plan how to take advantage of this third AI summer; however, it is not clear why or how. The latter is evident if we analyze global strategies, finding many focuses e.g. research, development, and ethics), governance (e.g. public, private, and hybrid), processes (e.g. top-down, bottom-up, and policy-maker– or academia-centered), etc.

This concern is understandable when we realize that AI is a general purpose technology that is heavily shaping (and being shaped by) society. In the next five to ten years, AI will drastically change the way we perceive and process information, work, interact with each other, and engage in many other fundamental components of our lives. Thus, policy-makers feel the urge to foster socioeconomic development and to regulate AI to protect people from harm. However, even in the face of this anxiety, little understanding is available of how to do it right.

When AI strategies are developed, the epistemic hierarchy, in which scientists and policy-makers try to safeguard their credentials and authority by demarcating their expert knowledge versus "lay" knowledge, emerges. This has proven to be problematic for democracy and frames policy construction within a deficit model of innovation in which the lack of R&D is the main obstacle. This framing can fail to recognize AI as a sociotechnical construct in which the main question should be how we will be as human beings along with it. Additionally, this framework might lead to policy instruments disconnected from a thorough policy discussion about the means and ends of AI policy.

In Chile, social riots in 2019 and the COVID-19 pandemic opened a window of opportunity to design a participatory methodology for building the AI National Policy, since they lowered resistance to public participation, especially among policy-makers and authorities. We developed an open call for self-convened roundtable discussions in which anyone anywhere could participate and contribute, the only prerequisite being the use of the proposed axis as a guide (i.e., first, enabling factors; second, development and adoption; and third, ethics, regulatory aspects and socioeconomic impacts). This process was both a coconstruction exercise toward a first draft and a learning space in which academia, industry, government and society interacted,

五十五

作为合作共建实践和学习空间的人工智能政策制定

何塞·古里迪·比斯托

全球所有国家都已经制定（或正在制定）AI 政策和战略，好似对如何充分利用第三个 AI 爆发期进行规划是某种当务之急，但是又对为何以及如何进行规划不甚了解。只要对全球的 AI 战略加以分析，就能明显察觉到后一个问题，因为你能看到许多重点（例如研究、开发和伦理）、治理措施（例如公共措施、私人措施和混合型措施）、流程（例如自上而下、自下而上、以政策制定者为中心和以学术为中心的流程）等。

考虑到 AI 是一种正对社会造成极大影响（并受到社会极大影响）且具有普遍用途的技术，所有的考量都是可以理解的。在未来的 5~10 年内，AI 将彻底改变我们的信息感知和处理方式、工作方式以及人际互动方式，并为我们生活中的许多其他基本要素带来极大的变化。因此，政策制定者迫切需要促进社会经济发展，并对 AI 实施监管，以防 AI 对人们造成伤害。但是，即便这种焦虑感确实存在，政策制定者对如何正确处理这一问题也并没有多少头绪。

制定 AI 战略时出现了名为“认知层次”的概念，科学家和政策制定者试图在这一概念的框架内通过区分自身掌握的专业知识和“非专业”知识来维护自己的资格和权威，而后者已被证明会对民主制度造成负面影响，并导致政策制定工作被限制在一种主要障碍为研发不足的创新赤字模型中。该框架可能没有意识到 AI 是一种以“作为人类，我们应当如何与 AI 共存”为主要问题的社会技术结构。此外，这种框架还可能导致政策工具与围绕 AI 政策的手段和目标进行的全方位政策讨论发生脱节。

智利以 2019 年发生在圣地亚哥的反政府抗议活动和此次的新冠肺炎疫情为契机设计参与性方法，为建立 AI 国家政策打开了一扇机会之窗，因为这两个事件减轻了公众参与的阻力，特别是政策制定者和有关当局在这方面的阻力。我们公开呼吁进行自发召集的圆桌讨论会，任何地方的人都可以参加并做出贡献，唯一的要求是：拟定、开发与采用有利因素，以伦理、监管方面和社会经济影响为轴作为指导。这一流程既是共同制定政策草案初稿的一次实践，又是一个学术界、产业界、政府和社会彼此互动、自专业知识中吸取经验，并相互学习的学习空间。

taught from their expertise, and learned from each other. More than 7,000 people participated in discussions and webinars and had the opportunity to contrast their discussions with a draft in a recently closed public consultation.

In thinking about AI governance for the subsequent decades, experiences such as the Chilean process should be analyzed and improved to design institutions that acknowledge the sociotechnical nature of technology. Countries, in particular emergent ones, should design open processes and build their own development models from their strengths and weaknesses, refraining from merely importing international experiences.

五十五

超过 7,000 人参加了相关讨论和网络研讨会，并得到了在最近刚刚闭幕的公众咨询会中将讨论内容与草案进行对比的机会。

思考未来几十年的 AI 治理时，应分析与智利的经历类似的经验并加以改进，以设计出承认技术的社会技术性质的制度。各个国家，尤其是新兴国家，应根据自身优势和不足，制定开放的流程，建立自己的发展模式，而不是一味复制国际上的经验。

56

The OECD AI Recommendation: A Global Reference Point for AI Governance

Jessica Cussins NEWMAN

At the end of 2018, Deep Mind co-founder Mustafa Suleyman predicted that 2019 would be the year we would build global arenas to support international and multistakeholder coordination that would facilitate the safe and ethical development of artificial intelligence (AI). Suleyman wrote that the arenas would need to be global because AI opportunities and challenges don't stop at national borders and don't respect organizational boundaries.

In many ways, Suleyman's predictions were realized; 2019 saw the emergence of several meaningful new global forums including the UN Secretary General's High-Level Panel on Digital Cooperation, the Global Partnership for AI, and the Organization for Economic Cooperation and Development (OECD) Principles and Policy Observatory.

The OECD AI Principles and Policy Observatory in particular represent significant progress in the global governance of AI. Released May 22, 2019, the principles and recommendations became the first intergovernmental standard for AI and a new "global reference point" for AI governance into the future.

All 36 OECD member countries signed onto the OECD AI Principles, as well as several non-member countries including Argentina, Brazil, Colombia, Costa Rica, Peru, and Romania. The European Commission additionally backed the Principles, and Ukraine was added to the list of signatories in October 2019. When the Group of Twenty (G20), released AI Principles one month later, it was noted that they were drawn from the OECD AI Principles. Notably, support from the G20 expanded the list of involved countries to include China.

The principles include detailed calls for inclusive growth, sustainable development and well-being; human-centered values and fairness; transparency and explainability; robustness, security and safety; and accountability. Moreover, the recommendations for national policies and international cooperation include investing in AI research and development; fostering a digital ecosystem for AI; shaping an enabling policy environment for AI; building human capacity and preparing for labor market transformation; and facilitating international cooperation for trustworthy AI. The OECD AI Principles represent widespread awareness of the need for global coordination and cooperation to facilitate trustworthy AI.

五十六

《经合组织人工智能原则》：人工智能治理的全球参考

杰西卡·库辛·纽曼

2018 年年底，DeepMind 的联合创始人穆斯塔法·苏莱曼（Mustafa Suleyman）预测，2019 年将是我们建立全球竞技场，支持国际和多利益相关方协调，促进人工智能安全和伦理发展的一年。苏莱曼写道，竞技场需要全球化，因为人工智能的机遇和挑战不会受国界的限制，组织边界对其也不适用。

苏莱曼的前瞻观点在很多方面都得以证实。2019 年，一些意义深远的新全球论坛相继出现，包括联合国秘书长数字合作高级别小组、人工智能全球伙伴关系、经济合作与发展组织（OECD）原则和政策观察站等。

经合组织的人工智能原则和政策观察站代表了全球人工智能治理的重大进展。该观察站于 2019 年 5 月 22 日发布的《经合组织人工智能原则》（以下简称《原则》），这是首个针对人工智能治理的政府间标准，并成为了未来人工智能治理的一个新的"全球参考点"。

所有 36 个经合组织成员国以及包括阿根廷、巴西、哥伦比亚、哥斯达黎加、秘鲁和罗马尼亚在内的几个非成员国都签署了《原则》。此外，欧盟委员会也对该原则表示支持，乌克兰则于 2019 年 10 月成为了其签署国之一。一个月后，当 20 国集团发布《人工智能原则》时，人们注意到这些原则是从《原则》中提取的。20 国集团的支持显著扩大了参与国的范围。

这些原则包括：对实现包容性增长、可持续发展和福祉的呼吁；以人为本的价值观与公平；透明性和可解释性；稳定性、保障性和安全性；以及可问责性。此外，针对国家政策和国际合作的建议包括：加大对人工智能研发的投资；培育人工智能数字生态系统；创造有利的政策环境；加强人才能力建设，为劳动力市场转型做准备；促进可信赖人工智能的国际合作。《原则》体现了人类的广泛共识，即促进可信赖人工智能的发展需要全球范围内的协调与合作。

56

The OECD is additionally building on this momentum and aims to help countries implement the principles and recommendations. The OECD launched the AI Policy Observatory at the end of 2019 to facilitate dialogue among global multi-stakeholder partners and provide evidence-based policy analysis on AI. The Observatory will publish practical guidance to implement the AI Principles and a live database of AI policies and initiatives globally. It will also compile metrics and measurement of AI development, and use its convening power to bring together the private sector, governments, academia, and civil society.

The OECD AI Recommendation achieved a feat few would have thought possible just one year previously. The United States signed on at a time of relative aversion to international coordination in other policy arenas. China and Russia were part of a consensus agreement to support the effort more broadly. Other countries are welcome to add their support. While details regarding implementation are still being finalized, 2020 will likely see more substantive AI governance commitments and engagement from a broader range of actors.

五十六

经合组织在这一趋势的基础上继续推进，致力于帮助各国落实这些原则和建议。经合组织于 2019 年年底启动了人工智能政策观察站计划，以促进全球多方利益相关者之间的对话，并提供有关人工智能的循证政策分析。观察站将向全球实时发布实施人工智能原则的实务指引，以及人工智能政策和举措的实时数据库。此外，它还将编制人工智能发展的指标和度量方法，并利用其号召力建立起私营部门、政府、学术界和民间团体之间的沟通桥梁。

《原则》完成了一项在一年前大多数人都认为难以实现的壮举。美国在签署《原则》时，对其他政策领域的国际协调相对反感。中国和俄罗斯已经达成共识，将在更大范围内支持《原则》的实施，也欢迎其他国家提供支持。虽然相关实施细节仍在敲定中，但在 2020 年，我们可能会看到更多实质性的人工智能治理承诺和更多行动者的参与。

57

AI Governance: Responsible Use of AI by Law Enforcement

Irakli BERIDZE

With the worst pandemic seen in more than a century, 2020 has undoubtedly been a life-changing year involving political, social, and cultural upheavals across the world. At the same time, years of technological advancements seemed to happen in mere months, and the first COVID-19 vaccines appeared in record time. In fact, artificial intelligence (AI) was one of the technologies responsible for that achievement, contributing to speeding the development of a messenger ribonucleic acid (mRNA)-based vaccine.

AI adoption was accelerated during the COVID-19 outbreak, not only in medical research but also to restrict population movement, causing some controversies. From contact-tracing apps to facial recognition cameras that monitored travelers' temperature, the use of AI for tracking and surveillance raised concerns about fundamental freedoms, such as the right to privacy. While technology applications can play an important role in containing the spread of the virus, the use of AI must remain proportionate, necessary and legitimate. To avoid potential pitfalls that could undermine fundamental rights or infringe on public trust in national institutions, governments should strive to advance AI governance and guarantee that this technology is developed for the good of society.

Attending to the specificities of each sector and the different technical solutions AI can provide, global AI governance cannot curb the possible harmful effects in all disciplines. Although the general principles of ethics, fairness, accountability and transparency must be cross-cutting, sectoral initiatives might be more useful and effective.

The Centre for AI and Robotics of the United Nations Interregional Crime and Justice Research Institute (UNICRI) seeks to support law enforcement agencies and other key stakeholders in the criminal justice system to understand the risks and benefits of AI and to explore its use in contributing to a future free of violence and crime.

The use of AI in law enforcement is often a highly sensitive and controversial subject, and no guidance specifically addresses this matter. Thus, the value of advancing AI governance for law enforcement becomes increasingly prominent. In this sense, the UNICRI Centre for AI and Robotics, together with INTERPOL's Innovation Centre, are developing an operationally oriented Toolkit for the Responsible Use of AI by Law Enforcement that can support and guide

五十七

人工智能治理：执法机构如何负责任地使用人工智能

伊拉克利·贝里泽

2020 年对许多人来说无疑是改变生活的一年。在该年，全球暴发了一个多世纪以来最严重的疫情，导致了世界范围的政治、社会和文化层面的剧变。同时，过去需要数年才能取得的技术进展似乎也在短短几个月的时间里相继出现，且第一批新冠肺炎疫苗以前所未有的速度被研发出来，创造了疫苗研发纪录。事实上，人工智能技术加快了信使核糖核酸（mRNA）疫苗的研发速度，是上述成就的驱动因素之一。

AI 应用的进度在新冠肺炎疫情期间着实有所加快，不但被用于医疗研究，而且还被用来限制人口流动，尽管这引发了一些争议。从接触者追踪应用到能监测旅客体温的人脸识别摄像头，AI 在追踪和监察方面的应用引发了人们对隐私权等基本自由和权利的担忧。虽然技术可在遏制病毒传播方面起到重要作用，但是 AI 的使用必须遵循适度、必要和合法的原则。为了避免可能侵犯到基本权利，以及损害民众对国家机构的信任的潜在隐患，各国政府应当努力推进 AI 治理，并确保 AI 技术朝着对社会有利的方向发展。

即使关注到各个行业的特点以及 AI 可提供的不同技术解决方案，全球性 AI 治理也无法遏制各学科领域受到的潜在负面影响。在道德性、公平性、可问责性和透明性层面，虽然存在适用于不同行业的通则，但面向不同行业的针对性举措可能更加实用和有效。

联合国区域间犯罪和司法研究所（UNICRI）人工智能与机器人中心致力于支持执法机构和刑事司法体系中的其他关键利益相关者了解 AI 的风险和效益，并探索如何通过 AI 助力实现没有暴力和犯罪的未来这一目标。人们公认执法机构对 AI 的使用通常是一个具有高度敏感性且富有争议的话题，而目前又没有具体的指导意见。在此背景下，推进 AI 治理为执法机构提供支持的重要性日益突显。从这个意义上来说，联合国区域间犯罪和司法研究所人工智能与机器人中心和国际刑警组织环球创新中心已开始着手合作开发注重操作性的工具包，以帮助执法机构负责任地使用 AI，并支持和引导负责任的 AI 设计、开发和部署。INTERPOL-UNICRI 全球 AI 执法会议汇聚全球专家展开了多次探讨，这些专家来自执法机构、学术界和产业界。

the responsible design, development and deployment of AI. This ambitious goal was initiated and fueled by several discussions at the INTERPOL–UNICRI Global Meetings on AI for Law Enforcement that brought together worldwide experts from law enforcement, academia and industry. This first-ever proposed global approach can be an important contribution to the law enforcement community, the technology providers behind AI technology, policy-makers and regulators, and civil society in this growing and important AI governance field.

With a long road and much work ahead, we are nevertheless moving in the direction of the responsible use of AI by law enforcement, which could revolutionize police work and practices and lead to a safer and better world.

五十七

随着人工智能治理领域的不断发展，这一首次提出的全球对策对于执法界、AI 技术供应商、政策制定者和监管者以及民间社会具有重要意义。

尽管前路漫长而艰苦，但我们仍在向着实现针对执法机构的负责任的 AI 迈进，这可能会彻底改变警方的工作和实践，创造更安全、更美好的世界。

58

Some Engineering Views of AI Development and Governance

GONG Ke

Artificial intelligence (AI) is now moving from scientific papers and technical labs into engineering applications and people's daily lives. This is a turning point in the historical development of AI. Engineering and engineers have become crucial players in AI applications and further development as well as in its governance to ensure AI for the good of all people and the planet.

1. AI is a new tool for human development, and the ultimate goal of its development and governance is to ensure that it is good for sustainable development.

Toolmaking is an important feature of humans and differentiates them from other animals. From simple stone tools and ironware to levers, pulleys, all kinds of machinery and electrical power and to computer and modern information networks, humans have used tools to extend their physical and intellectual strength and to increase their capacity to survive and their wellbeing. Hence, human history is often characterized by the progress of human-made tools, such as the Stone, Iron, Machine and Information Ages. In this regard, AI is a new tool for human development and is ushering humankind into the Intelligent Age.

The purpose of human inventions and the use of tools are to solve problems in survival and development. At present, the foremost problem facing humankind is the issue of sustainable development. Therefore, AI should become a powerful tool for human sustainable development. This is also the ultimate goal of AI development and governance. In 2020, a notable development is that the role of AI in achieving the sustainable development goals (SDGs) has been analyzed by researchers and has received attention from many international organizations. To guide AI development and support its governance, more comprehensive and insightful studies are urgently required to explore the relationship between AI and the SDGs.

2. Engineering society should shoulder the responsibility for and be an important part of the joint AI development and governance by multiple stakeholders.

The World Federation of Engineering Organizations (WFEO) realizes its responsibility for promoting AI for the good of people and the environment. An interdisciplinary working group with experts from industry and academia was established by its standing technical committee, Engineering for Innovative Technologies. On March 4th, 2020, at the first World Engineering Day for Sustainable Development, WFEO released its position paper on "Promoting the Responsible

五十八

从工程视角看人工智能的发展与治理

龚克

如今，人工智能已经从基于科学论文和技术实验室的研究，发展到工程应用阶段，进入了人们的日常生活。这无疑是 AI 历史发展的转折点。应用和工程师已经成为了影响 AI 应用进一步发展，以及 AI 治理的关键因素，对于确保 AI 能够造福地球和全人类而言至关重要。

1. AI是一种助力人类发展的新工具，AI发展和治理的最终目标是确保AI有利于可持续发展。

人类区别于其他动物的重要特征是能够制造工具。从简单的石器和铁器，到杠杆、滑轮、各类机械和电力，再到计算机和现代信息网络，人类已经利用这些工具提高了自身的劳动能力、智能水平、生存能力以及幸福指数。因此，人类历史通常是人造工具的进步史，人造工具则是时代的标志，例如石器时代、铁器时代、机器时代、信息时代等。从这个方面来看，AI 也不过是一个推动人类发展的新工具，正将人类带往智能时代。

必须要指出的是，人类发明和使用工具的目的在于解决生存和发展问题。目前，可持续发展是人类面临的最大问题。因此，AI 应该成为一种能推动人类可持续发展的有力工具。这同时也是 AI 发展和治理的最终目标。2020 年，AI 领域的主要进展在于，研究人员分析了 AI 在实现可持续发展目标方面的作用，而这种作用也已经引起了许多国际组织的关注。为了引导和支持 AI 发展与治理，我们亟须通过更加全面和富有见地的研究来探索 AI 和可持续发展目标之间的关系。

2. 工程界应担起责任，成为多利益相关者共同发展和治理 AI 的重要参与者。

世界工程组织联合会（WFEO）意识到了其有责任推动 AI 造福人类和环境，并通过其下属的创新技术委员会常务技术委员会成立了一个由产业界和学术界专家组成的跨学科工作小组。2020 年 3 月 4 日，WFEO 在首个促进持续发展世界工程日上发布了一份题为《促进大数据和 AI 创新与应用在工程中的责任管理方式》（*Promoting Responsible Conduct of Big Data and AI*

Conduct of Big Data and AI Innovation and Application in Engineering", in which 7 principles were proposed:

- Good for Humanity and the Environment
- Inclusiveness, Fairness, Public Awareness and Empowerment
- Openness and Sharing while Respecting Privacy and Data Integrity
- Transparency
- Accountability
- Peace, Safety and Security
- Collaboration

Many governments, NGOs, corporations, etc., have declared principles for AI applications. Although these principles are largely common, they are still far from sufficient to reach a global consensus. Generally, engineering has not yet played an important role in AI governance, and there is a shortage of crosstalk between different sectors and different societal groups. Global dialogs with multiple stakeholders are urgently needed.

3. The green development of AI should become a focus of AI development and its governance.

AI has incredible potential to improve the productivity, quality, safety and efficiency of various engineering projects so AI empowers and transforms every aspect of engineering.

It is exciting to see many AI applications for increasing energy efficiency in various productions and households, and the power efficiency of AI products is far behind that of human workers. However, green and lower carbon AI development have not yet been emphasized in AI R&D and applications. Therefore, there must be a call for a full understanding of the rigid constraints of AI development, and more attention must be paid to green AI development and application, which should also become one of the focuses of AI governance.

Additionally, much research and development work has been carried out for AI safety and security. In comparison with the antivirus software and services market approximately 20 years ago, when PC usage became widespread, products and services remain lacking for AI safety and security.

Innovation and Application in Engineering）的立场声明。该声明中提出了七项原则，分别是：

- 造福人类和人类的生存环境
- 确保包容性、公平性、公众意识和自主权
- 在尊重隐私和数据完整性的基础上实现开放共享
- 透明性
- 可问责性
- 和平、安全和保障性
- 合作

许多政府、非政府组织和公司等都已声明了AI应用原则。虽然这些原则在很大程度上是相同的，但我们仍需要通过大量努力达成全球共识。总体而言，工程尚未在AI治理中发挥重要作用，而不同行业和社会团体之间的交流也有所欠缺。为此，我们亟须开展涵盖多个利益 相关者的全球对话。

3. AI的绿色发展应成为AI发展和治理的重点。

AI在提高各类工程项目的生产力、质量、安全性和效率方面潜力惊人，因此可以说AI正在从各个方面增强和改变工程应用。

我们惊喜地看到，许多AI应用能够有效提高各类产品和家用电器的能源效率。然而，AI产品的功率效率要远低于人类员工也是众所周知的事实。但是，绿色和低碳发展尚未在AI研发和应用中得到重视。因此，必须呼吁业界充分了解AI开发的严格限制，并更加重视AI的绿色发展和应用，而这也应该成为AI治理的重点之一。

此外，还需要注意的是，虽然许多针对AI安全和保障性的研发工作已经展开，但是与大约20年前家用电脑在开始被大规模应用时所出现的与之配套的杀毒软件和服务市场相比，用于保障AI安全的产品和服务仍然缺乏。

59

Trustworthy AI and Corporate Governance

Don WRIGHT

"Organizations must create ethical systems and practices for the use of AI if they are to gain people's trust. This is not just a compliance issue, but one that can create a significant benefit in terms of loyalty, endorsement, and engagement."

– *Capgemini*

The proliferation of A/IS (autonomous and intelligent systems) presents a profoundly human moment. Collectively, we are standing in the nexus of history.

While it's always been essential to know your customer and their needs, the specific nuances of AI, where interacting with people demands a higher level of awareness around things like bias, identity, emotion, and cultural relevance, make obtaining and using this knowledge of the customer even more difficult. It also means recognizing that, outside of anyone's positive intentions for what they create, an end-user's experience is not fully up to the designer–it is up to each end-user. This is why IEEE created *Ethically Aligned Design*, 1st Edition and why it focused on end-users and how they and their values can be a part of AI design.

According to McKinsey Global Institute, "AI has the potential to deliver...global economic activity of around $13 trillion by the year 2030." While the monetary benefits of AI have increased in recent years, so have the concerns around its ethical implementation for people and society as a whole. Beyond the need to combat negative unintended consequences in the design of AI, the analysis, utilization, and honoring of end-user values in design is providing a growing trend of driving innovation in corporate governance.

As a way to highlight this trend, IEEE recently created the Ethically Aligned Design for Business Committee as part of its Global Initiative on Ethics of Autonomous and Intelligent Systems. Comprised of participants from Google, IBM, Intel, Salesforce, Microsoft, and others, the committee launched its first paper in Q1 of 2020 called A Call to Action for Businesses Using AI featuring:

- The Value and Necessity of AI Ethics;
- Creating a Sustainable Culture of AI Ethics; and,
- AI Ethics Skills and Hiring

五十九

可信赖人工智能和公司治理

唐·赖特

> 如果企业想要赢得人们的信任，就必须创建使用人工智能的伦理体系和实践。这不仅是一个合规性问题，而且能在忠诚度、认可度和参与度方面创造重大效益。
>
> ——凯捷管理顾问公司

A/IS（自主和智能系统）的普及对人类发展而言是一个具有深远意义的时刻，此时，我们都站在历史的交点。

对于软件系统和应用程序开发来说，了解客户及其需求一直是非常重要的。但人工智能的特别之处在于，与人进行互动时需要对偏见、身份、情感和文化相关性等问题有更高层次的认识，这使得获取和使用有关客户需求的信息更加困难。这也意味着我们要认识到，即使开发者创造产品是出于好意，终端用户的体验也并不完全取决于设计者，而是取决于每个终端用户。这就是 IEEE 发布《符合伦理的设计》（第一版），并关注终端用户及其价值观对人工智能设计的影响的原因所在。

据麦肯锡全球研究所透露，“到 2030 年，人工智能有望为全球带来价值约 13 万亿美元的经济活动。”近年来，人工智能所带来的经济效益不断增加，但其对人类和整个社会伦理方面的影响也引起了人们的担忧。除了需要应对人工智能设计中不经意所产生的负面影响外，设计中对终端用户价值观的分析、利用和尊重也是推动公司治理创新的重要因素。

电气和电子工程师协会（IEEE）最近发布了《针对商业委员会的合乎伦理设计指南》，作为其自主和智能系统伦理全球倡议的一部分，并在其中突出了上述趋势。该委员会由来自谷歌、IBM、英特尔、Salesforce、微软等公司的参与者组成，将在 2020 年第一季度发布第一份倡议文件，题为《呼吁企业使用人工智能》（A Call to Action for Businesses Using AI），具体包含以下内容：

- 人工智能伦理的价值和必要性；
- 创建可持续的人工智能伦理文化；
- 人工智能伦理技能和招聘。

59

While created with corporations in mind, much of its contents will also provide useful guidance for certain governments and NGOs. The paper also features an "AI Ethics Readiness Framework" allowing readers to assess where their organization, public or private, lies on a four-tiered scale highlighting issues such as training, leadership buy-in, organizational impact, and key performance indicators (KPIs) beyond financial metrics alone.

Corporate governance for AI cannot rely on simply adhering to basic compliance criteria regarding mandated legislation like the GDPR. Organizations need to proactively create and prioritize transparent and accountable practices that honor end-user values to establish genuine trust with their employees, customers, and all stakeholders throughout their value chain.

> *"We want to design healthy relationships with our users. The potential of AI is wrapped up in its longevity as a solution-meaning everything we design must address current and future needs for users. To truly understand those needs, we need an inclusive and ethical approach to the entire process. Globally, we are starting to see the repercussions that come when companies do not prioritize AI ethics in their solutions. We want to make sure that ethical practices are ingrained on our teams so they can then be embedded into the products themselves."*
>
> *– EAD for Business Committee Member Milena Pribec of IBM*

五十九

虽然该文件是针对企业撰写的，但其中的许多内容也能为某些政府和非政府组织提供有效指导。此外，文件还以“人工智能伦理成熟度框架”为特色，让读者能评估他们所在的公共或私营组织，确定其在四大层次中的哪个位置上。框架强调的问题包括培训、领导力认可度、组织影响和财务指标以外的关键绩效指标（KPI）等。

人工智能的公司治理不能仅仅依靠遵守相关法规（如《通用数据保护条例》(GDPR) 等）的基本合规标准实现。企业需要积极创建并优先考虑尊重终端用户价值观、透明和可问责的实践，从而与员工、客户和整个价值链中的所有利益相关者建立真正的信任关系。

> 我们希望与用户建立健康的关系。人工智能的潜力在于它作为解决方案的寿命，这意味着我们设计的一切都必须满足用户当前和未来的需求。为了真正理解这些需要，我们需要对整个进程采取包容和合乎伦理的做法。在全球范围内，我们开始看到当公司在解决方案中不优先考虑人工智能伦理时所产生的影响。我们希望确保伦理规范扎根于我们的团队中，以便可以将其嵌入到产品本身中。
>
> ——IBM 商业委员会成员米莱娜·普里贝克(Milena Pribec)(来自 EAD 工卡)

60

From Principles to Actions: Governing and Using AI for Humanity

Cyrus HODES

In 2020, global AI governance, or at least discussions in various fora on AI ethics, gathered momentum, and people are now (or should be) focusing on translating these principles into action.

As usual, one of the most active and globally influential platforms is the OECD, since the adoption of their principles by the G20 last year in Japan and reaffirmed this year at the Saudi Arabia S20. The launch of the AI observatory (OECD.AI) successfully brought together truly cross-disciplinary views; conducted deep dives into AI policy; explored countries' AI initiatives; and, very importantly, better assessed the impact of AI systems through a framework that understands contexts, data and input, AI models, and tasks and output.

In Europe, the EU Parliament's Panel for the Future of Science and Technology (STOA) has launched a partnership with the OECD Global Parliamentary Network, focused on the promotion of trustworthy and human-centered AI as well as shared reflections on future AI development. This initiative brings together members of parliament from 42 countries and represents an important step toward multilateral coordination on AI governance.

An important milestone in AI governance in 2020 was the launch of the UN Secretary–General's Roadmap for Digital Collaboration in May, based on the recommendations of the High-Level Panel on Digital Cooperation. In addition to Recommendation 3C on artificial intelligence, Recommendation 1B on digital public goods has validated and highlighted the work of the Global Data Access Framework (GDAF). In particular, it calls for the utilization of big data and artificial intelligence to create "digital public goods in the form of actionable real-time and predictive insights, critical for all stakeholders, including the United Nations, as they can serve to identify new disease outbreaks, counter xenophobia and disinformation and measure impacts on vulnerable populations, among other relevant challenges". However, the Secretary–General goes on to point out "efforts such as the Global Data Access Framework, which is aimed at developing technical infrastructure to enable and scale up the sharing of data in all modalities to speed up the processes for creating quality digital public goods".

The GDAF exercise is co-led by the UN Global Pulse initiative, the AI Initiative of The Future Society (TFS) and the Noble Intelligence Initiative of the McKinsey Global Institute and has over

六十

从原则到行动：造福人类的人工智能治理和应用

塞勒斯·霍德斯

2020 年，人工智能的全球治理，或者至少是各论坛上关于人工智能伦理的讨论，已成为大势所趋。如今，人们正在（或应在）致力于将这些原则付诸实践。

与往常一样，经合组织仍是最活跃、最具全球影响力的平台之一。自去年在日本举行的 G20 峰会采纳其原则以来，今年的沙特阿拉伯 S20 峰会又重申了这些原则。新推出的人工智能天文台（OECD.AI）不仅成功地汇集了真正跨学科的观点，深入研究了人工智能政策，探索了各国的人工智能倡议，甚至还通过一个契合背景、数据和输入、人工智能模型以及任务和输出的框架，更深入透彻地对人工智能系统的影响进行了评估。

在欧洲,欧洲议会未来与科学和技术小组(STOA)与经合组织全球议会网络建立了合作关系，重点推广值得信赖和以人为中心的人工智能，共同思考人工智能的未来发展。该倡议汇集了来自 42 个国家的议会成员，是人类在人工智能治理的多边合作方面迈出的重要一步。

2020 年 5 月，联合国秘书长根据数字合作高级别小组的建议发布了数字合作路线图，这是 2020 年人工智能治理的一个重要里程碑。除了关于人工智能的建议 3C 外，关于数字公共产品的建议 1B 也证实并强调了全球数据获取框架（GDAF）的工作。特别是，它呼吁利用大数据和人工智能，“以具有可操作性的实时和预测性见解的形式创造数字公共产品，这对包括联合国在内的所有利益相关者都至关重要,因为它们有助于确定新疾病的暴发、反制仇外心理和谣言、衡量对弱势群体的影响，以及应对其他相关挑战”。秘书长接着指出：“全球数据获取框架等措施旨在发展技术基础设施，以促进通过各种方式进行的数据共享并扩大其规模，从而加快创造优质数字公共产品的进程。”

GDAF 实践由联合国 Global Pulse 倡议、未来社会人工智能计划（TFS）和麦肯锡 Noble Purpose AI 共同领导，涉及超过 120 个利益相关者，包括主要技术公司、学术机构、非政府组织和联合国机构。我们的目标是在 2021 年第一季度发布一份蓝图，然后发布一个关于如何

120 stakeholders, including major technology firms, academic institutions, nongovernmental organizations and UN agencies. We aim to publish a blueprint in the first quarter of 2021, followed by a minimum viable product (MVP) of how various types of data could be shared or accessed to run AI systems to help us attain the sustainable development goals.

In 2020, the World Bank played an important role in helping emerging countries adopt and implement national AI strategies (and the AI Initiative was honored to take part in this exercise, the same way we are working on the Rwanda National AI Strategy and with GIZ and the World Economic Forum).

Another relevant platform advancing international AI governance is the Global Partnership on AI (GPAI), launched by France and Canada. The year 2020 saw this partnership consolidate its global role to discuss responsible AI, data governance, innovation, commercialization, and the future of work. A very timely subgroup was created under the topic of responsible AI to focus on AI-based solutions for the pandemic response. GPAI's 15 founding members are Australia, Canada, France, Germany, India, Italy, Japan, Mexico, New Zealand, the Republic of Korea, Singapore, Slovenia, the United Kingdom, the United States and the European Union. They were joined by Brazil, the Netherlands, Poland and Spain in December 2020. There is a strong drive to open GPAI to the Global South, and finding a mechanism to have China join as one of the world's leading AI powers only makes sense.

The Future Society has worked closely with GPAI and their members to publish two seminal reports on both the responsible AI group and the pandemic response; these can be accessed here: https://gpai.ai/projects/responsible-ai/ https://gpai.ai/projects/ai-and-pandemic-response/.

Part of the work on the pandemic, putting the OECD AI Principles into action, is the CAIAC (pronounced "kayak") project that I have the pleasure to colead, together with Stanford Human-Centered AI (HAI); Stability.ai; and various UN partners, starting with UNESCO and supported by the Patrick J. McGovern Foundation. CAIAC is a platform designed to increase our common knowledge about the COVID-19 virus and to offer unique decision-making support. It dynamically maps knowledge about the virus and its impact by connecting localized initiatives and interventions. Such a platform is important for policy-making, giving our leaders direct access to relevant knowledge based on human intelligence and augmented by AI. It also offers available datasets to tackle health aspects of the crisis as well as the social, economic and financial responses needed to emerge from this crisis in a globally coordinated fashion. We know other pandemics will emerge, and we face a dormant crisis highlighted by the UN Sustainable Development Goals, starting with climate change as a strong case that calls for globally coordinated actions, augmented by AI systems following up the CAIAC knowledge-gathering and knowledge-sharing model.

If anything, 2020 has highlighted the dire need for global coordination in times of crisis. One can only regret that partisan politics, instead of common sense, have limited global coordination

共享或获取各类数据的最简化可实行产品（MVP），以便运行人工智能系统，帮助我们实现可持续发展目标。

2020 年，世界银行在帮助新兴国家采纳和实施国家人工智能战略方面发挥了重要作用。人工智能倡议很荣幸能参加这项活动，我们也以同样的方式与德国国际合作机构（GIZ）和世界经济论坛合作制定卢旺达国家人工智能战略。

推动国际人工智能治理的另一个相关平台是法国和加拿大发起的全球人工智能伙伴关系（GPAI）。2020 年，该合作伙伴关系进一步发挥了其全球职能，促进了关于负责任的人工智能、数据治理、创新和商业化以及未来工作的更深入讨论。在此情形下，负责任的人工智能领域迅速成立了一个小组，重点关注基于人工智能的疫情应对方案。GPAI 的 15 个创始成员为澳大利亚、加拿大、法国、德国、印度、意大利、日本、墨西哥、新西兰、韩国、新加坡、斯洛文尼亚、英国、美国和欧盟。2020 年 12 月，巴西、荷兰、波兰和西班牙也加入其中。目前有一股强大的动力推动 GPAI 向发展中国家开放。我认为，寻找一种机制让作为世界领先的人工智能大国之一的中国加入其中具有显著意义。

未来社会组织与 GPAI 及其成员国密切合作，发表了两份关于负责任的人工智能小组和疫情应对措施的开创性报告，两者都可点击 https://gpai.ai/projects/responsible-ai/; https://gpai.ai/projects/ai-and-pandemic-response/ 查阅。

CAIAC（发音为“kayak”）项目是有关本次疫情的一项工作，很好地推动了经合组织人工智能原则的实施，我很荣幸能与斯坦福大学以人为中心的人工智能计划（HAI）、Stability.ai，以及各联合国合作伙伴共同领导这一由联合国教科文组织发起，并得到帕特里克·麦戈文基金会的支持的项目。CAIAC 是一个旨在增加我们对新冠病毒的认识，并提供独特决策支持的平台。它通过连接本地化的举措和干预措施，以一种动态的方式绘制有关病毒及其影响的知识图谱。这样一个平台对政策的制定非常重要，它使我们的领导人能够直接获得以人类智能为基础、经人工智能增强的相关知识和现有数据集，以应对本次危机中相关的健康问题，并制定以全球合作的方式摆脱这场危机所需的社会、经济和金融应对措施。我们知道以后还会出现其他疫情，同时也面临着联合国可持续发展目标所强调的潜在危机，首先是气候变化，这是一个明确而恰当的例子，它呼吁全球共同采取行动，并由遵循 CAIAC 知识收集和共享模式的人工智能系统提供增强性支持。

2020 年甚至凸显了危机时期对全球合作的迫切需要。人们只能遗憾地看到，是党派政治限制了通过重要的多边行为体（例如世卫组织）进行全球协调，而不是常识。但我们仍然抱有希望，

60

through essential multilateral actors (the WHO being a case in point), but we remain hopeful that in this decade of action for the UN SDGs, more AI for SDG initiatives will blossom. Examples include the AI4SDGs think tank from the Beijing Academy of Artificial Intelligence (BAAI), with the support of Baidu, Megvii, Yitu and Didi, or the Oxford Initiative on AI×SDGs led by Saïd Business School with the support of Facebook, Google and Amazon. This situation also clearly highlights the increased role of the UN in bringing together not only governments but also leading AI platforms in the East and the West to foster AI-based projects to tackle the complex systems that are the SDGs. Hopefully, 2021 will allow us to bring these projects together.

Finally, we have been working on a couple of impactful projects with world governments and UN partners (e.g., UNICRI) to deploy AI systems against human trafficking and to educate law enforcement agencies on existing AI tools to identify and eliminate Child Sexual Abuse Material (CSAM) online. These are very concrete, practical cases in which we can leverage the power of AI while helping governments and policy-makers tackle humanity's challenges. We hope that, as world leaders embrace the potential of AI systems and implement various AI principles, large-scale, ambitious AI for good programs will be deployed in 2021 with strong global coordination, emulating the collaborations of the CERN or ISSS programs.

六十

认为在努力实现联合国可持续发展目标的这十年中，会有更多旨在实现可持续发展目标的人工智能计划蓬勃发展，如获得百度、旷视、依图和滴滴支持的北京智源人工智能研究院（BAAI）的 AI4SDGs 智库，或由赛德商学院（Saïd Business School）领导、脸书、谷歌和亚马逊的支持的牛津 AI×SDG 计划。这也清楚地表明，联合国要发挥更大的作用，不但要将各国政府联系在一起，还要引导东西方的人工智能平台，去推进以人工智能为基础的项目，来应对可持续发展目标这一复杂情况。这是一项可持续发展目标。希望我们能在 2021 年把这些项目整合到一起。

最后，我们一直在与世界各国政府和联合国合作伙伴（联合国区域间犯罪和司法研究所）合作开展一些具有影响力的项目，部署人工智能系统打击人口贩卖、向执法机构提供关于现有人工智能工具的应用教育，以及删除网络上的儿童性虐待材料（CSAM）。这些都是非常具体的实际案例。针对这些案例，我们可以利用人工智能的力量，帮助政府和决策者应对人类面临的挑战。我们希望在 2021 年，世界各国领导人拥抱人工智能系统的潜力，并实施各种人工智能原则，我们能在坚实的全球合作下仿效 CERN 或 ISSS 项目的合作，大规模部署宏伟的人工智能造福人类项目。

APPENDIX: INDEX OF TERMS

A

Acceptable Intelligence with Responsibility Study Group	可接受的负责任人工智能研究小组	AIR
Act on the Protection of Personal Information	《个人信息保护法》	—
Ad Hoc Committee on Artificial Intelligence	人工智能特别委员会	CAHAI
AI Act	《人工智能法》	—
AI and Shared Prosperity Initiative	AI 与共享繁荣倡议	—
AI Commons	人工智能联盟	—
AI Ethics Guidelines Global Inventory	全球人工智能伦理指南清单	—
AI for social impact regional initiative	人工智能促进社会影响区域倡议	fAIr LAC
AI Initiative of the Future Society	未来社会人工智能计划	TFS
Algorithm Watch	算法监视	—
American Academy of Arts and Sciences	美国艺术与科学院	AAAS
American Association for the Advancement of Science	美国科学促进会	AAAS
American National Standards Institute	美国国家标准协会	ANSI
American Statistical Association	美国统计协会	—
Application Programming Interface	应用程序编程接口	API
Artificial General Intelligence	通用人工智能协会	AGI
Artificial Moral Agents	人工道德智能体	AMAs
Asilomar Principles	阿西洛马人工智能原则	—
Association for Electrical, Electronic & Information Technologies	电气、电子和信息技术协会	VDE
Association for the Advancement of Artificial Intelligence	人工智能促进协会	AAAI
Association of Computing Machinery	美国计算机协会	ACM
August Capital	奥格斯特资本	—
Automata Theory	自动机理论	—

B

Beijing Academy of Artificial Intelligence	北京智源人工智能研究院	BAAI
Beijing AI Principles	人工智能北京共识	—
Berkman Klein Center for Internet and Society	伯克曼·克莱因互联网与社会中心	BKC

C

Center for Human-Compatible AI	人类兼容人工智能中心	CHAI
Centre for the Governance of AI	AI 治理中心	GovAI
Centre for the Study of Existential Risk	生存风险研究中心	CSER
China Academy of Information and Communications Technology	中国信息通信研究院	CAICT
China Computer Federation	中国计算机学会	CCF
China National Computer Congress	中国计算机学会年会	CNCC
China's Center for Information and Industry Development	智库赛迪研究院	CCID
Chinese Academy of Science and Technology for Development	中国科学技术发展战略研究院	CASTED
Chinese Society for Dialectics of Nature	中国自然辩证法研究会	CSDN
Collective and Augmented Intelligence Against COVID-19	针对新冠肺炎疫情的集体和增强智能项目	CAIAC
Committee on Ethics and Professional Conduct	职业伦理与学术道德委员会	CEPC
Committee on Industry, Research and Energy	工业、研究和能源委员会	ITRE
Computer Aided Group	计算机辅助小组	CAP
Computer Science and Artificial Intelligence Laboratory	麻省理工学院计算机科学与人工智能实验室	CSAIL
Conference and Workshop on Neural Information Processing Systems	神经信息处理系统大会	NeurIPS
Coordinated Plan on AI	欧盟《人工智能协调计划》	—

附录：专业术语中英文对照表

D

Data Security Law	《数据安全法》	—
Deep Learning	深度学习	—
Deutsche Gesellschaft für Internationale Zusammenarbeit	德国国际合作机构	GIZ
Differential Privacy	差分隐私	DP

E

Economic and Social Research Council	经济与社会研究理事会	ESRC
Edward Elgar Publishing	爱德华·埃尔加出版社	—
Electroencephalogram	脑电图	EEG
Ethically Aligned AI Classical Ethics Committee	合乎伦理的人工智能伦理标准委员会	—
EU Ethics Guidelines for Trustworthy AI	欧盟可信赖人工智能的伦理准则	—
European Association of AI	欧洲人工智能协会	EurAI
European Social Simulation Association	欧洲社会模拟协会	ESSA

F

Food and Drug Administration	美国食品和药物管理局	FDA
Founders Space	创始人空间	—
Future of Life Institute	生命未来研究所	FLI
Future of Science and Technology	欧洲议会未来与科学和技术小组	STOA
Future Society	未来学会	—

G

G20 AI Principles	G20 人工智能原则	—
General Data Protection Regulation	通用数据保护条例	GDPR
Generic Names Supporting Organization	通用名称支持组织	GNSO
Global Data Access Framework	全球数据获取框架	GDAF
Global Governance of AI Forums	全球人工智能治理论坛	—
Global Governance of AI Roundtable	全球人工智能治理圆桌会议	GGAR
Global Initiative on Data Security	中国《全球数据安全倡议》	—
Global Partnership on AI	全球人工智能伙伴关系	GPAI
Global Public Policy Institute	德国全球公共政策研究所	GPPi
Graph Algorithm	图算法	—

H

High Level Expert Group on AI	欧盟内部的人工智能高级专家组	FDA
Homomorphic encryption	同态加密	HE

I

IEEE Robotics and Automation Society	IEEE 机器人与自动化协会	IEEE RAS
IEEE Standards Association	IEEE 标准协会	IEEE SA
IEEE Industry Standards and Technology Organization	行业标准和技术组织	IEEE-ISTO
Indian Institutes of Information Technology	印度信息技术研究所	IIIT

I

Information for All Programme	联合国教科文组织全民信息计划	IFAP
Institute for the Study of Science, Technology and Innovation	科学、技术与创新研究所	ISSTI
Institute of Electrical and Electronics Engineers	电气与电子工程师学会	IEEE
Inter-American Development Bank	美洲开发银行	IADB
International Center for Ethics in the Sciences and Humanities	科学与人文伦理国际中心	IZEW
International Committee for Information Technology Standards	国际信息技术标准委员会	INCITS
International Joint Conference on Artficial Intelligence	国际人工智能联席会议	IJCAI
International Studies Association	国际研究协会	ISA

J

Japan Deep Learning Association	日本深度学习协会	JDLA
Japanese Society for Artificial Intelligence	日本人工智能学会	JSAI
Johannes Gutenberg University	约翰内斯·古腾堡大学	JGU

L

Lethal Autonomous Weapon Systems	致命性自主武器系统	LAWS
Leverhulme Centre for the Future of Intelligence	莱弗哈姆未来智能中心	—

M

Ministry of Education	教育部	MOE
Ministry of Industry and Information Technology	中国工业和信息化部	MIIT
Montreal AI Ethics Institute	蒙特利尔人工智能伦理研究所	MAIEI

N

National Academy of Engineering	美国国家工程院	NAE
National Academy of Sciences	美国国家科学院	NAS
National AI Strategy	新加坡国家人工智能战略	NAIS
National Association of Software and Service Companies	印度软件和服务公司协会	NASSCOM
National Research Council	国家研究委员会	NRC
National Science Board	国家科学委员会	NSB
National Science Foundation	国家科学基金会	NSF
Non-Personal Data (NPD) Governance Framework	印度《非个人数据治理框架》	—

O

OECD Principles on AI	经合组织人工智能原则	—
OECD's Network of Experts on AI	经合组织人工智能专家网络	ONE AI
Order of the British Empire	大英帝国官佐勋章	OBE
Organization for Security and Co-operation in Europe	欧洲安全与合作组织	OSCE

P

Partnership on AI	人工智能合作组织	PAI
Patent Cooperation Treaty	专利合作条约	PCT
Proceedings of the National Academy of Sciences of the United States of America	美国国家科学院院刊	*Proc. Natl. Acad. of Sci.*

R

Robotics Society of Japan	日本机器人学会	RSJ
Routledge	劳特利奇出版社	—

S

Sciences Po Paris	巴黎政治学院	—
Sensyne Health	森西恩健康公司	—
Shanghai Institute for Science of Science	上海市科学学研究所	SISS
Singapore Management University	新加坡管理大学	SMU
Singapore University of Technology and Design	新加坡科技设计大学	SUTD
Social Principles of Human-Centric AI	日本《以人类为中心的人工智能社会原则》	—
Society for Industrial and Applied Mathematics	美国工业与应用数学学会	SIAM
Standard for Fail-Safe Design of Autonomous and Semi-Autonomous Systems	自主和半自主系统故障安全设计标准	IEEE P7009
Standardization Administration of the People's Republic of China	国家标准化管理委员会	SAC
Stanford Human-Centered AI	斯坦福大学以人为中心的人工智能计划	Stanford HAI

T

Technology & Innovation Sociology / Social Simulation Laboratory	美因兹大学技术与创新社会学 / 社会模拟实验室	TISSS
The Engineering Honor Society	美国工程荣誉协会	Tau Beta Pi
The National Institution for Transforming India	改造印度国家研究院	NITI
The Personal Data Protection	印度《个人数据保护法》	PDP
Transfer Learning	迁移学习	—
Trustworthy Ai	可信人工智能	—

U

United Nations Development Programme	联合国开发计划署	UNDP
United Nations Educational, Scientific and Cultural Organization	联合国教科文组织	UNESCO
United Nations Interregional Crime and Justice Research Institute	联合国区域间犯罪和司法研究所	UNICRI
US Federal Trade Commission	美国联邦贸易委员会	FTC

V

Vector Institute for Artificial Intelligence	多伦多人工智能矢量研究所	—

W

World Artificial Intelligence Conference	世界人工智能大会	—
World Economic Forum	世界经济论坛	WEF
World Federation of Engineering Organizations	世界工程组织联合会	WFEO
World Government Summit	世界政府首脑峰会	—

Y

Young Computer Scientists and Engineers Forum	中国计算机学会青年计算机科学家与工程师论坛	CCF YOCSEF

ACKNOWLEDGMENTS

We could never have presented this book to you without the support of numerous advisers and experts. Our sincere appreciation goes to John E. Hopcroft, who has extended his very generous offer in providing whole-process guidance to our work. In addition, we would like to express our gratitude to Stuart Russell, Eugenio V. Garcia and other experts for their valuable suggestions during the compilation, especially to Mr. Eugenio V. Garcia as all the South American authors in the two reports were referred to us by him. We are also thankful for the multifaceted support of Jaan Tallinn, Co-founder of Skype.

We are grateful to LI Xiuquan (Chinese Academy of Science and Technology for Development), Cyrus Hodes (The Future Society), Herbert Chia (Sequoia Capital China), DUAN Weiwen (Chinese Academy of Social Sciences), HE Jia, and other contributors for their valuable support in bringing all the contributors together. We would also like to thank Caroline Jeanmaire from the University of California, Berkeley, USA, Charlotte Stix from the Eindhoven University of Technology, the Netherlands, Angela Daly from the University of Strathclyde, UK, Dev Lewis from Digital Asia Hub, SUN Baoxue and HU Xiaomeng from Hunan Normal University, WU Junyi from Peking University, and ZHANG Dazhi from Central China Normal University for their considerable support and assistance in the compilation of the report, and we would like to express our special thanks to NIE Yunzhe from Columbia University in the City of New York, USA, who made many painstaking efforts to contact dozens of global experts.

The two-way English and Chinese translation is reliant on the review of numerous industry experts. WANG Xiangfeng (East China Normal University), WEN Xianqing (Hunan Normal University), XU Nuo (Shanghai Institute for Science of Science), ZHANG Chenchen (Synced), WU Yiying (Synced), and CHEN Zifu (Mind Education) reviewed the relevant professional contents; JI Caixuan (University of Oxford), ZHANG Kai (University of Oxford), LI Hailong (University of Birmingham), PU Xingyue (University of Oxford), CHEN Zhihao (East China University of Political Science and Law), etc. proofread the translation. WANG Yingchun, CHEN Qiuping, QU Jingjing, FENG Jingjing and ZHANG Chaoyun from Research Department of Science, Technology and Society at Shanghai Institute for Science of Science reviewed the first drafts of all articles, and interns ZHANG Jie, SONG Zhixian, SUN Hui, NI Jiawei, LIANG Xinyi, HUANG Siwei, XIAO Di, et al. also assisted in text proofreading.

The leading team and our colleagues at Shanghai Institute for Science of Science provided great and solid support in the setup, funding, and promotion of the project, and many other aspects.

We appreciate the support of all our partners, peers, and friends from all over the world! We are so honored to work with all of them on such a significant task.

致谢

本书的完成，依赖于众多顾问和专家的支持。真诚感谢约翰·霍普克罗夫特全程的顾问指导，感谢斯图尔特·拉塞尔、尤金尼奥·加西亚等专家在组稿过程中提出的宝贵建议，尤其要感谢尤金尼奥·加西亚先生帮助我们引荐了所有的南美作者。感谢 Skype 联合创始人让·塔林（Jaan Tallinn）的多方面支持。

感谢李修全（中国科技发展战略研究院）、Cyrus Hodes（未来社会）、Herbert Chia（红杉资本）、段伟文（中国社科院）及贺佳等人在邀请专家的过程中给予的关键性帮助。感谢来自美国加利福尼亚大学伯克利分校的林晨力（Caroline Jeanmaire）、荷兰埃因霍温理工大学的夏洛特·斯蒂克斯（Charlotte Stix）、英国思克莱德大学李安琪（Angela Daly）以及来自亚洲数字中心的戴逸司（Dev Lewis）、湖南师范大学的孙保学和胡晓萌、北京大学的吴君仪和华中师范大学的张达志，他们在报告编制过程中提供了大量的支持与帮助；还要特别感谢来自美国哥伦比亚大学的聂蕴哲，他为联络全球数十位专家投入了大量精力。

中英文版本互译也有赖于众多同行专家的审校。王祥丰（华东师范大学）、文贤庆（湖南师范大学）、徐诺（上海市科学学研究所）、张晨琛（机器之心）、仵翼颖（机器之心）、陈自富（世纪明德）对有关专业内容进行了审校；季采璇（牛津大学）、张凯（牛津大学）、李海龙（伯明翰大学）、蒲星月（牛津大学）、陈志豪（华东政法大学）等对翻译内容进行了校对。上海市科学学研究所科技与社会研究室的王迎春、陈秋萍、瞿晶晶、冯晶晶和张朝云是每一篇初稿的审稿人，实习生张洁、宋志贤、孙慧、倪佳炜、梁新怡、黄思伟、肖迪等在文字校对上也提供了帮助。

在本书的项目立项、资金支持、宣传推广等方方面面，上海市科学学研究所的领导团队和同事们都给予了坚定的支持。

很荣幸能与所有人一起合作，为如此重要的事业而共同奋斗。对所有全球同仁的帮助，我们一并致谢！

CONTRIBUTORS' LIST

John E. HOPCROFT

is the IBM Professor of Engineering and Applied Mathematics in Computer Science at Cornell University. From January 1994 until June 2001, he was the Joseph Silbert Dean of Engineering. After receiving both his M.S. (1962) and Ph.D. (1964) in electrical engineering from Stanford University, he spent three years on the faculty of Princeton University. He joined the Cornell faculty in 1967, was named professor in 1972 and the Joseph C. Ford Professor of Computer Science in 1985. He served as chairman of the Department of Computer Science from 1987 to 1992 and was the associate dean for college affairs in 1993. As an undergraduate alumnus of Seattle University, Hopcroft was honored with a Doctor of Humanities Degree, Honoris Causa, in 1990. Hopcroft's research centers on theoretical aspects of computing, especially analysis of algorithms, automata theory, and graph algorithms. He has coauthored four books on formal languages and algorithms with Jeffrey D. Ullman and Alfred V. Aho. His most recent work is on the study of information capture and access. He was honored with the A.M. Turing Award in 1986. He is a member of the National Academy of Sciences (NAS), the National Academy of Engineering (NAE), a foreign member of the Chinese Academy of Sciences, and a fellow of the American Academy of Arts and Sciences (AAAS), the American Association for the Advancement of Science, the Institute of Electrical and Electronics Engineers (IEEE), and the Association of Computing Machinery (ACM). In 1992, he was appointed by President Bush to the National Science Board (NSB), which oversees the National Science Foundation (NSF), and served through May 1998. From 1995-98, Hopcroft served on the National Research Council's Commission on Physical Sciences, Mathematics, and Applications. In addition to these appointments, Hopcroft serves as a member of the SIAM financial management committee, IIIT New Delhi advisory board, Microsoft's technical advisory board for research Asia, and the Engineering Advisory Board, Seattle University.

Bart SELMAN

is the Joseph C. Ford Professor of Engineering and Computer Science at Cornell University. Prof. Selman is the President of the Association for the Advancement of Artificial Intelligence (AAAI), the main international professional society for AI researchers and practitioners. He was also the co-Chair of a national study to determine a roadmap for AI research guiding US government research investments in AI. Prof. Selman was previously at AT&T Bell Laboratories. His research interests include artificial intelligence, computational sustainability, efficient reasoning procedures, machine learning, deep learning, deep reinforcement learning, planning, knowledge representation, and connections between computer science and statistical physics. He has (co-)authored over 150 publications, including six best paper awards and two classic paper awards. His papers have appeared in venues spanning Nature, Science, Proc. Natl. Acad. of Sci., and a variety of conferences and journals in AI and Computer Science. He has received the Cornell Stephen Miles Excellence in Teaching Award, the Cornell Outstanding Educator Award, an NSF Career Award, and an Alfred P. Sloan Research Fellowship. He is a Fellow of the American Association for Artificial Intelligence (AAAI), a Fellow of the American Association for the Advancement of Science (AAAS), and a Fellow of the American Association for Computing Machinery (ACM). He is the recipient of the inaugural IJCAI John McCarthy Research Award, the premier award for artificial intelligence researchers at mid-career stage.

Stuart RUSSELL

is a Professor of Computer Science at the University of California at Berkeley, holder of the Smith-Zadeh Chair in Engineering, and Director of the Center for Human-Compatible AI. His book Artificial Intelligence: A Modern Approach (with Peter Norvig) is the standard text in AI, used in 1500 universities in 135 countries. His research covers a wide range of topics in artificial intelligence, with a current emphasis on the long-term future of artificial intelligence and its relation to humanity. He has developed a new global seismic monitoring system for the nuclear-test-ban treaty with the United Nations and is currently working to ban lethal autonomous weapons. He is an Honorary Fellow of Wadham College, Oxford, an Andrew Carnegie Fellow, and a Fellow of the American Association for Artificial Intelligence, the Association for Computing Machinery, and the American Association for the Advancement of Science. He has served as an Adjunct Professor of Neurological Surgery at UC San Francisco and as Vice-Chair of the World Economic Forum's Council on AI and Robotics. He is a recipient of the Presidential Young Investigator Award of the National Science Foundation, the IJCAI Computers and Thought Award, the World Technology Award (Policy category), the Mitchell Prize of the American Statistical Association, the Feigenbaum Prize of the Association for the Advancement of Artificial Intelligence, and Outstanding Educator Awards from both ACM and AAAI. Stuart Russell obtained his B.A. with first-class honors in physics from Oxford University in 1982 and his Ph.D. in computer science from Stanford in 1986. In 2021, he received the OBE from Her Majesty Queen Elizabeth.

Caroline JEANMAIRE

researches international coordination models to ensure the safety and reliability of artificial intelligence systems at the Center for Human-Compatible AI (CHAI) at UC Berkeley. She also leads CHAI's partnership and external relations strategy, focusing on building a research community around AI safety and relationships with key stakeholders. Before working at CHAI, she was an AI Policy Researcher and Project Manager at The Future Society, a think tank incubated at Harvard's Kennedy School of Government. She notably supported the organization of the first and second Global Governance of AI Forums at the World Government Summit in Dubai. Before this, she participated in numerous climate negotiations and technical intersessions as a youth delegate, including with the French delegation for COP23 and COP24. Caroline

撰稿人简介

约翰·霍普克罗夫特

美国康奈尔大学计算机科学系工程与应用数学方向 IBM 教授，图灵奖获得者。霍普克罗夫特获得斯坦福大学电气工程硕士学位（1962 年）和博士学位（1964 年）后，曾在普林斯顿大学任教三年。他于 1967年加入康奈尔大学，1972 年被任命为教授。1985 年，霍普克罗夫特曾被任命为计算机科学系的约瑟夫·福德（Joseph C. Ford）教授，于 1987 年至 1992 年担任计算机科学系主任，并于 1993 年担任学院常务副院长。作为西雅图大学的本科生校友，霍普克罗夫特教授在 1990 年获得了人文荣誉博士学位。霍普克罗夫特教授的研究集中在计算理论方面，特别是算法分析、自动机理论和图算法。霍普克罗夫特教授与杰弗里·乌尔曼（Jeffrey D. Ullman）和阿尔弗雷德·阿霍（Alfred V. Aho）合著了四本关于形式语言和算法的著作。近来，他致力于研究信息的获取与访问。1986 年，霍普克罗夫特教授被授予图灵奖。他是美国国家科学院（NAS）院士、美国国家工程院（NAE）院士、中国科学院外籍院士、美国艺术与科学院（AAAS）院士、美国科学促进会院士、电气与电子工程师学会院士，以及美国计算机协会院士。1992 年，被时任美国总统布什任命为国家科学委员会成员 [负责监督国家科学基金会（NSF）]，任期至 1998 年 5 月。1995 年至 1998 年，霍普克罗夫特教授在国家研究委员会（National Research Council）的物理科学、数学和应用委员会任职。除上述任命，霍普克罗夫特教授还是美国工业与应用数学学会（SIAM）财务管理委员会、印度信息技术研究所新德里咨询委员会、微软亚洲研究院技术咨询委员会和西雅图大学工程咨询委员会的成员。

巴特·塞尔曼

美国康奈尔大学计算机科学与工程系约瑟夫·福德（Joseph C. Ford）教授，也是人工智能促进协会（AAAI）主席。AAAI 是面向 AI 研究人员和从业者的主要国际专业协会。此外，他还是一项国家级研究项目的联合主席，该项目旨在确定 AI 研究的路线图，以指导美国政府的 AI 科研投资。塞尔曼教授此前曾任职于贝尔实验室。他的研究领域包括人工智能、计算可持续性、高效推理程序、机器学习、深度学习、深度强化学习、线性规划、知识表征学习，以及计算机科学与统计物理学之间的关系。塞尔曼教授曾编著或合著超过 150 篇作品，其中 6 篇获得了最佳论文奖，3 篇获得了经典论文奖，这些论文发表于《自然》《科学》《美国国家科学院院刊》以及一系列有关人工智能和计算机科学的会议和期刊上。他曾获得康奈尔大学斯蒂芬·迈尔斯优秀教学奖、康奈尔大学杰出教育奖、美国国家科学基金会（NSF）事业奖和阿尔弗雷德·斯隆研究奖。塞尔曼教授是美国人工智能协会（AAAI）会员、美国科学促进会（AAAS）以及美国计算机协会（ACM）会员。他曾获得首届国际人工智能联席会议（International Joint Conference on Artficial Intelligence, IJCAI）约翰·麦卡锡研究奖，这是处于职业生涯中期的人工智能研究人员所能获得的最高奖项。

斯图尔特·拉塞尔

加州大学伯克利分校计算机科学系教授、史密斯 - 扎德工程学讲席教授，以及人类兼容人工智能中心主任。他与彼得·诺维格（Peter Norvig）合著的《人工智能：一种现代方法》（*Artificial Intelligence: A Modern Approach*）是人工智能领域的标准教材，被 135 个国家的 1500 所高校选用。拉塞尔的研究涉及多个人工智能领域，他目前的研究重点是人工智能的长远未来及其与人类的关系。拉塞尔已与联合国携手为《禁止核试验条约》开发了新的全球地震监测系统，目前致力于推行针对致命性自主武器的禁令。拉塞尔是牛津大学瓦德汉学院的荣誉院士、安德鲁·卡内基研究员、美国人工智能协会会员、美国计算机协会会员，以及美国科学促进会会员，曾在加州大学旧金山分校担任神经外科客座教授，还曾担任世界经济论坛人工智能和机器人委员会副主席。他曾获美国国家科学基金会总统青年研究员奖、国际人工智能联席会议（IJCAI）计算机与思维奖、世界技术奖（政策类）、美国统计协会米切尔奖、人工智能促进协会（AAAI）费根鲍姆奖，以及美国计算机协会（ACM）和人工智能促进协会颁发的杰出教育家奖。1982 年，斯图尔特·拉塞尔获得牛津大学物理学一等荣誉学士学位；1986 年，他获得斯坦福大学计算机科学博士学位；2021 年，他获得伊丽莎白女王颁发的大英帝国官佐勋章。

林晨力

在加州大学伯克利分校人类兼容人工智能中心（CHAI）从事旨在确保人工智能系统安全性和可靠性的国际协调模型的相关研究。此外，她还负责该中心的伙伴关系和对外关系战略，致力于建立一个围绕人工智能安全及其对关键利益相关者的意义的研究社区。在加入 CHAI 之前，林晨力曾是哈佛大学肯尼迪政治学院孵化的智库“未来学会”（Future Society）的人工智能政策研究员和项目经理，并为在迪拜世界政府首脑峰会上组织的第一届和第二届全球人工智能治理论坛提供了大力支持。在此之前，她还曾多次作为青年代表参加气候谈判和技术会议，包括随同法国代表团参加 2017 年及 2018 年联合国气候变化大会（COP23，COP24）。林晨力拥有北京大学国际关系硕士学位，以及巴黎政治学院国际公共管理硕士学位。

杨强

微众银行首席人工智能官、香港科技大学计算机科学与工程系的讲席教授和前系主任。他是国际人工智能界“迁移学习”（Transfer Learning）技术的开创者,同时提出“联邦学习”(Federated Learning)的研究新方向。他于 2013 年 7 月当选为人工智能促进协会(AAAI)院士，之后又于 2020 年 1 月当选 AAAI 2021 主席，2017 年 8 月当选国际人工智能联席会议（IJCAI）理事会主席。

has a master's degree in International Relations from Peking University and a master's degree in International Public Management from Sciences Po Paris.

YANG Qiang

is the Chief AI Officer at WeBank and a Chair Professor and former Head of the Department of Computer Science and Engineering of the Hong Kong University of Science and Technology. He is a leading researcher of "transfer learning" technology in the international AI community, and he is spearheading the new research direction of "federated learning". He was elected a fellow of the AAAI (Association for the Advancement of Artificial Intelligence) in July 2013 and the Conference Chair of AAAI 2021 conference. Between 2017 and 2019, he was elected the President of the Board of Trustees of IJCAI, the world's oldest and most popular AI society.

Roman V. YAMPOLSKIY

is a Tenured Associate Professor in the Department of Computer Science and Engineering at the Speed School of Engineering, University of Louisville. He is the founding and current director of the Cyber Security Lab and an author of many books including *Artificial Superintelligence: A Futuristic Approach*. Yampolskiy is a Senior Member of IEEE and AGI; and a Member of Kentucky Academy of Science. Dr. Yampolskiy's main areas of interest are AI Safety and Cybersecurity. Dr. Yampolskiy is an author of over 200 publications. Dr. Yampolskiy has been an invited speaker at 100+ events.

Allan DAFOE

is Associate Professor in the International Politics of AI, Senior Staff Research Scientist at DeepMind, and Founder of the Centre for the Governance of AI at the Future of Humanity Institute, University of Oxford. His research examines the causes of great power war and the global politics surrounding transformative technologies, in particular concerning the risks from artificial intelligence.

Alexis CARLIER

is the incoming Head of Strategy at the Centre for the Governance of AI. Previously, Alexis helped found the Consortium on the Landscape of AI Safety, and worked as a machine learning engineer at Sensyne Health.

SU Jun

is the Cheung Kong Scholar Chair Professor in the School of Public Policy and Management at Tsinghua University. He serves as the Dean of the Institute of Intelligence Society Governance (ISG), Tsinghua University; the Director of the Center for Science, Technology and Education Policy (CSTEP) and of the Think Tank Center of Tsinghua University; and the Deputy Director of the Advisory Committee of the Public Administration under the Ministry of Education. Su Jun has been awarded a special allowance from the State Council. In addition, Su Jun is an associate at Harvard Kennedy School and a senior research fellow at the Fletcher School of Law and Diplomacy, Tufts University. He is also the Chair of the First National Conference on Artificial Intelligence Social Experiment and the cochair of the Harvard–Tsinghua Workshop on Low Carbon Development and Public Policy (2014-2018).

Petra AHRWEILER

is Full Professor of Sociology of Technology and Innovation, Social Simulation, at Johannes Gutenberg University (JGU) at Mainz, Germany and leads its TISSS Lab. At Free University Berlin, Germany, she received her PhD for a study on Artificial Intelligence, and got her habilitation at the University of Bielefeld, Germany, for a study on simulation in Science and Technology Studies.

Brian CHRISTIAN

is a Visiting Scholar at the University of California, Berkeley and the bestselling author of three acclaimed books of nonfiction about the human implications of computer science: *The Most Human Human*, *Algorithms to Live By: The Computer Science of Human Decisions* (with Tom Griffiths), and *The Alignment Problem*. His books have been named a *New York Times* Editors' Choice, a Wall Street Journal bestseller, a New Yorker favorite book of the year, Amazon best science book of the year, and MIT Technology Review best book of the year, and have been translated into nineteen languages. Christian has lectured at Google, Facebook, Microsoft, the Santa Fe Institute and the London School of Economics, and holds degrees in philosophy, computer science, and poetry from Brown University and the University of Washington.

Danil KERIMI

is an experienced technology, public administration and corporate strategy executive with a track record of impactful projects on digital transformation, innovation policy, tech and economic diplomacy in developed, emerging and frontier markets. With experience spanning private, public and philanthropical organizations, he worked on international justice systems at the UN and OSCE, on technology governance at the World Economic Forum where he advanced the network of the Centres for the Fourth Industrial Revolution. After leaving WEF, Danil co-founded the Edgelands Institute and advised several governments, corporates and startups on their digital transformation, FDI and global competitiveness strategies. Danil is a graduate of Shandong University (LLB), Vienna Diplomatic Academy (MA), Global Leadership Fellowship (MA), affiliate of Berkman-Klein Center, Harvard and fellow, Arrell Food Institute and FuXi Institute for Digital Economy.

罗曼·亚姆波尔斯基

路易斯维尔大学计算机科学与工程系终身副教授，网络安全实验室的创始人和现任主任，著有多部著作，包括《超级人工智能：未来主义方法》（*Artificial Superintelligence: A Futuristic Approach*）。亚姆波尔斯基是电气与电子工程师学会（IEEE）和通用人工智能协会（AGI）的高级会员以及肯塔基州科学院的成员。他的主要研究领域是人工智能安全和网络安全，发表了 200 多篇论文，曾应邀在 100 多场活动中发表演讲。

艾伦·达福

牛津大学人类未来研究所人工智能国际政治学副教授，DeepMind 公司资深科学家，人工智能治理中心创立者。他主要研究大国战争的起因，以及围绕变革性技术，特别是关于人工智能风险的全球政治。

亚历克西斯·卡利尔

牛津大学人类未来研究所人工智能治理中心新任战略主管。此前，他协助创立了人工智能安全局势联盟。他还曾在森西恩健康公司（Sensyne Health）担任机器学习工程师。

苏竣

清华大学公共管理学院教授，教育部长江学者特聘教授。现任清华大学智能社会治理研究院院长、清华大学科教政策研究中心主任、清华大学智库中心主任，兼任教育部公共管理类学科专业教学指导委员会副主任，享受国务院特殊津贴。兼任哈佛大学肯尼迪政府学院兼职研究员、塔夫茨大学弗莱彻学院兼职高级研究员。任第一届全国人工智能社会实验学术会议主席，清华—哈佛低碳发展与公共政策国际研讨会（2014—2018）联席主席。

佩特拉·阿维勒

德国美因茨约翰内斯·古腾堡大学（JGU）技术与创新社会学、 社会模拟系全职教授。2013—2017 年，任职于德国巴特诺因阿尔的 JGU，并担任欧洲技术与创新评估学院的董事和首席执行官。2013 年之前，曾任爱尔兰都柏林大学迈克尔·斯穆菲特商学院技术与创新管理专业全职教授，并担任该校创新研究部门 IRU 的主管。此外，还担任美国麻省理工学院工程系统部研究员。佩特拉最初在德国汉堡大学学习社会科学。之后，获得了德国柏林自由大学的人工智能博士学位，并在德国比勒费尔德大学任教，主攻科学技术研究中的模拟研究。主要研究和教学方向是新技术与社会的相互关系、组织间创新网络以及社会科学研究方法中具有创新性的基于代理的模型。佩特拉获有各类研究奖项，在协调和完成国际研究项目（主要是欧洲的研究项目）方面有着丰富的经验。她在国际期刊上发表了多篇跨学科文章，并受到多个科学团体（包括德国技术科学院和德国杰出女科学家网络 Acaderianet）的嘉奖。

布莱恩·克里斯蒂安

加州大学伯克利分校访问学者，著有三部有关计算机科学人文意蕴的畅销纪实作品：《最有人性的“人”》（*The Most Human Human*）、《算法之美：指导工作与生活的算法》（*Algorithms to Live By: The Computer Science of Human Decisions*）[与汤姆·格里菲斯（Tom Griffiths）合著] 和《一致性问题》（*The Alignment Problem*）。他的书作被翻译成 19 种语言，入选《纽约时报》编辑推荐书目、《华尔街日报》畅销书、纽约人最喜爱的年度书籍、亚马逊年度最佳科学书籍，以及《麻省理工技术评论》年度最佳书籍。克里斯蒂安曾在谷歌、脸书、微软、圣塔菲研究所和伦敦政治经济学院举办讲座，拥有布朗大学和华盛顿大学的哲学、计算机科学以及诗歌方面的学位。

鲁子龙

是一名经验丰富的技术、公共管理和企业战略主管，曾在发达市场、新兴市场和前沿市场参与具有影响力的数字化转型项目、创新政策项目，以及技术与经济外交项目。鲁子龙拥有在私营、公共和慈善组织工作的经验，且曾在联合国及欧洲安全与合作组织（OSCE）负责国际司法系统事务，在世界经济论坛（WEF）负责技术治理事务。在世界经济论坛任职期间，鲁子龙推动了第四次工业革命中心的网络建设。离开世界经济论坛后，鲁子龙与他人合伙创办了艾德兰研究所，为多个政府、集团和初创企业提供数字化转型、国际直接投资（FDI）和全球竞争战略咨询服务。鲁子龙拥有山东大学法学学士学位、维也纳外交学院文学硕士学位和全球领袖伙伴计划文学硕士学位。此外，他还是哈佛大学伯克曼互联网与社会研究中心的成员，阿雷尔食品研究所和伏羲智库数字经济研究院的研究员。

马库斯·克纳夫

吉森大学实验心理学与认知科学学院教授兼前任院长。此前，他先后就职于德国弗莱堡大学、普林斯顿大学以及马克斯·普朗克生物控制论研究所。马库斯·克纳夫还曾任德国认知科学协会会长、《认知科学》（*Cognitive Science*）副主编，并曾主持于柏林召开的第 35 届认知科学协会年会。2011 至 2018 年，他担任“理性的新闻框架”优先项目计划主任，其中 15 项研究项目得到德国研究基金会资助，涵盖心理学、人工智能、哲学和逻辑学等多个领域，旨在了解人类理性的本质。他结合心理实验、计算模型和神经影像，从方法论的角度来了解认知与行为之间的神经关联性。他曾从事多年的 AI 项目研究，但之后因其发展逐渐违背心理学规律又重回人类认知领域。如今，他看到了重新对人工智能进行心理学研究的潜力（和必要性）。马库斯·克纳夫近期出版的著作包括《推理空间：人类思维

Markus KNAUFF

is Professor (and formally Chair) of Experimental Psychology and Cognitive Science at the University of Giessen. Prior to his current position, he worked at the University of Freiburg, Princeton University, and the Max Planck Institute for Biological Cybernetics. He has been President of the German Cognitive Science Society, Associate Editor of *Cognitive Science*, and Chair of the 35th Annual Meeting of the Cognitive Science Society in Berlin. From 2011 to 2018, he was Director of the Priority Program News Frameworks of Rationality, in which the German Research Foundation (DFG) funded 15 research projects from psychology, AI, philosophy, and logic to understand the nature of human rationality. Knauff's research focuses on reasoning and rationality in natural and artificial cognitive systems. Methodologically he combines psychological experiments, computational modeling, and neuroimaging to understand the neural correlates of cognition and behavior. He worked on AI projects for many years, but then returned to human cognition as AI became increasingly anti-psychological. Now he sees the potential (and need) of re-psychologizing AI. His most recent publications include: *Space to Reason: A Spatial Theory of Human Thought* (2013) and *The Handbook of Rationality* (2021, together with the Philosopher W. Spohn), both with MIT Press.

Gillian K. HADFIELD

B.A. (Hons.) Queens, J.D., M.A., Ph.D. (Economics) Stanford, is Professor of Law and Professor of Strategic Management at the University of Toronto and holds the Schwartz Reisman Chair in Technology and Society. She is the inaugural Director of the Schwartz Reisman Institute for Technology and Society. Her research is focused on innovative design for legal and dispute resolution systems in advanced and developing market economies; governance for artificial intelligence; the markets for law, lawyers, and dispute resolution; and contract law and theory. Professor Hadfield is a Faculty Affiliate at the Vector Institute for Artificial Intelligence in Toronto and at the Center for Human-Compatible AI at the University of California Berkeley and Senior Policy Advisor at OpenAI in San Francisco. Her book Rules for a Flat World: Why Humans Invented Law and How to Reinvent It for a Complex Global Economy was published by Oxford University Press in 2017.

Thilo HAGENDORFF

is working for the "Ethics and Philosophy Lab" at the "Machine Learning: New Perspectives for Science" Excellence Cluster at the University of Tuebingen, Germany. Moreover, he works for the "AI Ethics Impact Group" of the technical-scientific association VDE (Association for Electrical, Electronic & Information Technologies). His research focusses on ethics in machine learning as well as broader questions in the field of media and technology ethics. Furthermore, he works as a research associate at the University of Tuebinge's International Center for Ethics in the Sciences and Humanities (IZEW). He is also a lecturer at the University of Potsdam's Hasso Plattner Institute.

WANG Guoyu

is a Professor of Philosophy at Fudan University. She is also Distinguished Professor of "Chang Jiang Scholars" of MOE. She serves as the Director of the Center for Biomedical Ethics and Applied Ethics at Fudan University. Prof. Wang is also Vice President of the Committee on the Ethics of Science Technology and Engineering of the Chinese Society for Dialectics of Nature (CSDN), the cochair of the CCF Committee on Ethics and Professional Conduct (CEPC), and Director of the Ethics Committee of the International Human Phenotype Group Project. Wang Guoyu has long been engaged in high-tech ethics and governance research. She conducts several National Key Projects as a PI.

Nathalie SMUHA

is a researcher at the KU Leuven Faculty of Law and the Leuven.AI Institute, where she examines legal and ethical questions around Artificial Intelligence (AI) and other new technologies. Her research focuses particularly on the impact of AI on human rights and societal values. Nathalie regularly advises governments and international organizations on AI-related policy matters. She is involved in the Council of Europe's Ad Hoc Committee on Artificial Intelligence (CAHAI) as an independent expert, and a member of the OECD's Network of Experts on AI (ONE AI). She also worked at the European Commission (DG Connect) where she coordinated the work of the High-Level Expert Group on Artificial Intelligence and contributed to EU policy-making on AI. Nathalie is a qualified attorney at the New York Bar, and worked as a lawyer in an international law firm. She holds degrees in Law and Philosophy from the KU Leuven, and an LL.M. from the University of Chicago School of Law.

Robin WILLIAMS

is Professor of Social Research on Technology at The University of Edinburgh, where he is Director of the Institute for the Study of Science, Technology and Innovation (ISSTI). Since his recruitment to Edinburgh in 1986 to lead its Centre under the ESRC Programme on Information and Communications Technologies, he has developed an interdisciplinary research programme into "the social shaping of technology" through over 50 externally funded projects. He is developing with co-authors, the Biography of Artefacts perspective to address the design and implementation of information infrastructures. Recent books include Social Learning in Technological Innovation: Experimenting with Information and Communication Technologie (Edward Elgar: 2005) with James Stewart and Roger Slack, Software and Organisations: The Biography of the Enterprise-Wide System Or how SAP Conquered the World (Routledge: 2009) with Neil Pollock, and How Industry Analysts Shape the Digital Future (Oxford University Press: 2016) with Neil Pollock.

LI Xiuquan

is now Research Fellow for the Chinese Academy of Science and Technology for Development (CASTED) and Deputy Director of the

的空间理论》(*Space to Reason: A Spatial Theory of Human Thought*, 2013) 和《理性手册》[The Handbook of Rationality, 2021, 与哲学家沃尔夫冈·斯波恩 (Wolfgang Spohn) 合著], 均由麻省理工学院出版社出版。

吉莉安·哈德菲尔德

女王大学 (荣誉) 文学学士, 斯坦福大学文学硕士、法学博士、经济学博士, 多伦多大学法学教授、战略管理教授, 施瓦茨·赖斯曼技术与社会研究所所长。她的研究重点是发达经济体和发展中经济体中法律和争端解决制度的创新设计; 人工智能治理; 法律、律师和争端解决的市场机制; 以及合同法和合同理论。哈德菲尔德教授是多伦多人工智能矢量研究所 (Vector Institute for Artificial Intelligence) 研究员、加州大学伯克利分校人类兼容人工智能中心研究员, 以及 OpenAI 高级政策顾问。2017 年, 其著作《扁平世界的规则: 人类为何发明法律, 又如何再造法律以应对复杂的全球经济》(Rules for a Flat World: Why Humans Invented Law and How to Reinvent It for a Complex Global Economy) 由牛津大学出版社出版。

希洛·哈根多夫

任职于德国图宾根大学"机器学习: 科学新视角"卓越集群的伦理和哲学实验室。他是电气、电子和信息技术协会 (VDE) AI 伦理影响小组的成员。他的研究聚焦于机器学习中的伦理问题以及媒体和技术伦理领域更宽泛的问题。此外, 希洛·哈根多夫博士还是图宾根大学科学与人文伦理国际中心 (IZEW) 副研究员, 在图宾根大学和波茨坦大学哈索普拉特纳研究所担任讲师。

王国豫

复旦大学哲学学院教授, 复旦大学应用伦理学中心、复旦大学生命医学伦理研究中心主任, 博士生导师。教育部长江学者特聘教授。兼任中国自然辩证法研究会科学技术与工程伦理专业委员会副主任, 中国计算机学会职业伦理与学术道德委员会共同主席, 国际人类表型组计划伦理委员会主任。王国豫长期从事高科技伦理与治理研究, 是国家社会科学基金重大项目"高科技伦理问题研究"首席专家, 国家重点研发计划重点专项"精准医疗的伦理政策法规框架研究"首席科学家。

娜塔莉亚·苏姆哈

比利时鲁汶大学法学院和鲁汶大学人工智能研究院研究员, 负责研究人工智能和其他新技术的法律和伦理问题。其研究关注人工智能对人权和社会价值观的影响。娜塔莉亚定期会就人工智能相关政策问题向各国政府和国际组织提供咨询建议。她是欧洲委员会人工智能特别委员会 (CAHAI) 的独立专家, 也是经合组织人工智能专家网络 (ONE AI) 的成员。她还曾在欧盟委员会通信网络、内容和技术总局 (DG Connect) 任职, 负责协调人工智能高级专家组的工作, 并协助制定欧盟的人工智能政策。另外, 娜塔莉亚还是一名纽约律师公会 (New York Bar) 的执业律师, 曾在一家国际律师事务所任职。她拥有鲁汶大学的法律和哲学学位, 以及芝加哥大学法学院的法学硕士学位。

罗宾·威廉姆斯

爱丁堡大学科技社会研究教授, 科学、技术与创新研究所 (ISSTI) 所长。自 1986 年起, 威廉姆斯任爱丁堡大学英国经济与社会研究理事会 (ESRC) 信息和通信技术中心主任, 他通过 50 多个外部资助项目开发了一个跨学科研究计划, 研究"技术的社会塑造作用"。他还在与合著者一起, 从"人工制品传记"的视角探讨信息基础设施的设计和实施。威廉姆斯的最新著作包括与詹姆斯·斯图尔特 (James Stewart) 和罗杰·斯莱克 (Roger Slack) 合著的《技术创新中的社会学习: 信息和通讯技术试验》(Social Learning in Technological Innovation: Experimenting with Information and Communication Technologies) (爱德华·埃尔加出版社: 2005 年), 以及与尼尔·波洛克 (Neil Pollock) 合著的《企业系统传记, 又名 SAP 如何征服世界》(The Biography of the Enterprise Wide-System Or how SAP Conquered the World) (劳特利奇出版社: 2009 年) 和《行业分析师如何塑造数字未来》(How Industry Analysts Shape the Digital Future) (牛津大学出版社: 2016 年)。

李修全

中国科学技术发展战略研究院研究员, 科技部新一代人工智能发展研究中心副主任。毕业于清华大学计算机系, 德国汉堡大学信息学科学系联合培养博士, 在多维时序数据建模与预测、基于脑电图 (electroencephalogram, EEG) 的脑控机器人系统等领域有多年研究经历。目前主要关注大数据与人工智能技术预测、产业技术路线图、人工智能创新政策研究等, 对于智能化变革的前沿趋势和对研发、产业、治理等经济社会各方面的创新政策需求具有浓厚研究兴趣。李修全主持我国"智能经济与智能社会发展的重大战略问题研究""国内外人工智能前沿趋势与政策研究"等研究课题 10 余项。

杨庆峰

2003 年获得复旦大学哲学博士。现为复旦大学应用伦理研究中心、发展研究院教授。现担任中国自然辩证法研究会技术哲学专业委员会常务理事、上海市自然辩证法研究会秘书长。美国达特茅斯学院、斯维本科技大学访问学者。主要研究方向为技术哲学、数据伦理、记忆哲学与人工智能伦理等。

New Generation Artificial Intelligence Development Research Center of the Ministry of Science and Technology. He received his PhD in Computer Science from Tsinghua University. He is also a joint PhD in Information Science, University of Hamburg, Germany. He has many years of research experience in AI fields, such as multidimensional time series data-modeling and prediction and brain-controlled robot systems based on EEG. His current research area is big data and AI technology foresight and evaluation, industrial technology roadmaps and AI innovation policy research. He has a strong interest in the study of the frontier trend of intelligent transformation and the demand for innovative policies in various aspects of AI development, such as research, industry and governance. He has presided over 10 research projects, such as "Research on the Major Strategic Issues of Chinese Intelligence Economy and Intelligence Society Development" and "Research on the Leading Trends and Policies of Artificial Intelligence at Home and Abroad".

YANG Qingfeng

received his PhD from Fudan University in 2003. Currently, he is a professor at the Center for Applied Ethics and Fudan Development Institute of Fudan University. He also serves as the Executive Director of the Technology Philosophy Committee of the Chinese Society for Philosophy of Nature and the Secretary General of Shanghai Nature of Dialectics Association in China. He is a visiting scholar at Dartmouth College, USA, and Swinburne University of Technology, Australia. His current research includes the philosophy of technology, data ethics, the philosophy of memory and AI ethics.

CHEN Dingding

is Professor of International Relations; Associate Dean of the Institute for 21st Century Silk Road Studies at Jinan University, Guangzhou, China; Non-Resident Fellow at the Global Public Policy Institute (GPPi) Berlin, Germany; Vice-President of International Studies Association (Asia Pacific region); and Senior Research Fellow for the Center for Global Studies at Tsinghua University. He is also the Founding Director of the Intellisia Institute, a newly established independent think tank focusing on international affairs in China. His research interests include Chinese foreign policy, Asian security, Chinese politics, and human rights.

Malavika JAYARAM

is a Practice Assistant Professor and Lee Kong Chian Fellow at the SMU School of Law, Singapore. She is also a Faculty Associate at the Berkman Klein Center for Internet and Society at Harvard University (BKC) and the inaugural Executive Director of the Digital Asia Hub, an independent research think tank incubated by BKC. A technology lawyer for over 15 years, she practiced law at Allen & Overy and was Vice President and Technology Counsel at Citigroup, both in London. A graduate of the National Law School of India, Malavika has an LL.M. from Northwestern University, Chicago. She was a Visiting Scholar at the Annenberg School for Communication, University of Pennsylvania, and has had fellowships at the University of Sydney and the Institute for Technology & Society, Rio de Janeiro. She taught India's first course on information technology and law in 1997. Malavika was previously a member of the Executive Committee of the IEEE Global Initiative on the Ethics of Autonomous and Intelligent Systems and an Associate Fellow with Chatham House (the Royal Institute of International Affairs) as part of its Asia-Pacific Programme. She was also a member of the High-level Expert Advisory Group to the OECD project, "Going Digital: Making the Transformation Work for Growth and Well-being".

Marie-Therese PNG

is a PhD candidate at the Oxford Internet Institute, researching AI governance and contestations led by technology activists and civil society. She was previously Technology Advisor to the UN Secretary General's High Level Panel on Digital Cooperation, leading multi-stakeholder coalition building and strategic geographic representation. Marie-Therese has worked with Google DeepMind on AI value alignment, and is a member of the IEEE Ethically Aligned AI Classical Ethics Committee. Her research includes facial recognition systems in Singapore's smart city ecosystem, neurotechnology ethics at the MIT Media Lab, and international AI policy with the Harvard AI Initiative.

WANG Xiaohong

received her PhD in the Philosophy of Science and Technology from Peking University in 2004. She is Fulbright Visiting Research Scholar (IU, 2006-2007). Presently, she works in the Department of Philosophy at Xi'an Jiaotong University as the codirector and is a professor in the Research Center for Computational Philosophy. She also serves as a member of the Big Data & AI Working Group of World Federation of Engineering Organizations (WFEO) (since 2019) and an executive committee member of the China Scientific Methodology Commission (since 2011). Professor Wang's research concerns the philosophy of cognitive science. She is particularly interested in the philosophy of AI machine discovery, computational analyses of Chinese philosophy, information ethics and the integration of science and the humanities.

Anand S. RAO

Anand is a Partner in PwC Advisory, with over 32 years of experience in industry and in research. He leads PwC's Artificial Intelligence efforts globally and is the Innovation Lead for the Emerging Technology Group. He is responsible for a team of practitioners who work with C-level executives, advising them on a range of topics including global growth strategies, marketing, sales, distribution and digital strategies, behavioral economics and customer experience, risk management and statistical and computational analytics. His experience spans primarily financial services, insurance, telecommunications, and healthcare. He lived and worked at clients in Asia, Australia, Europe and Americas. Anand is responsible for research and commercial relationships with academic institutions and start-ups focused on new and innovative big data and analytic techniques. With his PhD and research career in Artificial Intelligence and subsequent experience in

陈定定

暨南大学国际关系学院教授，博士研究生导师，21 世纪丝绸之路研究院副院长。著名社会智库海国图智研究院创始人兼院长。曾任国际研究协会（ISA）亚太区副会长（2014—2018），现兼任德国全球公共政策研究所客座研究员、清华大学全球化研究中心高级研究员。研究方向包括中国外交政策、亚洲安全、中国政治和人权。

马拉维卡·杰亚拉姆

新加坡管理大学法学院的执业助理教授和李光前法学研究员。她还是哈佛大学伯克曼·克莱因互联网与社会中心（BKC）的教员和 BKC 孵化的独立研究智库数字亚洲研究中心的首届执行董事。她拥有超过 15 年的技术律师从业经验，曾在伦敦安理国际律师事务所执业，还曾任花旗集团伦敦办事处的副总裁兼技术顾问。马拉维卡毕业于印度德里国立法律大学，拥有芝加哥西北大学的法学硕士学位。她曾是宾夕法尼亚大学安嫩伯格传播学院的访问学者，还曾在悉尼大学和里约热内卢技术与社会研究所担任研究员。1997 年，她负责教授印度首次开设的信息技术与法律课程。马拉维卡曾是 IEEE 全球自主和智能系统伦理倡议执行委员会的委员，以及查塔姆研究所（英国皇家国际事务研究所）亚太项目的副研究员。她还是经合组织项目“走向数字化：通过数字化转型促进经济增长和福利水平”高级专家顾问组成员。

方淑霞

牛津互联网研究所博士生，主要研究技术活动家和民间社会主导的人工智能治理及其讨论。她曾是联合国秘书长数字合作高级别小组的技术顾问，领导多方利益相关者联盟的建立和战略地域代表性的实现。方淑霞曾与谷歌 DeepMind 公司在人工智能价值一致性方面展开合作。此外，她还是电气与电子工程师学会合乎伦理的人工智能伦理标准委员会成员。方淑霞曾对新加坡智慧城市生态系统中的人脸识别系统展开研究，曾在麻省理工学院媒体实验室研究神经技术伦理以及哈佛人工智能倡议的国际人工智能政策。

王小红

北京大学科学技术哲学博士（CSSS，2004），富布赖特高级访问学者（IU，2006—2007），现任职西安交通大学哲学系，计算哲学研究中心主任、教授。兼任世界工程组织联合会（WFEO）“大数据和 AI 工作组”专家（2019 年至今）、中国自然辩证法研究会方法论委员会常务理事（2011 年至今）。主要研究领域是认知科学哲学，尤其是人工智能机器发现哲学、中国哲学文本的计算建模分析，也关注信息伦理学、科学人文融合。

安纳德·劳

普华永道咨询公司合伙人之一，拥有超过 32 年的行业经验和研究经验，负责领导普华永道的全球人工智能工作，是新兴技术小组的创新负责人。安纳德负责带领一个与高层管理人员合作的专业团队，为他们提供有关全球增长战略、营销、销售、分销和数字战略、行为经济学和客户体验、风险管理，以及统计和计算分析等一系列主题的咨询建议。他曾在亚洲、澳大利亚、欧洲和美洲工作和生活，从业经验主要涵盖金融服务、保险、电信和医疗健康领域。安纳德负责与专注于新型创新大数据和分析技术的学术机构与初创企业建立研究和商业关系。凭借其人工智能博士学位和人工智能研究经验，以及后续获得的管理咨询经验，他独到地结合了商业领域的经验与统计和计算分析专业知识，对“数据科学”理论和实践拥有独特的见解。在开始从事战略咨询服务前，他曾引导并有效使用了针对空战建模、空中交通管制、客户服务决策支持和电信网络管理的创新人工智能方法。此外，他还在墨尔本大学负责教授和指导博士生，并担任智能决策系统中心的项目主任。安纳德与他人合编过 4 本著作，并在各类会议和期刊上发表过 50 多篇同行评议论文。他经常在关于分析学、人工智能、行为经济学和创新等主题的技术和商业论坛上发表演讲，也曾在国际期刊、会议和研讨会的组织计划委员会任职。

阿布辛克·库布塔

蒙特利尔人工智能伦理研究所(MAIEI)创始人，微软机器学习工程师，微软商业软件工程(CSE)负责任的人工智能董事会成员。他的著作《可操作的人工智能伦理》（*Actionable AI Ethics*）即将出版，该作将成为人工智能伦理的实用操作指南。阿布辛克是美国国务院国际访问者领导项目的人工智能伦理访问研究员、美国西北高校委员会数据咨询委员会的负责任 AI 主管、道森学院人工智能咨询委员会成员，Linux 基金会下属人工智能基金会（LF AI）准会员，以及歌德大学法兰克福大数据实验室教员。其研究侧重于应用技术和政策方法，在不同领域使用人工智能来解决伦理、安全和包容性问题。他建立了世界上最大的社区驱动型人工智能伦理公共咨询小组，为负责任人工智能领域中许多倡议的制定做出了重大贡献。

贾里德·布朗

生命未来研究所（FLI）政府事务高级顾问，全球灾难风险研究所政府事务特别顾问。他致力于研究公共政策和风险管理的交叉领域，此前曾在美国国会研究服务局担任应急管理和国土安全政策分析师，并在美国交通部担任国土安全分析师。贾里德拥有乔治城大学公共政策硕士学位和加州大学圣地亚哥分校社会心理学学士学位。

management consulting, he brings a unique combination of business domain experience, statistical, and computational analytics expertise to generate unique insights into the theory and practice of "data science". Prior to his strategic consulting career, he has led and managed innovative artificial-intelligence based approaches for air-combat modeling, air-traffic management, customer service decision support, and telecommunications network management. He has also taught and supervised doctoral students at the University of Melbourne and served as the Program Director of the Center for Intelligent Decision Systems. He has co-edited four books, published over fifty peer-reviewed papers in conferences and journals. He frequently speaks at technology and business forums on analytics, AI, behavioral economics, and innovation; served on the Organizing and Program Committees of International Journals, Conferences, and Workshops.

Abhishek GUPTA

is the founder of the Montreal AI Ethics Institute (MAIEI) and a Machine-Learning Engineer at Microsoft, where he serves on the CSE Responsible AI Board. He is the author of the forthcoming book *Actionable AI Ethics*, which will be a practical and hands-on guide for operationalizing AI ethics. He is a Visiting AI Ethics Researcher in the Future of Work in the International Visitor Leadership Program with the U.S. Department of State, the Responsible AI Lead at the Data Advisory Council for the Northwest Commission on Colleges and Universities, AI Advisory Board Member for Dawson College, Associate Member of the LF AI Foundation at The Linux Foundation, and Faculty Associate in the Frankfurt Big Data Lab at Goethe University. Abhishek's research focuses on applied technical and policy methods to address ethical, safety and inclusivity concerns using AI in different domains. He has built the largest community-driven, public consultation group on AI ethics in the world that has made significant contributions to the development of many initiatives in the domain of responsible AI. More information about his work can be found at https://atg-abhishek.github.io.

Jared BROWN

is the Senior Advisor for Government Affairs at the Future of Life Institute. He is also a Special Advisor for Government Affairs at the Global Catastrophic Risk Institute. He has spent his career working at the intersection of public policy and risk management, having previously served as an Analyst in Emergency Management and Homeland Security Policy at the U.S. Congressional Research Service and in homeland security at the U.S. Department of Transportation. He has earned a Master of Public Policy from Georgetown University and a B.S. in Social Psychology from the University of California, San Diego.

Irene SOLAIMAN

is a Public Policy Manager at OpenAI. She leads policymaker engagement and conducts social impact and fairness analysis. Prior to OpenAI, she was a fellow at Harvard's Berkman Klein Center as part of the Assembly Student Fellowship researching the ethics and governance of AI. Irene holds a Master in Public Policy from the Harvard Kennedy School and a B.A. in International Relations from the University of Maryland where she was elected Phi Beta Kappa.

YIN Qi

is a cofounder and CEO of Megvii Technology Limited, a world-class AI company with core competencies in deep learning. He chairs the company's board-level AI Ethics Committee, which is committed to positively contributing to society with Megvii's AI technology. Yin is a member of the National New Generation Artificial Intelligence Governance Expert Committee, an expert committee established by China's Ministry of Science and Technology engaged in research on AI-related laws, ethics, standards and social issues and international exchanges and cooperation on AI-related governance. Yin was a member of the 2019 Young Global Leaders of the World Economic Forum. He was named in Fortune's "40 under 40" list of Chinese elites for three consecutive years and was ranked No. 1 on Forbes Asia's "30 under 30" Enterprise Technology entrepreneurs. The MIT Technology Review has also included him in their global "Innovators under 35" list.

YANG Fan

is currently Vice President, Co-Founder and Chairman of the AI Ethics & Governance Committee of SenseTime, where he is in charge of the planning and development of SenseTime's ecosystem and integration with other industries. Before joining SenseTime, he worked at Microsoft Research Asia (MSRA) for many years. At MSRA, he was actively engaged in the research and development of new technologies, many of which are widely applied in Microsoft's flagship products worldwide. He has accumulated rich experience in planning and implementing the commercialization of cutting-edge technologies. Since the foundation of SenseTime, Yang Fan has led the company to successfully practice the innovative business model of "AI+Industry" in industries such as smartphones, retailing, and smart cities and has empowered the engineering and tech team of SenseTime to develop a comprehensive methodology that covers the full cycle from the underlying fundamental architecture to technological industrialization. In industrial practice, he spearheaded AI commercialization in financial technology and internet entertainment; masterminded the overall AI layout and its exponential growth in the smart city industry; and was the first to put forward and implement the concept of a city-level video analysis center, leading SenseTime to become the pacesetter in this field. In terms of business promotion, he led a team in establishing major cooperation with strategic customers such as China Mobile, Huawei, Xiaomi, and Honda. It was also his decisiveness and leadership that lead to SenseTime's successfully applying for the intelligent vision project of China's National Open Innovative Platform for Next-generation AI. Mr. YANG is an engineering PhD candidate at the Innovation Leadership Program at Tsinghua University, where he also received his bachelor's and master's degrees from the Department of Electronic Engineering. He holds 13 PCT patents, 2 Chinese invention patents, and 2 Chinese utility model patents. He is currently an expert with the Industry Expert Consultant Library of Shenzhen Stock Exchange and the AI Expert Library of MIIT, Member of the Overall Expert Group on AI Social Experimentation of MOST, Managing Director of the Chinese Association for Artificial Intelligence, Vice President of the

艾琳·索拉曼

OpenAI 政策研究员，负责引导政策制定者参与相关事务，并进行社会影响和公平性分析。在加入 OpenAI 之前，她是哈佛大学伯克曼·克莱因中心（BKC）的研究员，作为大会学生奖学金的成员研究人工智能的伦理和治理问题。艾琳拥有哈佛大学肯尼迪学院公共政策硕士学位和马里兰大学国际关系学士学位，她在马里兰大学被选为美国大学优等生协会会员。

印奇

旷视科技联合创始人兼首席执行官。旷视科技是一家世界级的人工智能企业，深度学习是企业的核心竞争力。他还担任公司董事会下设人工智能道德委员会主席一职，确保旷视技术为社会带来积极的影响。印奇是科技部组织成立的国家新一代人工智能治理专业委员会委员，委员会旨在进一步加强人工智能相关法律、伦理、标准和社会问题研究，并深入参与人工智能相关治理的国际交流合作。印奇曾获评世界经济论坛“2019 年全球青年领袖”，并连续三年入选《财富》“中国 40 位 40 岁以下的商界精英”，入选福布斯“30U30 亚洲青年领袖”，以及《麻省理工科技评论》“全球 35 岁以下科技创新 35 人”等榜单。

杨帆

商汤科技副总裁、联合创始人，商汤科技 AI 伦理与治理委员会主席。目前负责商汤的生态体系与产业协同的规划建设。加入商汤前，杨帆曾长期就职于微软亚洲研究院，其间参与研发的技术均被广泛应用于微软全球主要产品中，积累了丰富的尖端技术产品化的路径规划经验和实践经验。自商汤成立以来，杨帆带领团队在手机、零售、智慧城市等行业成功实践“AI+ 产业”的创新业务模式，并赋能商汤工程技术团队沉淀从组建基础架构到技术产业化的整体方法论。行业实践中，他主导推动 AI 在金融科技领域及互联网娱乐领域的产品化过程，决策推动 AI 在智慧城市行业裂变增长的整体布局，首提并落地城市级视频分析中心概念，成功打造行业第一品牌。商务推进中，杨帆带领团队先后与中国移动、华为、小米、本田等战略客户达成重大合作，并决策主导集团成功申请智能视觉国家新一代人工智能开放创新平台项目。清华大学创新领军工程博士在读，本科硕士毕业于清华大学电子工程系，在研发领域，拥有国际专利（PCT）13 项，国内发明专利 2 项，实用新型专利 2 项。现任深圳证券交易所行业咨询专家库专家，工信部人工智能专家库专家，科技部人工智能社会实验总体专家组专家，中国人工智能学会常务理事，中国青年科技工作者协会副会长，中国电子学会中国数字经济百人会执行委员，中国电子学会虚拟 / 增强现实技术与产业分会委员。他亦于 2016 年当选“北京市优秀青年人才”。

贺尚安

莱弗哈姆未来智能中心（Leverhulme Centre for the Future of Intelligence）“人工智能：未来与责任计划（AI：FAR）”负责人，该中心是一个探索人工智能机遇与挑战的跨学科中心。AI：FAR 计划重点关注与人工智能有关的远见、安全和治理问题。同时，他还是剑桥大学生存风险研究中心（CSER）联合主任，该研究中心致力于研究新兴的全球风险和长期挑战。贺尚安的研究涉及于人工智能和其他新兴技术的影响、愿景扫描和预见，以及这些技术带来的全球风险。2011—2015 年，他在牛津大学人类未来研究所领导开展了关于这些课题的研究项目，2014—2019 年，他担任剑桥大学生存风险研究中心的创始执行主任，参与创立了战略人工智能研究中心和莱弗哈姆未来智能中心。他与史提芬·凯夫（Stephen Cave）合著的论文《人工智能竞赛：益处与风险》（An AI Race: Rhetoric and Risks）最近在首届人工智能伦理与社会会议上获得了最佳论文奖。此外，他拥有都柏林三一学院基因组进化学博士学位。

张建伟

德国汉堡大学信息学科学系教授及多模态技术研究所（TAMS）所长。他于 1986 年以优异的成绩获得清华大学计算机系工程学士学位、于 1989 年获得该系的工程硕士学位，此后又于 1994 年获得德国卡尔斯鲁厄大学计算机系实时计算机系统与机器人研究所的博士学位。其研究方向包括认知传感器融合、稳定机器人感知、智能机器人架构、多模态人机交互、机器人的灵巧操作以及类脑机器学习等。他在这些领域发表了超过 400 篇期刊论文、会议论文和技术报告，并出版过 6 本著作。他在智能组件和系统领域拥有超过 40 项专利。他的研究成果已被应用于现实场景中的机器人系统，例如医疗助理系统、康复系统、先进 3C 组装系统、工业流程在线质量监控系统等。张建伟是德国研究联合会（DFG）与国家自然科学基金委员会（NSFC）联合发起的跨区域合作研究中心 SFB/TRR169“跨模态学习”项目，以及一些欧盟、德国和工业 AI 项目的协调人，获有多项最佳论文奖。他是 2012 年电气与电子工程师学会（IEEE）多传感器融合与集成智能系统国际会议、2015 年智能机器人与系统国际会议，以及 2018 年以人为本的机器人与系统国际研讨会的大会主席。此外，他还是德国汉堡科学院的终身院士。

奥马·科斯提拉·雷耶斯

麻省理工学院计算机科学与人工智能实验室（CSAIL）计算机辅助小组（CAP）研究科学家，医学工程与科学研究所（IMES）研究员，大脑与认知科学学院研究员。他的研究领域涵盖医疗保健、人工智能、教育和拉丁美洲。他是麻省理工学院博士后协会现任副主席。在目前着手进行的研究中，他专注于设计经过数字验证的新一代人工智能医疗保健解决方案。雷耶斯拥有英国曼彻斯特大学博士学位，他的博士论文主要研究人工智能在医疗保健和生物测定领域的应用。他创立了人工智能拉丁美洲峰会并担任主席，该峰会的目标是激励拉美地区政府、工业界和学术界的领导人投资和开发人工智能，以造福社会。

潘竞宏

新加坡科技设计大学（SUTD）李光耀创新型城市中心主任，同时也是该校战略规划高级主管。潘竞宏是世界经济论坛城市与城市化专

Chinese Association of Young Scientists and Technologists, Executive Committee Member of China Committee of 100 of Digital Economy of the Chinese Institute of Electronics, and Committee Member of the VR/AR Technology and Industry Branch of the Chinese Institute of Electronics. He was awarded "Beijing Outstanding Young Talent" in 2016.

Seán Ó hÉigeartaigh

is the Director of the AI: Futures and Responsibility programme (AI: FAR) at the Leverhulme Centre for the Future of Intelligence (CFI), an interdisciplinary centre that explores the opportunities and challenges of artificial intelligence. The AI: FAR programme focuses on foresight, security and governance related to artificial intelligence. He is also the Co-Director of Cambridge's Centre for the Study of Existential Risk (CSER), a research centre focused on emerging global risks and long-term challenges. Seán's research spans the impacts of artificial intelligence and other emerging technologies, horizon-scanning and foresight, and global risk. He led research programmes on these topics at the Future of Humanity Institute (Oxford) from 2011-2015, was founding Executive Director of the Centre for the Study of Existential Risk from 2014-2019, and co-developed both the Strategic AI Research Centre, and the Leverhulme Centre for the Future of Intelligence. His paper An AI Race: Rhetoric and Risks (with Stephen Cave) recently won joint best paper at the inaugural AI Ethics and Society Conference. He has a PhD in genome evolution from Trinity College Dublin.

ZHANG Jianwei

is a professor at and director of TAMS, Department of Informatics, University of Hamburg, Germany. He received both his Bachelor of Engineering (1986, with distinction) and Master of Engineering (1989) from the Department of Computer Science of Tsinghua University, Beijing, China, and his PhD (1994) at the Institute of Real-Time Computer Systems and Robotics, Department of Computer Science, University of Karlsruhe, Germany. His research interests are cognitive sensor fusion, robust robot perception, intelligent robot architecture, multimodal human–robot interaction, dexterous robot manipulation, brain-inspired machine learning, etc. In these areas, he has published over 400 journal and conference papers and technical reports as well as six books. He holds more than 40 patents on intelligent components and systems. His research results have been applied in robotic systems for real-world scenarios such as medical assistance, rehabilitation, advanced 3C assembly, online quality monitoring of industrial processes, etc. ZHANG Jianwei is coordinator of the DFG/NSFC Transregional Collaborative Research Centre SFB/TRR169 "Crossmodal Learning" and several EU, German and industrial AI projects. He has received multiple best paper awards. He is the General Chair of IEEE MFI 2012, IEEE/RSJ IROS 2015, and the International Symposium of Human-Centered Robotics and Systems 2018. He is a life-long Academician of the Academy of Sciences in Hamburg, Germany.

Omar COSTILLA-REYES

is a research scientist at the computer aided group (CAP) of the computer science and artificial intelligence laboratory (CSAIL) of the Massachusetts Institute of Technology (MIT). He was a researcher at the Institute for Medical and Engineering Science (IMES) and the Brain and Cognitive Sciences Department at MIT. Omar's interests are in digital health care, artificial intelligence, education, and Latin America. He was the vice-president of the MIT postdoctoral association. In his current research, Omar focuses on designing the next generation of artificial intelligence methodologies for digital health care. Omar obtained his PhD from the University of Manchester in England. His PhD thesis focused on deep learning in health care and biometrics in gait analysis. He is the founder and president of the Artificial Intelligence Latin American Summit. The goal of the summit is to incentivize leaders of the Latin American region in government, industry, and academia to invest in and develop artificial intelligence for social benefit.

POON King Wang

is the Director of the Lee Kuan Yew Centre for Innovative Cities at the Singapore University of Technology and Design (SUTD). He is concurrently Senior Director of Strategic Planning at SUTD. He is on the World Economic Forum's Expert Network on Cities and Urbanisation, Konrad Adenauer Stiftung's Strong Cities 2030 Network, and Global Partnership on AI's Future of Work working group. He was on two national taskforces on the future of adult learning, and on future digital economy services. He co-authored Living Digital 2040: Future of Work, Education, and Healthcare, which was also translated into Korean.

Steven HOFFMAN

or Captain Hoff as he is called in Silicon Valley, is the Chairman & CEO of Founders Space (FoundersSpace.com), one of the world's leading incubators and accelerators. He is also an angel investor, limited partner at August Capital, serial entrepreneur, and author of several award-winning books. These include Make Elephants Fly (MakeElephantsFly.com), Surviving a Startup (SurvivingAStartup.com), and The Five Forces (FiveForcesBook.com).

LUAN Qun

joined the China Center for Information Industry Development in 2011 as the Director of the Institute of Policy and Law, holding a PhD in Civil and Commercial Law from the China University of Political Science and Law. He is an industry expert in civil and commercial law and industrial economy and policy and leads the Legal Services Centre for Industry and Informatization. His recent consulting work has centered on industry strategy, business development and supervision, with a special focus on autonomous vehicles, industrial data and manufacturing. He has carried out successful projects for industrial development planning and the interpretation of industrial policy in Inner Mongolia, Henan and Shandong Provinces. He has published more than 50 articles in Learning Times, China Economy and Informatization, Modern Industrial Economy, Economic Daily, China Electronic Journal, and other magazines and newspapers.

家网络、德国阿登纳基金会强大城市 2030 网络，以及人工智能全球伙伴关系未来工作工作组的成员。他还曾是新加坡未来成人教育工作组和未来数字经济服务工作组的成员。此外，他还与人合著了《2040 数字生活：工作、教育和医疗健康的未来》（Living Digital 2040: Future of Work, Education, and Healthcare），该书也被翻译成韩文。

史蒂文·霍夫曼

在硅谷被称为霍夫曼船长（Captain Hoff），是全球领先的孵化器和加速器公司创始人空间（Founders Space）的董事长兼首席执行官。同时，他还是天使投资人、奥格斯特资本（August Capital）的有限合伙人和连续创业者。史蒂文·霍夫曼著有多本备受赞誉的著作，其中包括《让大象飞》（Make Elephants Fly）、《穿越寒冬》（Surviving A Startup）以及《五种力量》（The Five Forces）。

栾群

中国政法大学民商法博士，于 2011 年加入中国电子信息产业发展研究院，现任政策法规研究所所长。工业经济政策和法规方面的行业专家，并主管工业和信息化法律服务中心。近来咨询工作主要集中在行业战略、产业发展和行业监管方面，特别关注自动驾驶汽车、工业数据和制造业。他曾在内蒙古、河南、山东等地成功开展产业发展规划和产业政策解读项目。在《学习时报》、《中国经济与信息化》、《现代产业经济》、《经济日报》、《中国电子报》等报刊杂志上发表文章 50 余篇。

郭锐

中国人民大学法学院副教授，未来法治研究院研究员，社会责任和治理研究中心主任。郭锐博士的研究包括公司法、金融法、人权法、人工智能伦理与治理等。他毕业于中国政法大学（法学学士、硕士）和哈佛大学法学院（法学硕士、法学博士）。他担任国家信息标准化委员会人工智能专业委员会委员、全国标准化委员会人工智能总体组社会伦理研究负责人，他参与了中国第一个以人工智能标准化为主题的白皮书的写作并撰写“安全、隐私和伦理”部分（《人工智能标准化白皮书（2018）》已于 2018 年发布），并主持撰写了国家标准委人工智能总体组《人工智能伦理风险研究》报告（2019 年 5 月发布）。

傅莹

清华大学战略与安全研究中心主任、第十三届全国人大外事委员会副主任委员。傅莹 1978 年进入中国外交部，曾长期从事亚洲事务方面的工作，在外交部任亚洲司处长、参赞等职，1992 年参加联合国在柬埔寨的维和行动，1997 年任驻印度尼西亚使馆公使衔参赞，1998 年任驻菲律宾大使，2000 年任外交部亚洲司司长，2004 年任驻澳大利亚大使，2007 年任驻英国大使，2009—2013 年任外交部副部长，先后负责欧洲和亚洲事务。2013 年，傅莹当选为第十二届全国人大代表；2018 年当选为第十三届全国人大代表。2013 年至 2018 年任第十二届全国人大外事委员会主任委员和第十二届全国人大第一次至第五次会议新闻发言人。2018 年任第十三届全国人大外事委员会副主任委员。2018 年兼任清华大学战略与安全研究中心主任、清华大学兼职教授。2020 年受聘为清华大学人工智能国际治理研究院名誉院长。

赵志耘

经济学博士，研究员，博士生导师，现任科技部中国科学技术信息研究所党委书记，兼任科技部新一代人工智能发展研究中心主任，国务院政府特殊津贴获得者。她是著名的经济理论和政策、科技管理和政策方面的领军人才。她对新兴技术和产业发展具有独特见解。她非常重视人工智能治理问题，并致力于推动中国与其他国家的相关研究与合作。她在理论体系的建设、技术进步的促进和相关学科建设方面都取得了突出成就。出版学术专著 30 余部，译著 4 部，发表学术论文 130 余篇。作为首席研究员，主持国家、省部级科研项目近 30 项，包括国家重点研发项目、国家科技支撑计划项目、国家软科学重大项目。

段伟文

中国社科院哲学所科技哲学研究室主任、研究员，中国社科院科学技术和社会研究中心主任，中国社科院大学特聘教授；主要研究领域为科学哲学、信息技术哲学，近年来关注大数据与人工智能的哲学、伦理和社会研究；曾赴牛津大学、科罗拉多矿业大学、匹兹堡大学访问研究；现任国际期刊《社会中的信息、通信与伦理杂志》、《负责任创新杂志》编委，中国大数据专家委员会副主任委员；主持多项社科基金研究项目，目前为国家社科基金重大项目“智能革命与人类深度科技化前景的哲学研究”首席专家，著有《可接受的科学：当代科学基础的反思》、《网络空间的伦理反思》、《被捆绑的时间：技术与人的生活世界》等。

王迎春

博士，现为上海市科学学研究所科技与社会研究室主任，主要研究领域为创新变革与创新治理、科学技术与社会。他牵头组织了由多学科专家参与的人工智能研究组，对人工智能进行系统研究。承担了多项科技部和上海市委托的咨询项目，多次参与政府人工智能相关工作调研和政策起草。参与策划组织了上海世界人工智能大会治理论坛。目前同时负责上海国家新一代人工智能创新发展试验区专家咨询委员会秘书处工作。

GUO Rui

is Associate Professor of Law at Renmin University of China, researcher at RUC's Institute of Law and Technology, and Director of the Center for Social Responsibility and Governance. Dr. Guo Rui studies corporate law, financial regulations, human rights, and the ethics of AI. He graduated from China University of Political Science and Law (LL. B & LL. M) and Harvard Law School (LL. M & S.J.D). Professor Guo Rui is a member of the Subcommittee of User Interface, National Standardization Committee of Information Technology, and the Lead Expert for the Research Group on the Ethics of Artificial Intelligence appointed by the Artificial Intelligence Working Group, Standardization Administration of the People's Republic of China (SAC). He helped draft the first AI standardization white paper (published in 2018) and led the drafting of the AI Ethical Risks of AI Research Report (published in May 2019 by Artificial Intelligence Working Group, SAC).

FU Ying

is Chairperson, Center for International Security and Strategy, Tsinghua University (CISS). She is Vice-Chairperson of the Foreign Affairs Committee of China's 13th National People's Congress (NPC). Fu Ying started her career with China's Ministry of Foreign Affairs (MFA) in 1978 and has long engaged in Asian affairs. She served successively as Director of Division and Counselor in Asian Affairs Department of MFA. In 1992, she joined the UN peace-keeping mission in Cambodia. She was appointed Minister Counselor at the Chinese Embassy in Indonesia in 1997, Chinese Ambassador to the Philippines in 1998, and Director General of the Asian Department of MFA in 2000. She was then appointed Ambassador to Australia (2004-2007) and Ambassador to the United Kingdom (2007-2009). She served as Vice Minister of Foreign Affairs for European Affairs and then for Asian Affairs (2009-2013). Fu Ying was elected deputy to China's 12th (2013) and then 13th (2018) National People's Congress (NPC). She was the Chairperson of the Foreign Affairs Committee and spokesperson of the 12th NPC (2013-2018). She is now Vice-Chairperson of the Foreign Affairs Committee of China's 13th NPC (2018-2023). Fu Ying has also served as the Chair for the Center for International Security and Strategy (CISS) since 2018 and was appointed an adjunct professor at Tsinghua University in 2018. She was appointed the Honorary Dean of the Institute for AI International Governance of Tsinghua University (I-AIIG) in 2020.

ZHAO Zhiyun

is a PhD in Economics, Professor, Doctoral Supervisor, the Party Committee Secretary of the Institute of Science and Technology Information of China (ISTIC), Director of New-Generation Artificial Intelligence Development Research Center of Ministry of Science and Technology of the People's Republic of China (MOST). Zhao Zhiyun works under the Special Government Allowance provided by the State Council. She is a leading talent in economic theories and policies as well as S&T management and policies. In particular, she has unique insights into emerging technology and industrial development. She pays great attention to the issue of AI governance and focuses on promoting related research and cooperation between China and other countries. She has won outstanding achievements in the construction of theoretical systems, in the promotion of technological progress, and in related disciplinary constructions. She has published more than 30 academic monographs, 4 Chinese translations, and more than 130 academic papers. As a principal investigator, she is in charge of nearly 30 national, provincial and ministerial research projects, including the National Key Research and Development Project, National Sci-Tech Support Plan and National Soft Science Major Project.

DUAN Weiwen

is the Director and Professor of the Department of Philosophy of Science and Technology at the Institute of Philosophy, Chinese Academy of Social Sciences (CASS), and he is a Distinguished Professor at the University of CASS and the Director of the Research Center for Science, Technology and Society, CASS. He holds a Bachelor of Science in Physics from Central China Normal University and a Master of Philosophy and PhD in the Philosophy of Science and Technology from Renmin University of China. He specializes in the philosophy of science, the philosophy of information technology, etc. In recent years, he has focused on the philosophical, ethical and social research of big data and AI. He was a visiting scholar at Oxford University (with Luciano Floridi), the Colorado School of Mines (with Carl Mitcham), and the University of Pittsburgh (with Edouard Machery). He is on the editorial board of the Journal of Information, Communication and Ethics in Society and the Journal of Responsible Innovation, and he is one of the deputy chairmen of the Committee of Big Data Experts of China. He is now the chief researcher and project leader of several important and general social science fund research projects, including Philosophical Studies on Intelligence Revolution and Deepening Techno-scientific of Human Being (2017-2022), which is supported by the National Social Sciences Founding of China (NSSFC). He is the author of several books, including Acceptable Science: Reflection on the Foundation of Contemporary Science, Ethical Reflection on Cyberspace, and Truss up Time: Technology and Life World.

WANG Yingchun

is a PhD and Head of Research, Department of Science, Technology and Society at Shanghai Institute for Science of Science; his areas of expertise include innovation transformation and innovation governance and science, technology and society. He initiated and organized a multidisciplinary AI research group to conduct systematic research on AI. He has undertaken a number of consulting projects entrusted to him by the Ministry of Science and Technology and the government of Shanghai municipality and has continuously participated in the research and policy drafting of the government's AI policy. He led the organizing work of the Governance Forum under World AI Conference in Shanghai. He is also responsible for managing the Secretariat of the Expert Advisory Committee of the National New-generation AI Innovation and Development Pilot Zone in Shanghai.

Arisa EMA

is Assistant Professor at the University of Tokyo and Visiting Researcher at the RIKEN Center for Advanced Intelligence Project in Japan. She

江间有沙

东京大学助理教授，日本理化学研究所高级情报项目中心访问研究员。她是一名科学技术学（STS）研究者，主要工作是通过组织一个跨学科研究小组来研究人工智能的效益和风险。她是可接受的负责任人工智能研究小组（AIR）的联合创始人，该小组成立于 2014 年，旨在应对人工智能和社会之间的新兴问题和关系。江间有沙是日本人工智能学会（JSAI）伦理委员会的成员，该学会于 2017 年发布了 JSAI 伦理指南。她还是日本深度学习协会（JDLA）董事会的成员，担任人工智能治理研究小组的主席。此外，她也是日本内阁府以人类为中心的人工智能社会原则委员会成员，该委员会于 2019 年发布了《以人类为中心的人工智能社会原则》。她拥有东京大学博士学位，此前曾任京都大学白眉（Hakubi）高级研究中心助理教授。

高丹青

联合国秘书长数字合作高级别小组技术顾问。她的主要研究方向是技术伦理、地缘政治、治理、安全和保障之间的交叉领域。此前，她曾是日本东京庆应大学全球研究所网络文明研究中心的项目助理教授。高丹青是自主和半自主系统故障安全设计标准（IEEE P7009）的主持人，并在 IEEE 全球自主和智能系统伦理倡议执行委员会任职。她是剑桥大学莱弗哈姆未来智能中心副研究员，普林斯顿大学信息技术政策中心成员。

吴亦涵

新加坡管理大学法学教授。他的主要研究集中在合同法和侵权法，其次是对法定解释原则和法律程序的研究。他在国际上和新加坡国内出版了大量著作、文章和期刊论文，并被新加坡法院和马来西亚联邦法院多次引用。他被任命为新加坡最高法院的高级律师，以及新加坡上诉法院和新加坡高等法院的法庭之友。为了表彰他对新加坡法律的发展和进步的突出贡献，新加坡法律学会在 2013 年为他颁发了新加坡法律功勋奖，使其成为第五位，也是最年轻的获奖者。2006 年，他在大学本科奖学金的资助下以优异的成绩从新加坡国立大学毕业，并获得法学学士学位（一等荣誉）。2010 年，他又在新加坡国立大学海外研究生奖学金的资助下获得了哈佛大学法学学位。

尼地·阿莫林

新加坡管理大学兼职教授，人工智能和数据治理中心的研究助理，拥有斯坦福大学法学硕士学位，苏黎世大学的法学博士生，拥有十多年的金融服务行业的经验。尼地是苏黎世大学瑞士金融科技创新实验室成员，还是哥伦比亚银行（Grupo Bancolombia）的政策事务经理、经济合作与发展组织（OECD）的高级顾问，以及美国苏利文·克伦威尔律师事务所（纽约办事处）的外籍律师。她曾在美国、亚洲、欧洲和拉丁美洲多个学术机构任教或演讲，包括国际货币基金组织（IMF）、国际证券监督管理委员会组织（IOSCO）、美国证券交易委员会（SEC）和新加坡金融管理局（MAS）。她的主要工作和学术研究领域包括金融和银行监管、证券监管、金融科技、法律科技，以及法律、金融和技术的交叉领域。

乌尔瓦希·阿内贾

跨学科研究网络数字未来实验室主任，该实验室致力于研究发展中国家中技术与社会因素之间复杂相互作用。目前，她的研究重点是人工智能伦理与政策、大型科技企业与平台管理，以及数字零工经济下的员工福利。此外，乌尔瓦西还是查塔姆研究所亚太项目的副研究员，以及孟买印度理工学院的研究员。她的研究成果已被全国乃至全球领先的媒体出版物引用，而她本人也受印度政府委任，担任多个人工智能和前沿技术专家委员会的委员。

拉杰·谢卡尔

AI 政策交流所的创始人兼执行董事。AI 政策交流所是由从事 AI 和公共政策交叉领域工作的个人和机构组成的国际合作协会，致力于提供有助于创造 AI 文化社会，并制定更好 AI 政策的成果。作为印度软件和服务公司协会（NASSCOM）数据科学和人工智能卓越中心（K-Tech）的负责任人工智能主管，拉吉一直在推动 NASSCOM 的工作，为在印度广泛推广和采用负责任的人工智能制定路线图。此外，拉吉还是未来协会成员，施普林格·自然集团下属的《人工智能和伦理》（AI and Ethics）的创始期刊编委会的成员。在加入 NASSCOM 之前，拉吉是芝加哥大学国际创新小组（IIC）的数据和 AI 顾问，为金融公司——IDFC Institute 和 IIC 发起的开放数据工作小组（ODWG）倡议的运营，和由 IIC 和电子与信息技术部共同参与，旨在通过实施相关政策和项目来建立数据和 AI 创新能力的工作提供支持。拉杰还是加州大学伯克利分校社会利益信息技术研究中心政策实验室的关联学者，与布兰迪·农内克（Brandie Nonnecke）博士（创办负责人）合作进行有关 AI 治理的研究。2020 年，拉吉作为负责任技术生态系统的领导者出现在由非营利组织——All Tech Is Human 与纽约大学公共利益技术联盟合作推出的《负责任技术指南》（Responsible Tech Guide）中。2021 年，拉吉被 DataEthics4All 宣布为 DIET 捍卫者，以表彰他对团队和技术中的数据和多样性、包容和影响、道德和公平（DIET）的贡献。拉吉拥有拉姆·马诺哈尔·洛希亚（Ram Manohar Lohiya）博士国立法学院的法律和人文综合学士学位，以及印度大学国家法律学院公共政策研究所的公共政策硕士学位。

伊娃·凯利

欧洲议会议员，自 2014 年以来一直是希腊科技发展代表团成员。她是欧洲议会未来科技小组（STOA）和人工智能中心（C4AI）主席，以及欧洲议会工业、研究和能源委员会（ITRE）、经济和货币事务委员会（ECON）、预算委员会（BUDG）和数字时代人工智能特别委

is a researcher in Science and Technology Studies (STS), and her primary interest is to investigate the benefits and risks of artificial intelligence by organizing an interdisciplinary research group. She is a cofounder of the Acceptable Intelligence with Responsibility Study Group (AIR) established in 2014, which seeks to address emerging issues and relationships between artificial intelligence and society. She is a member of the Ethics Committee of the Japanese Society for Artificial Intelligence (JSAI), which released the JSAI Ethical Guidelines in 2017. She is also a board member of the Japan Deep-Learning Association (JDLA) and chairs AI governance study group. She was also a member of Council for Social Principles of Human-centric AI, The Cabinet Office, which released Social Principles of Human-Centric AI in 2019. She obtained her PhD from the University of Tokyo and previously held a position as Assistant Professor at the Hakubi Center for Advanced Research, Kyoto University.Professor at the Hakubi Center for Advanced Research, Kyoto University.

Danit GAL

is Technology Advisor to the UN Secretary General High-level Panel on Digital Cooperation. She is interested in the intersections between technology ethics, geopolitics, governance, safety, and security. Previously, she was Project Assistant Professor at the Cyber Civilizations Research Center at the Keio University Global Research Institute in Tokyo, Japan. Danit chairs the IEEE P7009 standard on the Fail-Safe Design of Autonomous and Semi-Autonomous Systems and serves on the executive committee of The IEEE Global Initiative on Ethics of Autonomous and Intelligent Systems. She is an Associate Fellow at the Leverhulme Centre for the Future of Intelligence at the University of Cambridge, and an Affiliate at the Center for Information Technology Policy at Princeton University.

GOH Yihan

is a Professor of Law of Singapore Management University. Goh's research focuses primarily on the law of contract and torts, with a secondary interest in the principles of statutory interpretation and the legal process. He has published numerous books, chapters and journal articles internationally and in Singapore, which have been cited on multiple occasions by the Singapore courts and the Federal Court of Malaysia. He has been appointed Senior Counsel of the Supreme Court of Singapore. He has also been designated amicus curiae before the Singapore Court of Appeal and the Singapore High Court. In recognition of his invaluable contributions to the development and advancement of Singapore law, he became the youngest recipient of the pentennial Singapore Academy of Law Singapore Law Merit Award in 2013. He obtained his LL.B. (First Class Honours) from the National University of Singapore on a University Undergraduate Scholarship, where he graduated as the top student in 2006. He subsequently obtained a LL.M. from Harvard University in 2010 on a NUS University Overseas Graduate Scholarship.

Nydia REMOLINA

is a Research Associate at the Singapore Management University's Centre for AI and Data Governance and an Adjunct Faculty at Singapore Management University. She holds a Master of the Science of Law from Stanford University, is a PhD in Law Candidate at the University of Zurich, and has more than ten years of experience in the financial services industry. Nydia is a member of the Swiss Fintech Innovation Lab at the University of Zurich. She has been the manager of policy affairs at Grupo Bancolombia, a financial conglomerate headquartered in Latin America, a senior advisor to the Organization for Economic Cooperation and Development (OECD), and Foreign Attorney at Sullivan & Cromwell LLP (New York Office). She has taught or delivered lectures at several academic institutions in the United States, Asia, Europe, and Latin America, and at various organizations, including the International Monetary Fund (IMF), the International Organization of Securities Commissions (IOSCO), the U.S. Securities and Exchange Commission (SEC), and the Monetary Authority of Singapore (MAS). Her main areas of work and academic research include financial and banking regulation, securities regulation, fintech, legaltech, and the intersections of law, finance and technology.

Urvashi ANEJA

Is the Director of the Digital Futures Lab, a multidisciplinary research network that examines the complex interactions between technology and society in the Global South. Her current work examines the ethics and politics of artificial intelligence, big tech and platform governance, and labor well-being in digital gig economies. Urvashi is also an Associate Fellow at the Asia Pacific Program at Chatham House and a Fellow at the Indian Institute of Technology, Mumbai. Her research has been cited in leading global and national media publications, and she has served on expert committees appointed by the Indian government on artificial intelligence and frontier technologies.

Raj SHEKHAR

is the Founder and Executive Director at AI Policy Exchange, an international cooperative association of individuals and institutions working at the intersection of AI and public policy, with the mission of producing deliverables that can create an AI–literate society and inform better AI policies. As Responsible AI Lead at K-Tech Centre of Excellence for Data Science & Artificial Intelligence at the National Association of Software and Service Companies (NASSCOM), Raj has been driving NASSCOM's efforts at defining a roadmap for an extensive roll-out and adoption of responsible AI in India. Raj is also an Affiliate at The Future Society and sits on the Founding Editorial Board of Springer Nature's AI and Ethics journal. Prior to joining NASSCOM, Raj served as Consultant (Data, AI) at International Innovation Corps (IIC) of The University of Chicago, supporting operations of the Open Data Working Group (an initiative by IDFC Institute and IIC to advance India's open data aspirations) and IIC's engagement with the Ministry of Electronics and Information Technology, Government of India, aimed at building capacity for data and AI innovation through policy and program implementation. Raj has also been an Affiliated Scholar at CITRIS Policy Lab, University of California, Berkeley, collaborating with Dr. Brandie Nonnecke (Founding Director) on research related to AI governance. In 2020, Raj was featured as a leader in the Responsible Tech ecosystem in the Responsible Tech Guide produced by All Tech Is Human in partnership

员会（AIDA）的委员。伊娃是非加太 - 欧盟（ACP-EU）联合议会大会（DACP）、阿拉伯半岛代表团（DARP）和北大西洋议会代表团（DNAT）的成员。伊娃一直尽己所能，致力于推动创新，以此推动欧洲数字单一市场的建设。她是区块链技术、在线平台、大数据、金融科技、人工智能和网络安全领域多项法案的起草人、容克计划（Juncker plan）欧洲战略投资基金 2.0（EFSI 2）的起草人，以及最近的欧盟投资计划（InvestEU）的起草人。伊娃还是欧洲议会驻北约巴勒斯坦代表团的团长，主要负责欧洲的防务和安全。在此之前，作为泛希腊社会主义运动党（PASOK）的一员，她曾被选为 2007-2012 年希腊议会成员。在从政之前，伊娃还曾是记者和新闻播音员。她拥有建筑学和土木工程学士学位，以及欧洲政治学研究生学位。

夏洛特·斯蒂克斯

是一名经验丰富的技术政策专家，专攻 AI 治理。她是埃因霍温理工大学研究员，致力于以批判的态度研究考察 AI 的伦理、治理和监管注意事项。针对该研究领域，她还是剑桥大学利弗休姆未来智能研究中心的成员。最近，夏洛特就任世界经济论坛全球未来神经技术理事会专家、联合国教科文组织（UNESCO）人工智能伦理原则专家，以及欧盟委员会人工智能高级别专家组协调员。此前，她曾任剑桥大学利弗休姆未来智能研究中心的研究员、世界经济论坛 AI 委员会的研究员以及国际 AI 初创企业——Element AI 的政策顾问，且曾在欧盟委员会机器人和人工智能部门担任政策官，监管的项目总金额超过 1800 万美元。夏洛特曾入选 2020 年福布斯 30 位 30 岁以下（欧洲）精英榜，并被世界经济论坛评为全球杰出青年。

李安琪

苏格兰思克莱德大学法学院的高级讲师（副教授）和网络法律和政策中心的主任，意大利马塞拉塔大学的客座教授。她是一名研究新数字技术的社会法律学者，专攻欧盟、英国和澳大利亚的数据保护、电信监管、知识产权、竞争法和人权问题。她曾在香港中文大学、昆士兰科技大学、斯文本科技大学和英国通信监管机构（OFCOM）工作。她著有《从社会法律角度看 3D 打印革命》（Socio-Legal Aspects of the 3D Printing Revolution）（帕尔格雷夫麦克米伦出版社，2016 年）和《私人权力、在线信息流和欧盟法律：注意差距》（Private Power, Online Information Flows and EU Law: Mind the Gap）（哈特出版社，2016 年）等学术专著，同时也是《良好数据》（Good Data）（INC 出版社，2019 年）的联合编辑。她目前的研究重点是欧盟、美国、中国和印度的公共和私人机构在人工智能方面的法律、伦理声明和政策方面做出的努力。

尤金尼奥·加西亚

外交官，巴西利亚大学国际关系学博士，AI 与全球治理领域研究者，目前担任巴西驻几内亚共和国科纳克里大使馆公使衔参赞兼临时代办。他曾于 2018—2020 年间担任纽约联合国大会主席办公室和平与安全事务高级顾问，也曾先后就职于巴西驻伦敦、墨西哥城和亚松森大使馆以及纽约巴西常驻联合国代表团。此外，他还在巴西外交部任职不同岗位，包括有关亚太事务和外交政策规划的各项职务、外交部部长顾问（2005—2009）和外交部副部长（2014—2015），并在 2015—2018 年间担任联合国司司长。他在 2005—2009 年间担任牛津大学客座副研究员，在 2004—2005 年间担任墨西哥国立自治大学拉美研究学院教授。加西亚共计出版过 7 本有关对外政策和国际事务的著作，曾在 1985 年获得巴西青少年象棋锦标赛冠军。他的主要学术研究领域包括 AI、新技术对和平与安全的影响，以及多边组织的作用。

维克多·法姆波德

现任电气与电子工程师学会自主与智能系统伦理全球倡议（P7003 对算法偏见的考量）项目委员会委员，是 AI 治理和政策方面的专家，致力于帮助政府机构构建数据治理框架。他拥有媒体、政府和咨询领域的工作经验，主要致力于确保在技术领域实现更好的公共政策方案。

奥尔迦·卡瓦利

阿根廷布宜诺斯艾利斯大学经济学院教授，她专注于研究互联网基础设施。她是南方互联网治理学校（SSIG）主任，曾参与编辑《拉丁美洲的互联网治理与监管》（Internet Governance and Regulations in Latin America）一书，并多次投稿发表有关自己专业领域的论文和章节书。她曾任物联网与智慧城市研究小组主席（2015—2017），并被国际电信联盟（ITU）认可为该领域的创新先驱。在 2007 年至 2014 年期间，她得到联合国秘书长的器重，被选为互联网治理论坛多利益相关者咨询小组（MAG）的成员。奥尔迦还积极参与互联网名称与数字地址分配机构（ICANN）的相关事务，并且在最近被任命为通用名称支持组织（GNSO）理事会的成员。奥尔迦参加过国家人工智能战略发展小组。她目前的研究包括人工智能和 5G 技术对拉丁美洲国家发展的影响。奥尔迦拥有商科博士学位、工商管理硕士学位、电信监管硕士学位和电子电气工程学位。她精通西班牙语、英语、葡萄牙语和德语，能听懂法语和意大利语。

埃德森·普雷斯特

巴西南大河州联邦大学（UFRGS）信息学研究所教授。他在 1996 年获得巴西亚马逊帕拉联邦大学计算机科学学士学位，在 1999 年和 2003 年分别获得了巴西南大河州联邦大学计算机科学硕士学位和博士学位。埃德森是 IEEE 机器人与自动化协会（IEEE RAS）和 IEEE 标准协会（IEEE SA）的资深会员。在过去的几年里，他一直致力于投身于与标准化、人工智能、机器人和伦理相关的各种倡议。

with the NYU Alliance for Public Interest Technology. In 2021, Raj was declared a DIET Champion by DataEthics4All for his demonstrated commitment to Data and Diversity, Inclusion and Impact, Ethics and Equity in Teams and Technology (DIET). Raj holds an integrated Bachelors in Law and Humanities from Dr. Ram Manohar Lohiya National Law University, Lucknow, and a Masters in Public Policy from the Institute of Public Policy, National Law School of India University, Bengaluru.

Eva KAILI

is a member of the European Parliament, part of the Hellenic S&D Delegation since 2014. She is the Chair of the Future of Science and Technology Panel in the European Parliament (STOA) and the Centre for Artificial Intelligence (C4AI), Member of the Committees on Industry, Research and Energy (ITRE), Economic and Monetary Affairs (ECON), Budgets (BUDG), and the Special Committee on Artificial Intelligence in a Digital Age (AIDA). Eva is a member of the delegation to the ACP-EU Joint Parliamentary Assembly (DACP), the Delegation for relations with the Arab Peninsula (DARP), and the Delegation for relations with the NATO Parliamentary Assembly (DNAT). In her capacity, she has been working intensively on promoting innovation as a driving force of the establishment of the European Digital Single Market. She has been the draftsperson of multiple pieces of legislation in the fields of blockchain technology, online platforms, big data, fintech, AI and cybersecurity, as well as the ITRE draftsperson on Juncker plan EFSI 2 and more recently the InvestEU program. She has also been the Chair of the Delegation to the NATO PA in the European Parliament, focusing on Defence and Security of Europe. Prior to that, she has been elected as a Member of the Hellenic Parliament (2007- 2012), with the PanHellenic Socialist Movement (PASOK). She also worked as a journalist and newscaster prior to her political career. She holds a Bachelor degree in Architecture and Civil Engineering, and Postgraduate degree in European Politics.

Charlotte STIX

is an experienced technology policy expert with a specialization in AI governance. She is a researcher at the Eindhoven University of Technology where she critically examines ethical, governance and regulatory considerations around artificial intelligence. In that context, she also serves as Fellow to the Leverhulme Centre for the Future of Intelligence, University of Cambridge. Most recently, Charlotte held an Expert role at the World Economic Forum's Global Future Council on Neurotechnologies, served as an Expert to the UNESCO's AI Ethics Principles, and was the Coordinator of the European Commission's High-Level Expert Group on Artificial Intelligence. Formerly, she was a Researcher at the Leverhulme Centre for the Future of Intelligence, University of Cambridge, a Fellow to the World Economic Forum's AI Council, a Policy Advisor for international AI start-up Element AI and worked as a Policy Officer at the European Commission's Robotics and AI Unit where she managed over 18m in projects. Charlotte is awarded as a 2020 Forbes' 30 under 30 (Europe) and was named a Young Global Shaper by the World Economic Forum.

Angela DALY

is Senior Lecturer (Associate Professor) and Co-Director of the Centre for Internet Law & Policy in Strathclyde University Law School (Scotland) and Visiting Professor at the Università degli Studi di Macerata (Italy). She is a socio-legal scholar of new digital technologies, with particular expertise in data protection, telecoms regulation, intellectual property, competition law and human rights in the European Union, the United Kingdom and Australia. She has previously worked at the Chinese University of Hong Kong, Queensland University of Technology, Swinburne University of Technology and the UK communications regulator OFCOM. She is the author of academic monographs Socio-Legal Aspects of the 3D Printing Revolution (Palgrave 2016) and Private Power, Online Information Flows and EU Law: Mind the Gap (Hart 2016), and the co-editor of Good Data (INC 2019). Her current research examines the emergence of law, ethics statements and policy from public and private actors in the EU, US, China and India on artificial intelligence (AI).

Eugenio V. GARCIA

is a diplomat, a PhD in International Relations from the University of Brasilia, and a researcher on artificial intelligence and global governance. He is currently Minister–Counsellor and Chargé d'affaires ad interim in the Brazilian Embassy in Conakry, Republic of Guinea. He was a former senior adviser on peace and security, Office of the President of the United Nations General Assembly, New York (2018-2020). He worked previously in the Brazilian Embassies in London, Mexico City, Asuncion, and in the Permanent Mission of Brazil to the United Nations in New York. He has held different positions in the Ministry of Foreign Affairs, including on Asia–Pacific affairs, diplomatic planning, as adviser to the Foreign Minister (2005-2009) and the Deputy Foreign Minister (2014-2015) and as Head of the United Nations Division (2015-2018). He is a visiting research associate at the University of Oxford (1999-2000) and professor at the College of Latin American Studies, National Autonomous University of Mexico (2004-2005). He has published seven books on foreign policy and international affairs. He is the former Brazilian junior chess champion (1985). His main areas of academic research include AI, the impact of new technologies in peace and security, and the role of multilateral organizations.

Victor FAMUBODE

is currently a committee member for IEEE Global Initiative for Autonomous and Intelligent Systems—P7003 Algorithms bias and considerations. He is an AI governance and policy specialist with a focus on helping government institutions design data governance frameworks. His experience cuts across media, government and consulting with a primary focus on ensuring better public policy choices are made within the technology sphere.

Olga CAVALLI

is a Professor of Internet Infrastructure at the Economy School of University of Buenos Aires in Argentina. She is director of the South School

埃德森是联合国秘书长数字合作高级别小组成员、联合国教科文组织人工智能伦理特别专家组成员、IEEE 技术伦理计划南美大使、IEEE RAS/SA 7007—伦理驱动机器人和自动化系统本体标准工作组主席、IEEE 自主和智能系统伦理全球倡议成员、未来学会顾问、卡内基道德与国际事务委员会卡内基人工智能和平等倡议顾问、联合国教科文组织全民信息计划（IFAP）信息无障碍工作组成员，以及 IEEE RAS 工业活动委员会的前任副主席。

康斯坦萨·戈麦斯蒙特

是一名社会影响战略家和实践者,她将政府、公司、跨国组织和当地社区聚集在一起,共同制定相关倡议,加速显现新兴技术的积极影响。康斯坦萨是 C Minds 的创始人兼总裁，这是一家由女性领导的行动机构，致力于新技术、社会和环境的融合。作为 C Minds 领导层的一员，她已在新兴经济体的数字经济、人工智能和社会创新政策和倡议制定领域深耕超过 12 年，特别关注拉丁美洲。此外，她还是人工智能改善气候全球倡议的联合创始人。康斯坦萨对建立社区和创建区域平台充满热情，这促使她成为了世界经济论坛人工智能造福人类全球未来理事会人工智能治理工作组的领导者；为 IEEE 国际战略提供咨询；受邀加入联合国教科文组织人工智能伦理全球文书草案高级小组；并协助美洲开发银行（IDB）建立人工智能促进社会影响区域倡议（fAIr LAC）；以及其他关键倡议。康斯坦萨的成就贡献曾被国际媒体报道，并得到了巴黎和平论坛、世界经济论坛和英国政府等机构的认可。

让·加西亚·佩里希

GENIA Latinoamérica 联合创始人及首席政府关系官。 GENIA Latinoamérica 是一个区域研发（R&D）平台， 其使命是将拉丁美洲纳入全球人工智能开发体系。让·加西亚·佩里希还是美国国家航空航天局埃姆斯研究中心 奇点大学的研究员，担任公共部门高级官员的顾问和战略远见研究员。他也是政治创新中心主席，国际人工智能集团全球顾问委员会成员，全球人工智能伦理研究所执行委员会成员，以

何塞·古里迪·比斯托

智利经济、发展和旅游部经济与中小企业部的副部长顾问。此前，他曾任科学、技术、知识和创新部未来团队顾问，带头制定了智利人工智能国家政策。同时，何塞还是智利天主教大学工程学院客座教授。他是经合组织人工智能专家网络、国际投资发展银行 fAIr LAC 倡议及未来协会分支机构的成员。他拥有智利天主教大学工业和系统工程硕士学位（工程学位）。

杰西卡·库辛·纽曼

是加州大学伯克利分校长期网络安全中心的研究员，这是一个研究人工智能对全球安全的影响的跨学科中心，她在此领导了人工智能安全计划。她还是未来生活研究所的人工智能政策专家和未来社会的研究顾问。杰西卡是哈佛大学贝尔弗中心 2016-2017 年度国际和全球事务研究员，曾在哈佛大学科技与社会中心项目、未来研究所和遗传学与社会中心担任研究员。杰西卡获有哈佛大学肯尼迪学院公共政策硕士学位、加州大学伯克利分校人类学学士学位，并获得最高荣誉。她通过《山丘》、《洛杉矶时报》、《药学杂志》和美国消费者新闻与商业频道（CNBC）等多种渠道发表了数十篇关于新兴技术的影响的文章。杰西卡是中美高级网络技术研讨会（CNAS）人工智能工作组的成员，也是人工智能全球伙伴关系公平、透明和可问责人工智能专家小组的成员。

伊拉克利·贝里泽

在领导多边谈判，与各国政府、联合国机构、国际组织、私营公司和企业、智库、民间团体、基金会、学术界以及其他国际合作伙伴制定利益相关者参与计划方面拥有 20 多年的经验。贝里泽先生正在就与国际安全、科技发展、新兴技术、创新和新技术的颠覆性潜力有关的许多问题，特别是预防犯罪、刑事司法和安全问题，向各国政府和国际组织提供建议。他从 AI 相关的战略、行动计划、路线图和政策文件等方面出发，为各国政府提供支持。2014 年，贝里泽发起了联合国首批 AI 项目之一，并管理至今。此外，他还在联合国大会和其他国际组织中发起并组织了一些高级别活动。他发现了传统威胁和风险的协同作用，并制定了 AI 帮助实现联合国可持续发展目标的解决方案。他是世界经济论坛全球人工智能委员会、联合国数字合作高级别小组，以及欧盟委员会人工智能高级专家小组等多个国际工作小组的成员。他经常发表有关技术发展、指数技术、人工智能和机器人以及国际安全主题的演讲。他在国际期刊和杂志上发表了大量文章，媒体在谈到有关 AI 的问题时，经常引用他的文章。贝里泽还是国际性别平等捍卫者（International Gender Champions，IGC）成员，支持 IGC 专家小组的平等宣言。2013 年，他代表禁止化学武器组织接受了诺贝尔和平奖。

龚克

世界工程组织联合会（WFEO）主席，中国新一代人工智能发展战略研究院执行院长。龚教授是信息通信技术方面的专家，获有奥地利格拉茨技术大学的电工电子系通讯与电波传播专业博士。他曾于 1987—2006 年在清华大学任职，担任清华大学副校长及信息科学技术国家研究中心主任；此后，他又先后任职天津大学校长（2006—2011）和南开大学校长（2011—2018）。龚教授于 2009 年加入 WFEO，工作至今，曾先后任职信息和传播委员会主席和创新技术委员会主席。2019 年，他当选 WFEO 主席，任职至今。自 2017 年中国工程院与天津市政府联合成立中国新一代人工智能发展战略研究院以来，龚教授一直领导着该院的发展。2013—2017 年，龚克教授曾任联合国秘书长潘基文的科学顾问委员会的委员。此外，他还曾在中国科学技术协会等组织机构担任过重要的行政职位。

on Internet Governance SSIG. She coedited the book Internet Governance and Regulations in Latin America and is a frequent contributor to papers and chapters in books on her areas of expertise. She was chair of the Study Group on Internet of Things and Smart Cities (2015-2017). The ITU has recognized her as an innovator in this field. During 2007-2014, she was distinguished by the United Nations Secretary General and was chosen to be a part of the Internet Governance Forum's Multistakeholder Advisory Group, MAG. Olga is very active in ICANN, where she has recently been appointed a GNSO Council Member. Olga participated in the National AI Strategy development group. Her current research includes the impact of AI and 5G on the development of countries in Latin America. Her education includes a PhD in Business Direction, a masters degree in Business Administration, a masters degree in Telecommunications Regulation, and a degree in Electronic and Electric Engineering. She is fluent in Spanish, English, Portuguese and German and is familiar with French and Italian.

Edson PRESTES

Is a Professor at Institute of Informatics of the Federal University of Rio Grande do Sul (UFRGS), Brazil. He received his BSc in Computer Science from the Federal University of Pará (1996), Amazon, Brazil, and MSc (1999) and PhD (2003) in Computer Science from UFRGS. Edson is a Senior Member of the IEEE Robotics and Automation Society (IEEE RAS) and IEEE Standards Association (IEEE SA). In recent years, he has worked in different initiatives related to standardization, artificial intelligence, robotics and ethics. For instance, Edson is Member of the United Nations Secretary–General's High-level Panel on Digital Cooperation, Member of the UNESCO Ad Hoc Expert Group for the Recommendation on the Ethics of Artificial Intelligence, South America Ambassador at IEEE TechEthics, Chair of the IEEE RAS/SA 7007–Ontological Standard for Ethically Driven Robotics and Automation Systems Working Group, Member of the IEEE Global Initiative on Ethics of Autonomous and Intelligent Systems, Adviser at The Future Society, Adviser at the Carnegie AI & Equality Initiative at Carnegie Council for Ethics in International Affairs, Member of UNESCO IFAP Information Accessibility Working Group and Past Associate Vice President on the IEEE RAS Industrial Activities in International Affairs.

Constanza GÓMEZ-MONT

is a social impact strategist and practitioner who brings governments, companies, multinational organizations, and local communities together to codesign initiatives that accelerate the positive impact of emerging technologies. She is the founder and president of C Minds, a women-led action tank that works at the intersection of new technologies, society, and the environment. Through C Minds leadership, she has worked for over 12 years in the development of policies and initiatives in the field of digital economy, AI, and social innovation in emerging economies, with a special focus on Latin America. Moreover, she is cofounder of the global initiative AI for Climate. Her passion for building communities and creating regional platforms has led her to lead the AI Governance Working Group of WEF's Global Future Council on AI for Humanity; advise IEEE's international strategy; be invited as part of the High-Level Group for the drafting of UNESCO global instrument on AI ethics; and assist the Inter-American Development Bank (IDB) in the founding of the AI for social impact regional initiative, fAIr LAC, among other key initiatives. Her work has been featured in international media and has been recognized by the Paris Peace Forum, the WEF and the Government of the United Kingdom, among others.

Jean García PERICHE

is the cofounder and Chief Government Officer of GENIA Latinoamérica, a research and development (R&D) regional platform including LATAM for global AI development. Jean is a Fellow from Singularity University at NASA Ames Research Center and works as an adviser to senior-level officials in government. He is also the President of the Centre for Political Innovation, a member of the Global Advisory Board of the International Group of Artificial Intelligence, part of the Executive Board of the Global AI Ethics Institute, and an AI Policy Affiliate at The Future Society.

José Guridi BUSTOS

is the Chief of the Future and Social Adoption of Technology Unit at the Chilean Ministry of Economy, Development and Tourism. Previously, he served as an adviser at the Future Team of the Ministry of Science, Technology, Knowledge and Innovation, where he led the creation of Chile's Artificial Intelligence National Policy. José is also an adjunct professor at the School of Engineering at Pontificia Universidad Católica de Chile. José is part of the OECD network of experts on AI, the fAIr LAC initiative of the InterAmerican Development Bank and an affiliate of The Future Society. He holds an engineering degree with a Master of Sciences in Industrial and System Engineering from Pontificia Universidad Católica de Chile.

Jessica Cussins NEWMAN

is a Research Fellow at the UC Berkeley Center for Long-Term Cybersecurity, where she leads the AI Security Initiative, a hub for interdisciplinary research on the global security impacts of artificial intelligence. She is also an AI Policy Specialist with the Future of Life Institute and a Research Advisor with The Future Society. Jessica was a 2016-17 International and Global Affairs Student Fellow at Harvard's Belfer Center, and has held research positions with Harvard's Program on Science, Technology & Society, the Institute for the Future, and the Center for Genetics and Society. Jessica received her master's degree in public policy from the Harvard Kennedy School and her bachelor's in anthropology from the University of California, Berkeley with highest distinction honors. She has published dozens of articles on the implications of emerging technologies in outlets including The Hill, The Los Angeles Times, The Pharmaceutical Journal, and CNBC. Jessica is a member of the CNAS AI Task Force and a member of the Partnership on AI Expert Group on Fair, Transparent, and Accountable AI.

Irakli BERIDZE

has more than 20 years' experience leading multilateral negotiations and developing stakeholder engagement programs with governments, UN agencies, international organizations, private industry and corporations, think tanks, civil society, foundations, academia, and other

唐·赖特

信息和通信技术标准化咨询公司 Standards Strategies 总裁。他曾是利盟国际（曾属 IBM）全球标准部的主管，在标准、工程、软件开发和市场营销方面拥有超过 40 年的经验。赖特先生是电气与电子工程师学会（IEEE）高级会员，曾任 IEEE 标准协会主席（2017-2018）和 IEEE 董事会成员（2017-2018），曾担任计算机协会标准副总裁、电气与电子工程师学会标准协会（IEEE Standards Association，IEEE-SA）主席、IEEE-SA 财务主管、IEEE-SA 奖励和认可委员会主席（IEEE Awards and Recognition Chair）、IEEE 高级评审委员会主席（IEEE Admission and Advancement Chair），以及 IEEE 奖励委员会成员。他是计算机学会、通信学会、消费电子学会、技术社会影响学会和技术与工程管理学会的成员。他是行业标准和技术组织（IEEE-ISTO）董事会成员，并曾担任董事长。他还曾担任国际信息技术标准委员会（INCITS）执行董事会主席、国际标准化组织和国际电工委员会的联合技术委员会（ISO/IEC JTC 1）美国总部和两届美国国家标准协会（ANSI）董事会成员。唐·赖特毕业于路易斯维尔大学，获有电子工程学士学位和电气工程硕士学位。此外，他还是美国工程荣誉协会——Tau Beta Pi 和 IEEE 国际荣誉协会——Eta Kappa Nu 的成员。

塞勒斯·霍德斯

最近担任阿联酋总理办公室人工智能办公室主任顾问，过去 3 年一直负责领导迪拜世界政府首脑峰会的全球人工智能治理圆桌会议（GGAR）。塞勒斯是硅谷跨阶段风险投资公司——FoundersX Ventures 合伙人。他还是哈佛大学肯尼迪学院孵化的未来社会（一个非营利组织）的人工智能倡议联合创始人及主席。他在该项目中与众多全球利益相关者一起研究、探讨并构建人工智能治理框架。在人工智能倡议方面，塞勒斯遵循联合国主要机构的建议，与斯坦福大学以人为本人工智能研究院（Stanford HAI）共同领导针对新冠肺炎疫情的集体和增强智能（CAIAC）项目，并与联合国可持续发展目标（Global Pulse）行政办公室和麦肯锡（Noble Purpose AI）共同领导全球数据获取框架（GDAF）项目。塞勒斯是全球人工智能伙伴关系（GPAI）、经合组织人工智能专家组（ONE AI）、欧洲议会未来与科学和技术小组（STOA）、联合国秘书长数字合作高级别小组建议 1B（数字公共产品）和 3C（人工智能）、全球扩展智能理事会（MIT-IEEE）的成员，也是 IEEE《人工智能设计的伦理准则》的共同作者之一。塞勒斯是人工智能联盟（AI Commons）指导委员会的成员，是其数据倡议的领导者，是智慧迪拜人工智能伦理委员会的成员，也是上海市科学学研究所（SISS）的人工智能治理顾问。塞勒斯曾就读于巴黎政治学院，后担任该院国际安全讲师，获得巴黎第二大学国防、地缘政治学和工业动力学荣誉硕士学位，以及哈佛大学肯尼迪政治学院硕士学位。

partners on an international level. Mr. Beridze advises governments and international organizations on numerous issues related to international security, scientific and technological developments, emerging technologies, innovation and the disruptive potential of new technologies, particularly on the issue of crime prevention, criminal justice and security. He supports governments worldwide in AI strategies, action plans, roadmaps and policy papers. Since 2014, he has initiated and managed one of the first United Nations Programmes on AI, initiating and organizing a number of high-level events at the United Nations General Assembly and other international organizations, finding synergies with traditional threats and risks, and identifying solutions where AI can contribute to the achievement of the United Nations Sustainable Development Goals. He is a member of various international task forces, including the World Economic Forum's Global Artificial Intelligence Council, the UN High-level panel for digital cooperation, and the High-Level Expert Group on Artificial Intelligence of the European Commission. He frequently lectures and speaks on subjects related to technological development, exponential technologies, artificial intelligence and robotics and international security. He has numerous publications in international journals and magazines and is frequently quoted in the media on issues related to AI. Irakli Beridze is an International Gender Champion supporting the IGC Panel Parity Pledge. He also received the Nobel Peace Prize on behalf of the OPCW in 2013.

GONG Ke

is President of the World Federation of Engineering Organizations (WFEO) and Executive Director of the Chinese Institute of New Generation Artificial Intelligence Development Strategies. By training, Prof. Gong is an engineer in information communication technology. After obtaining the degree of Doctor of Technical Science from Technical University of Graz, Austria, he worked at Tsinghua University from 1987-2006, where he served as the director of the Chinese National Research Center of Information Science and Technology and the Vice President of the university. Later, he was appointed President of Tianjin University (2006-2011) and President of Nankai University (2011-2018). Prof. Gong has worked with the WFEO since 2009 and chaired the Committees of Information and Communication and then the Committee on Engineering for Innovative Technologies. He was elected as the 2019 President. Prof. Gong has directed the Chinese Institute of New Generation Artificial Intelligence Development Strategies since it was cofounded in 2017 by the Chinese Academy of Engineering and the Tianjin Municipal Government. From 2013 to 2017, Prof. Gong Ke was a member of the Scientific Advisory Board to UN Secretary–General Ban Ki-moon. He has also served in executive positions for the China Association of Science and Technology.

Don WRIGHT

is the President of Standards Strategies, LLC, an ICT Standardization consulting firm. He is the retired Director of Worldwide Standards for Lexmark International and previously IBM and has over 40 years of experience in standards, engineering, software development and marketing. Mr. Wright is a Senior Member of the IEEE and served as President of the IEEE Standards Association (2017-2018), and a member of the IEEE Board of Directors (2017-2018). He previously served as Computer Society VP of Standards, IEEE-SA Standards Board Chair, IEEE-SA Treasurer, IEEE-SA Awards and Recognition Chair, IEEE Admission and Advancement Chair, and on the IEEE Awards Board. He is a member of the Computer Society, Communications Society, Consumer Electronics Society, Society on the Social Implications of Technology, and Technology and Engineering Management Society. He is a member of the Board of Directors of the IEEE-ISTO and previously served as Chairman. He previously served as Chair of the INCITS Executive Board, US HoD to ISO/IEC JTC 1, and two terms as a member of the Board of Directors of ANSI. He graduated from the University of Louisville with BSEE and MEng EE degrees. He is a member of Tau Beta Pi and Eta Kappa Nu.

Cyrus HODES

recently served as the Advisor to the Minister of Artificial Intelligence at the UAE Prime Minister's Office and for the past 3 years has led the Global Governance of AI Roundtable (GGAR) at the World Government Summit in Dubai. He is a Partner at FoundersX Ventures, a cross-stage venture capital firm based in Silicon Valley. Cyrus is the co-founder and Chair of the AI Initiative at The Future Society—a 501(c)3 that began at Harvard Kennedy School—where he engages a wide range of global stakeholders to study, discuss and shape AI governance. At the AI Initiative, Cyrus coleads the Collective and the Augmented Intelligence Against COVID-19 (CAIAC) project, together with Stanford HAI, advised by leading UN agencies, and coleads the Global Data Access Framework (GDAF) project with the Executive Office of the UN SG (Global Pulse) and McKinsey (Noble Purpose AI). He is part of the Global Partnership on AI (GPAI), a member of the OECD Expert Group on AI (ONE AI), a member of the EU Parliament Panel for the Future of Science and Technology (STOA), a Constituent of Recommendations 1B (Digital Public Goods) and 3C (AI) of the UN Secretary–General's High-level Panel on Digital Cooperation, a member of the Council on Extended Intelligence (MIT–IEEE), and is a coauthor of IEEE Ethically Aligned Design. Cyrus is part of the steering committee of AI Commons and is its Data Initiative lead, is a member of the AI Ethics Board of Smart Dubai, and is an AI Governance Adviser at the Shanghai Institute for Science of Science (SISS). Cyrus was educated at Sciences Po Paris, where he was later a Lecturer in International Security. He holds an M.A. (Hons) from Paris II University in Defense, Geostrategy and Industrial Dynamics and an M.P.A. from Harvard Kennedy School of Government.

图书在版编目（CIP）数据

全球视野下的人工智能治理．第一辑：汉英对照 / 石谦主编；李辉，谢旻希副主编．-- 上海：同济大学出版社，2022.8

ISBN 978-7-5765-0333-3

Ⅰ．①全… Ⅱ．①石… ②李… ③谢… Ⅲ．①人工智能－应用－社会管理－研究－世界－汉、英 Ⅳ．①C916-39

中国版本图书馆 CIP 数据核字 (2022) 第 148339 号

全球视野下的人工智能治理（第一辑）

A Global Perspective of AI Governance (Vol. I)

石谦 主编 李辉 谢旻希 副主编

上海市科学学研究所 策划

Chief Editor SHI Qian Vice Chief Editors LI Hui Brian TSE

Curated by Shanghai Institute for Science of Science (SISS)

策划编辑：高晓辉

责任编辑：袁佳麟

助理编辑：阮璐瑶

装帧设计：刘青

责任校对：徐逢乔

出版发行：同济大学出版社

地址：上海市杨浦区四平路 1239 号

电话：021- 65985622

邮政编码：200092

网址：http://www.tongjipress.com.cn

经销：全国各地新华书店

印刷：上海安枫印务有限公司

开本：710 mm x 1000 mm 1/16

字数：340 000

印张：17

版次：2022 年 8 月第 1 版

印次：2022 年 8 月第 1 次印刷

书号：ISBN 978-7-5765-0333-3

定价：78.00 元